O N E

The seasons are passing at a ferocious pace!

—ONE

Manga creator ONE began *One-Punch Man* as a webcomic, which quickly went viral, garnering over 10 million hits. In addition to *One-Punch Man*, ONE writes and draws the series *Mob Psycho 100* and *Makai no Ossan*.

Y U S U K E   M U R A T A

I believe I can solve 90 percent of my problems through sheer force of will.

—Yusuke Murata

A highly decorated and skilled artist best known for his work on *Eyeshield 21*, Yusuke Murata won the 122nd Hop Step Award (1995) for *Partner* and placed second in the 51st Akatsuka Award (1998) for *Samui Hanashi*.

ONE-PUNCH MAN | 28

ONE + YUSUKE MURATA

☆THE STORIES, CHARACTERS, AND INCIDENTS

MENTIONED IN THIS PUBLICATION
ARE ENTIRELY FICTIONAL.

STORY BY ONE ART BY YUSUKE MURATA

ONE-PUNCH MAN

28

INTO THE ABYSS

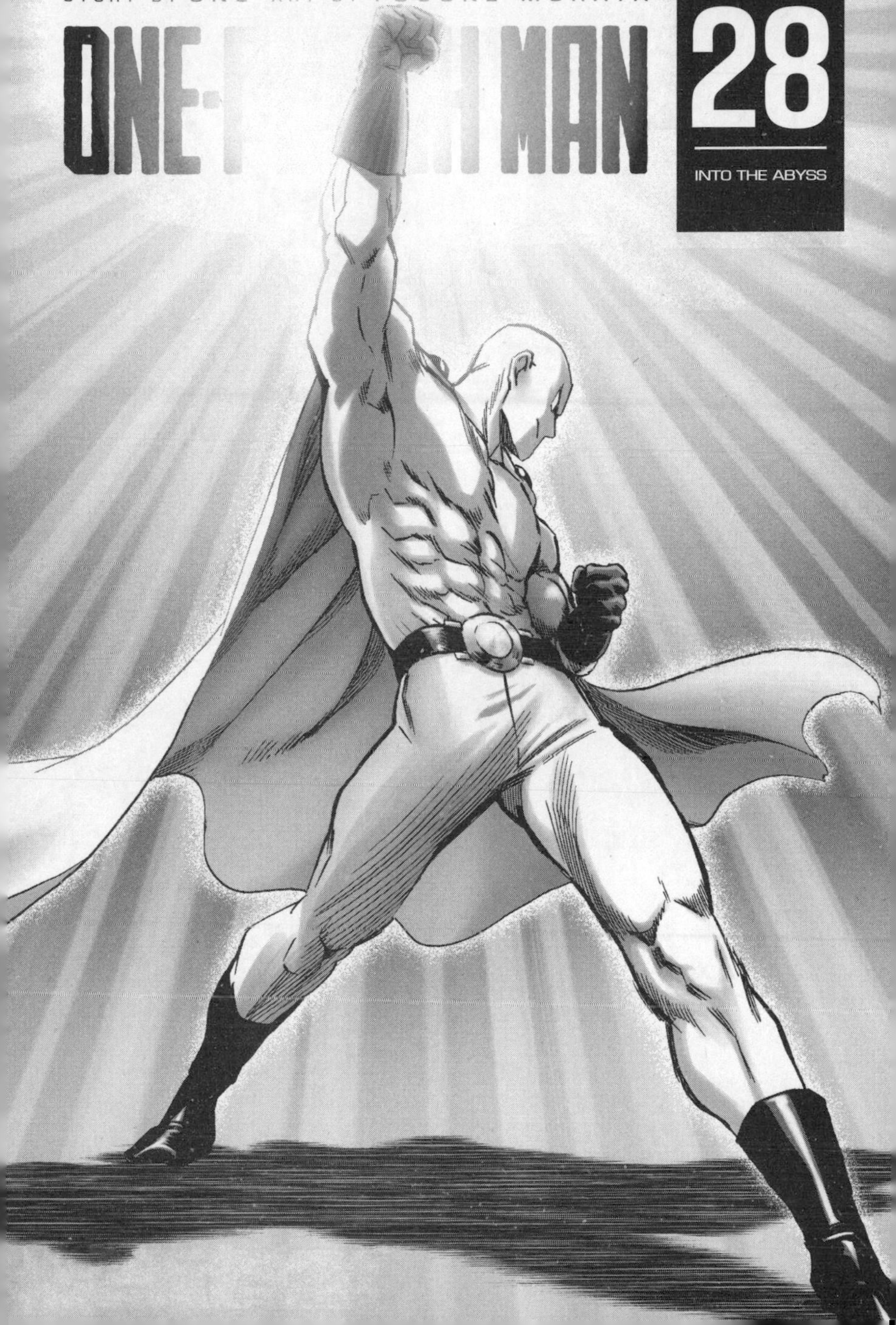

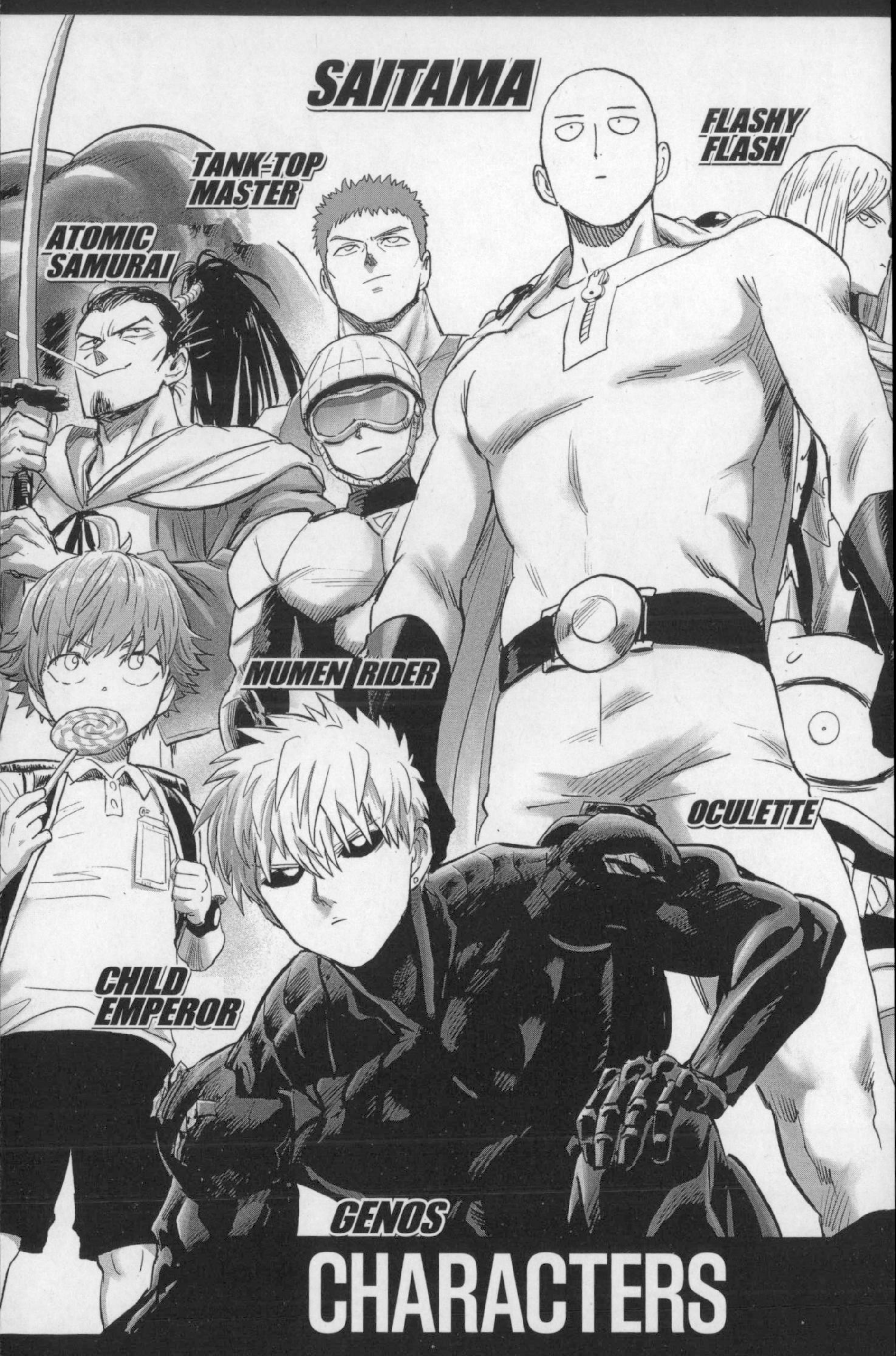
SAITAMA
FLASHY FLASH
TANK-TOP MASTER
ATOMIC SAMURAI
MUMEN RIDER
OCULETTE
CHILD EMPEROR
GENOS

CHARACTERS

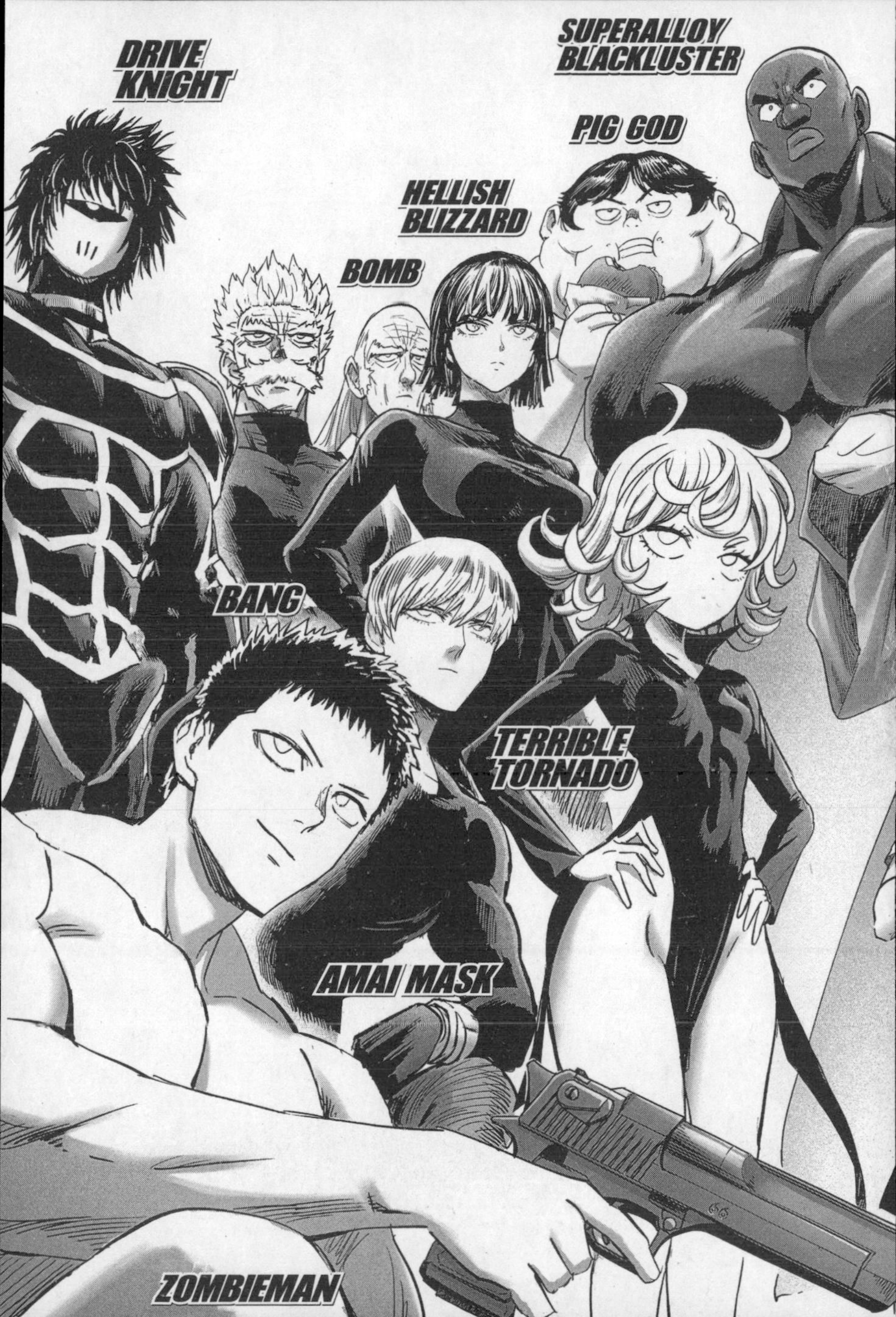
SUPERALLOY BLACKLUSTER
DRIVE KNIGHT
PIG GOD
HELLISH BLIZZARD
BOMB
BANG
TERRIBLE TORNADO
AMAI MASK
ZOMBIEMAN

CONTENTS

ONE-PUNCH MAN VOL. 28

STORY

Gyoro-Gyoro, the supposed brains of the Monster Association, is revealed to be a decoy for the psychic Psychos, the true mastermind. Finding herself on the losing end of a fierce battle against Tornado, Psychos fuses with the Monster King Orochi and accesses unbelievable power. A frightful battle between psychics ensues. Seeing an opening, Psychos delivers a grievous wound to Tornado.

However, Genos arrives to assist Tornado, thereby earning Psychos's wrath. Meanwhile, Saitama is digging out Flashy Flash from a mound of rubble in the underground labyrinth...

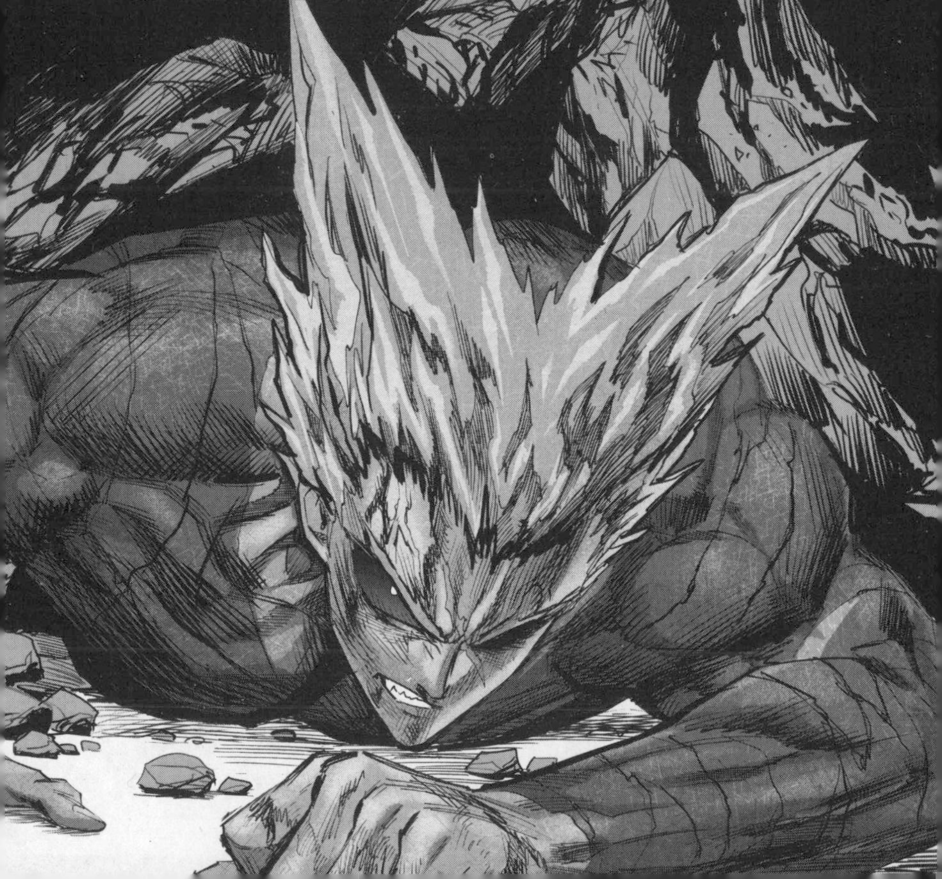

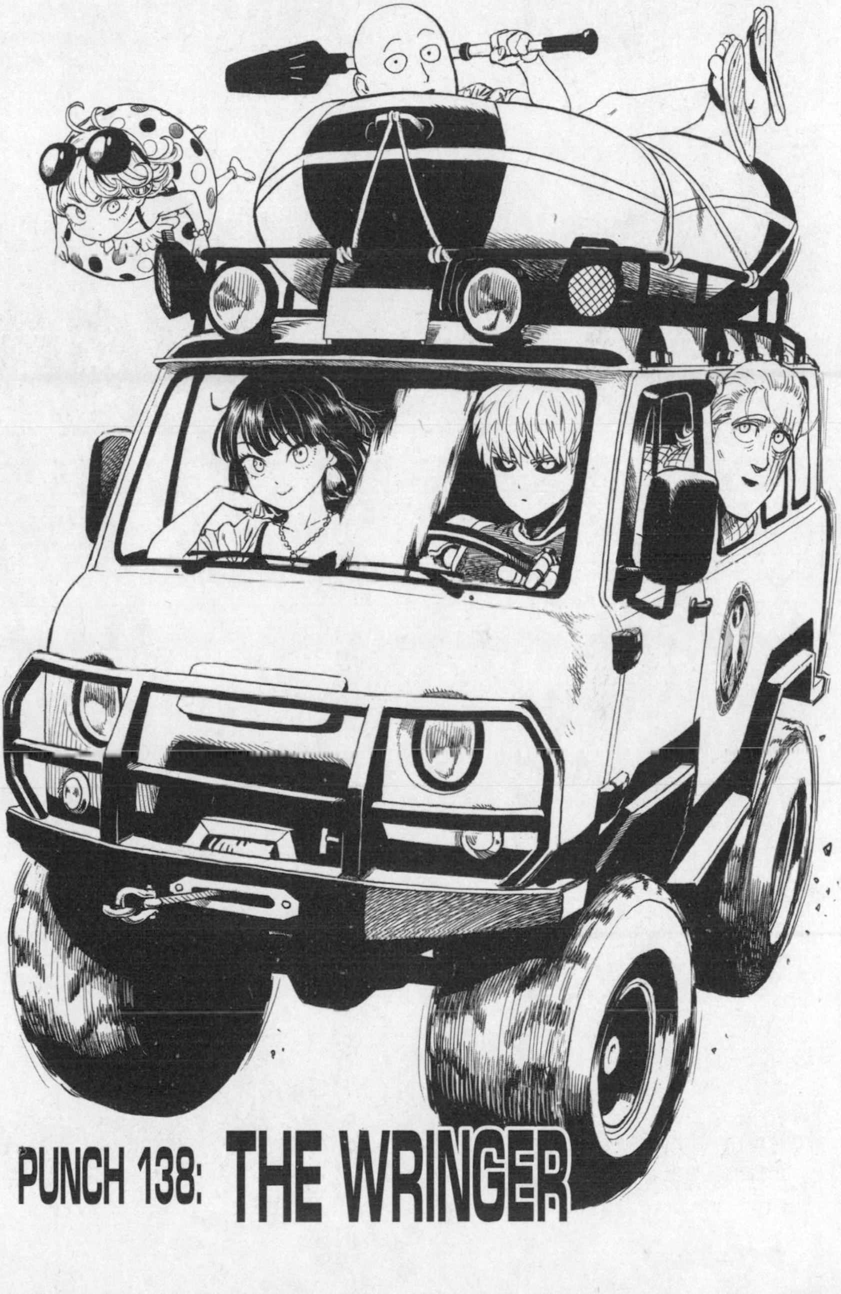

PUNCH 138: THE WRINGER

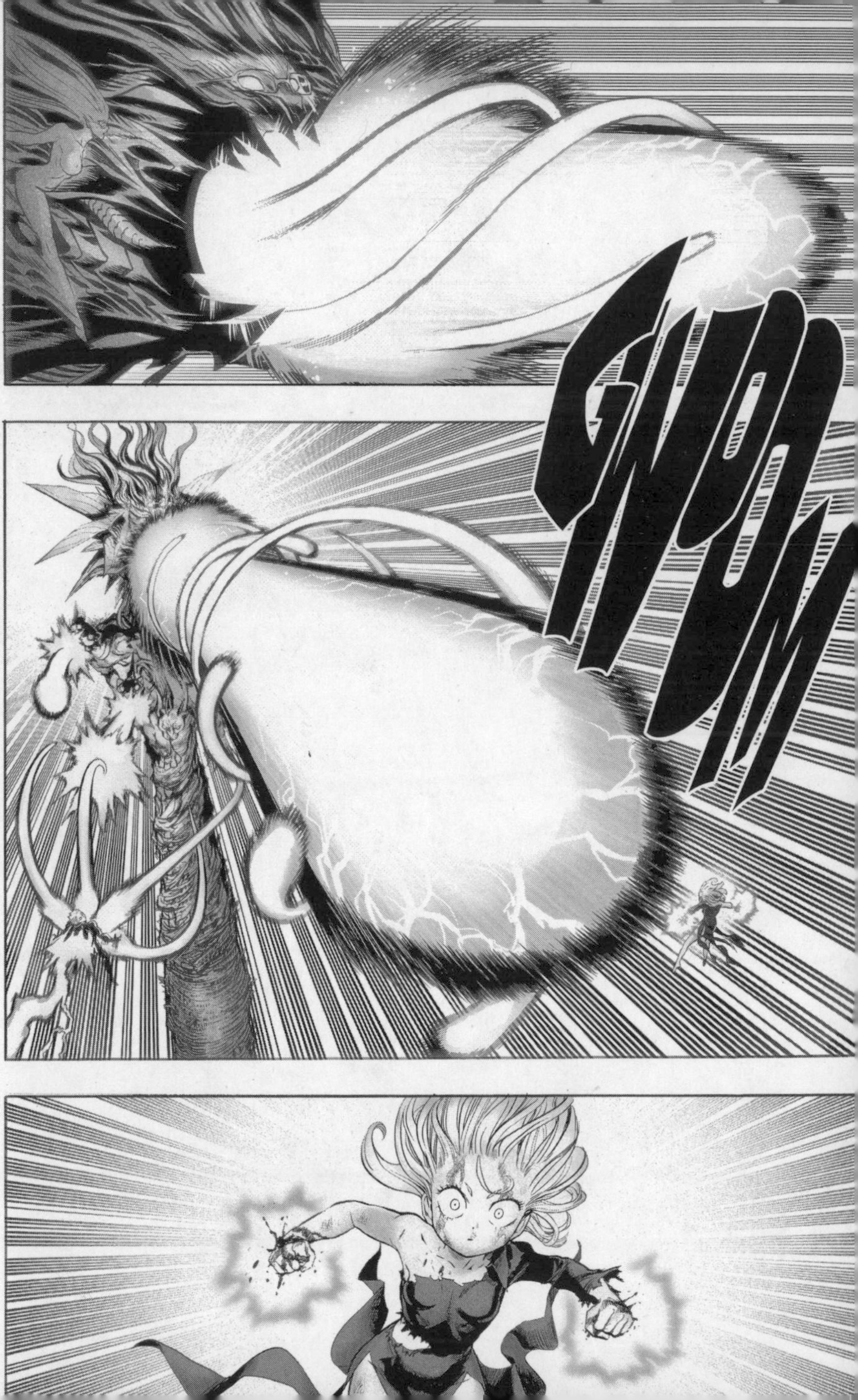

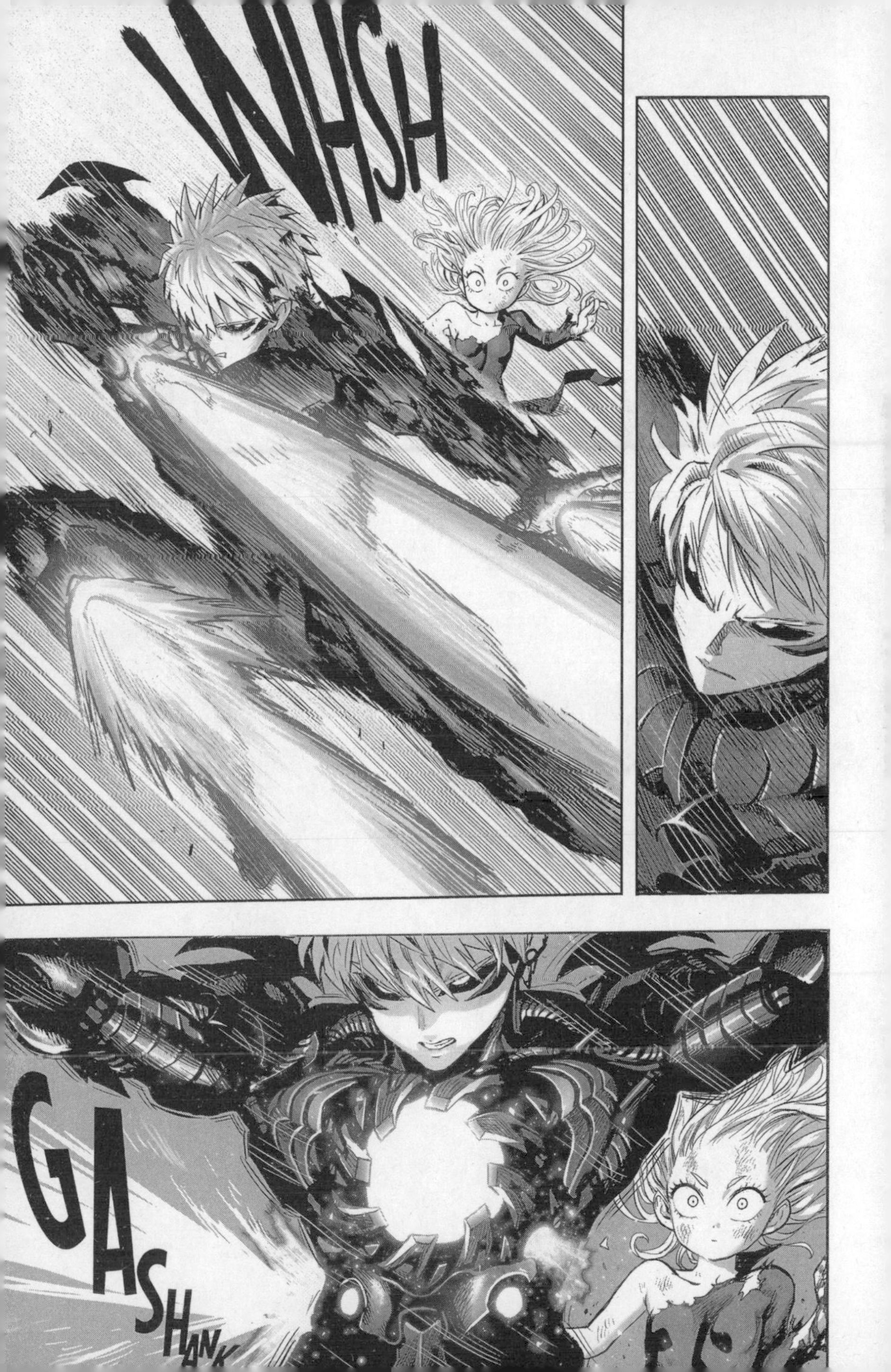
WHSH
GASHANK

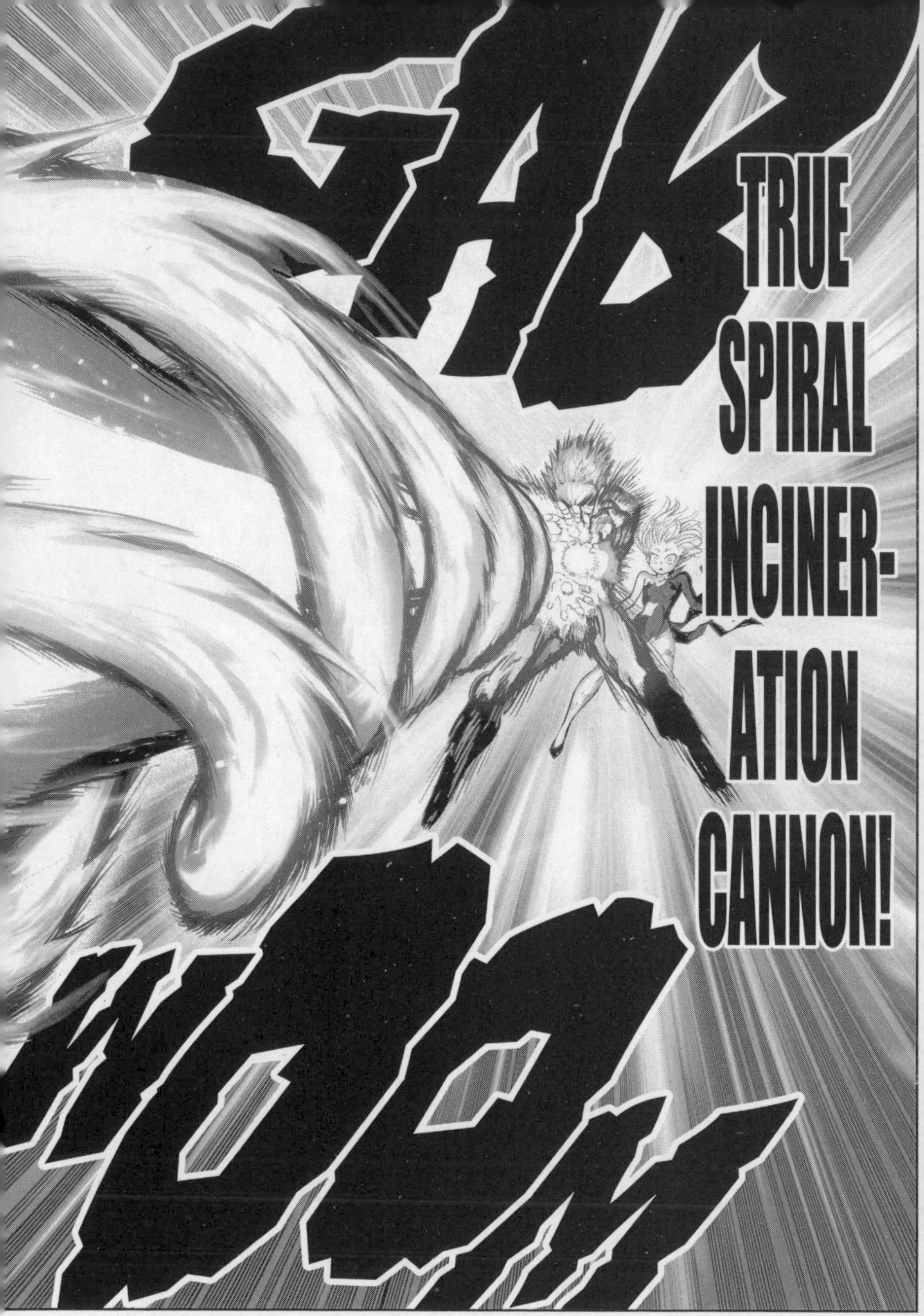
TRUE SPIRAL INCINER-ATION CANNON!

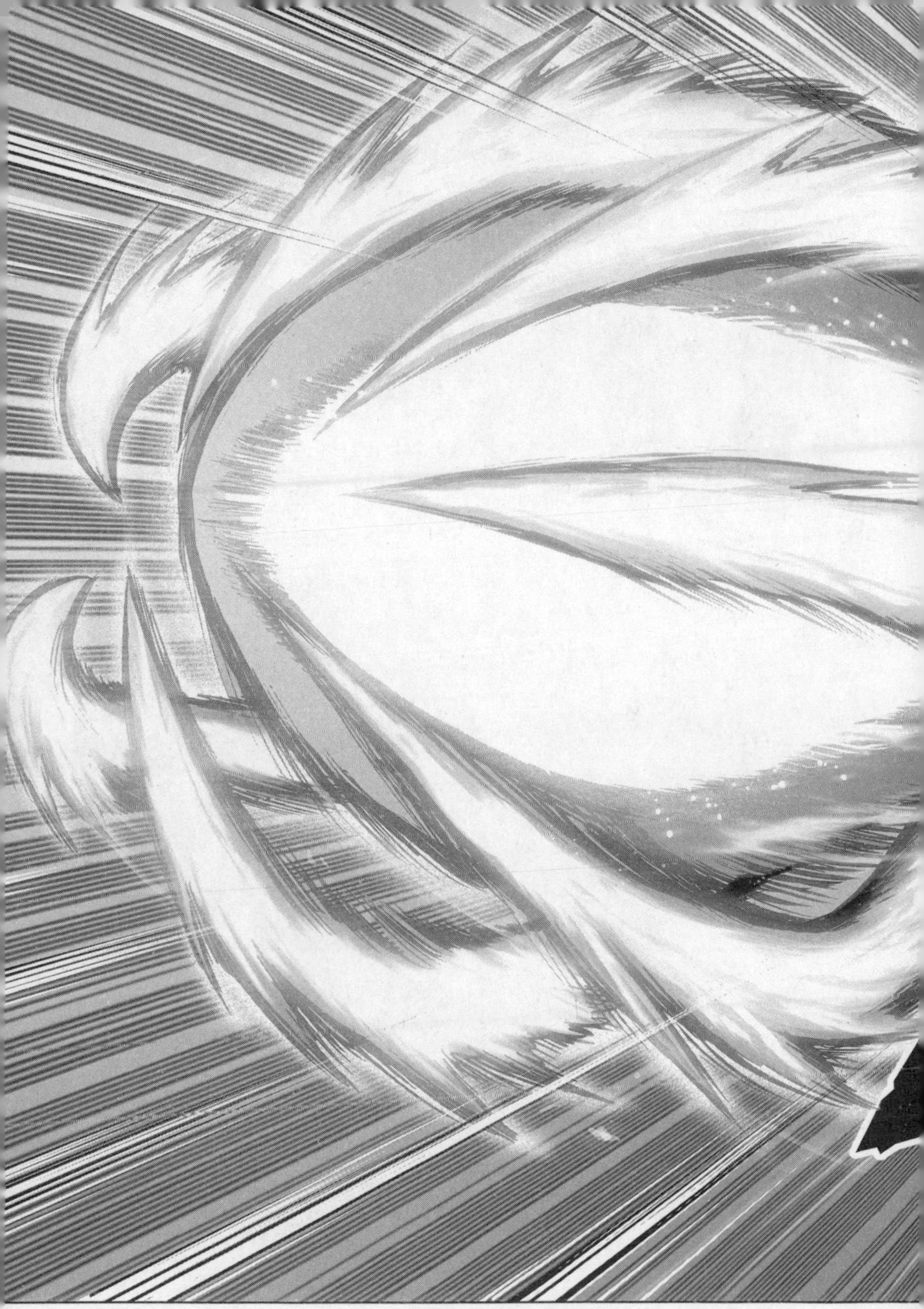

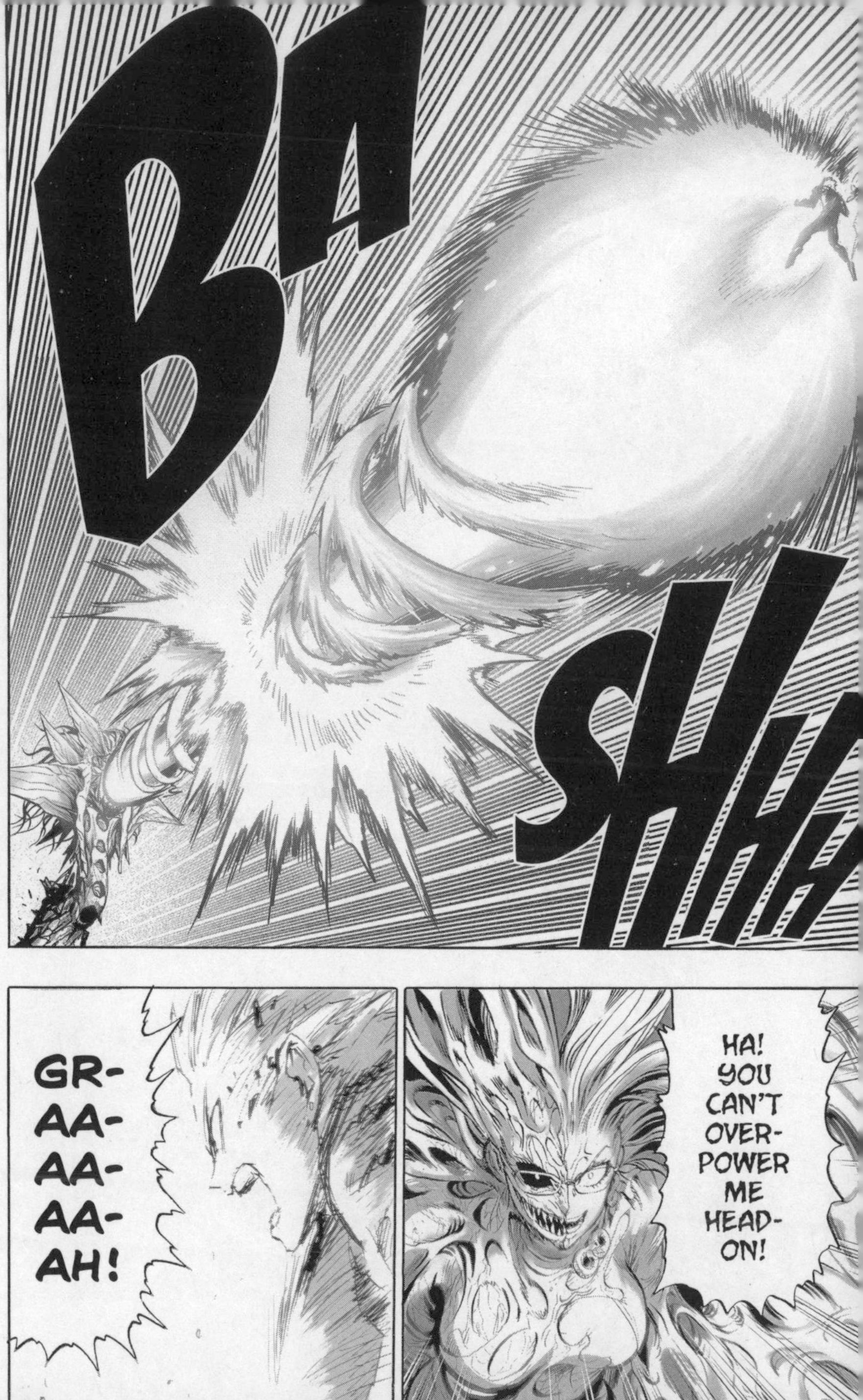
BA
SHH
HA! YOU CAN'T OVER-POWER ME HEAD-ON!
GR-AA-AA-AA-AH!

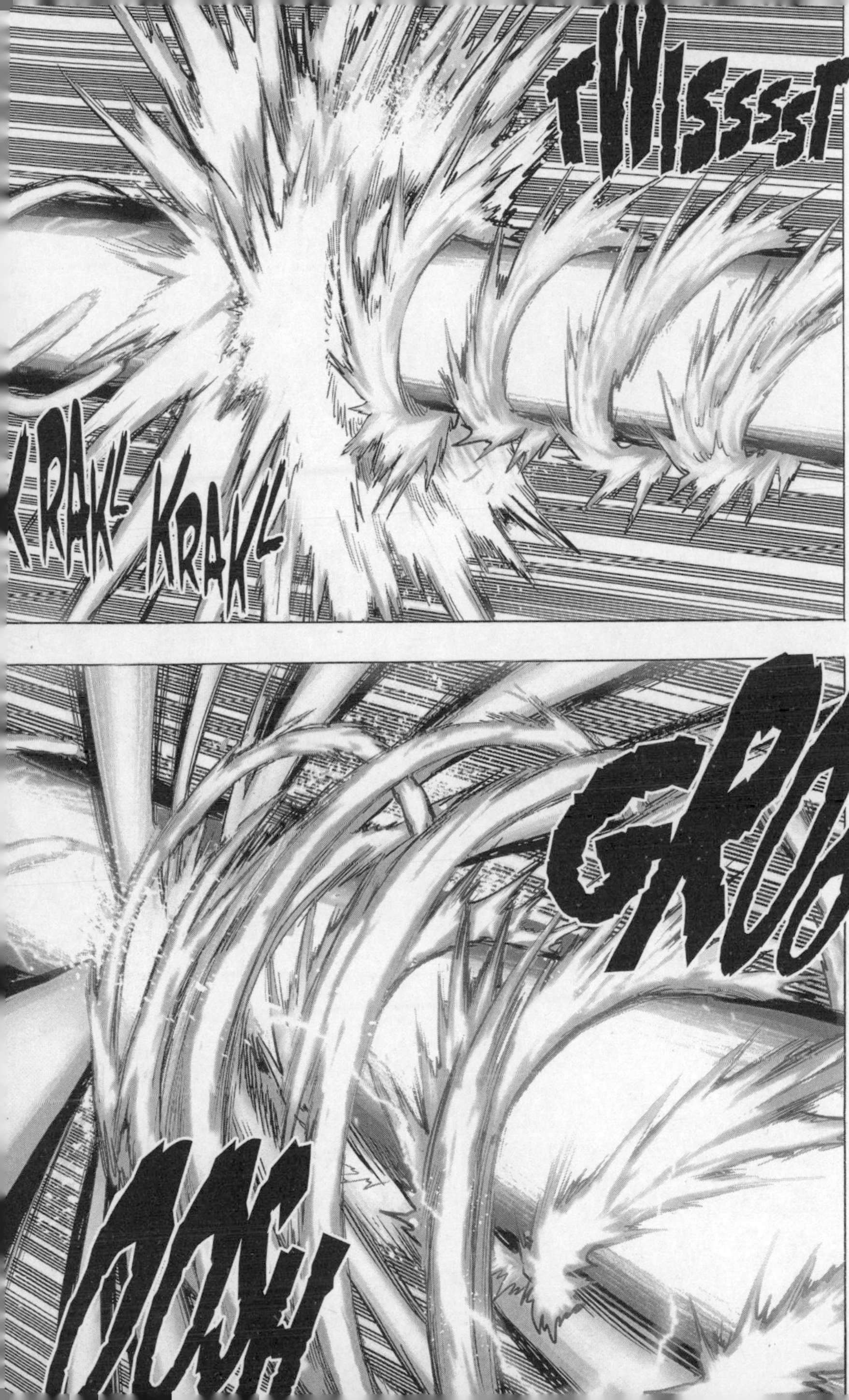
TWISSST
KRAKL KRAKL
GROO

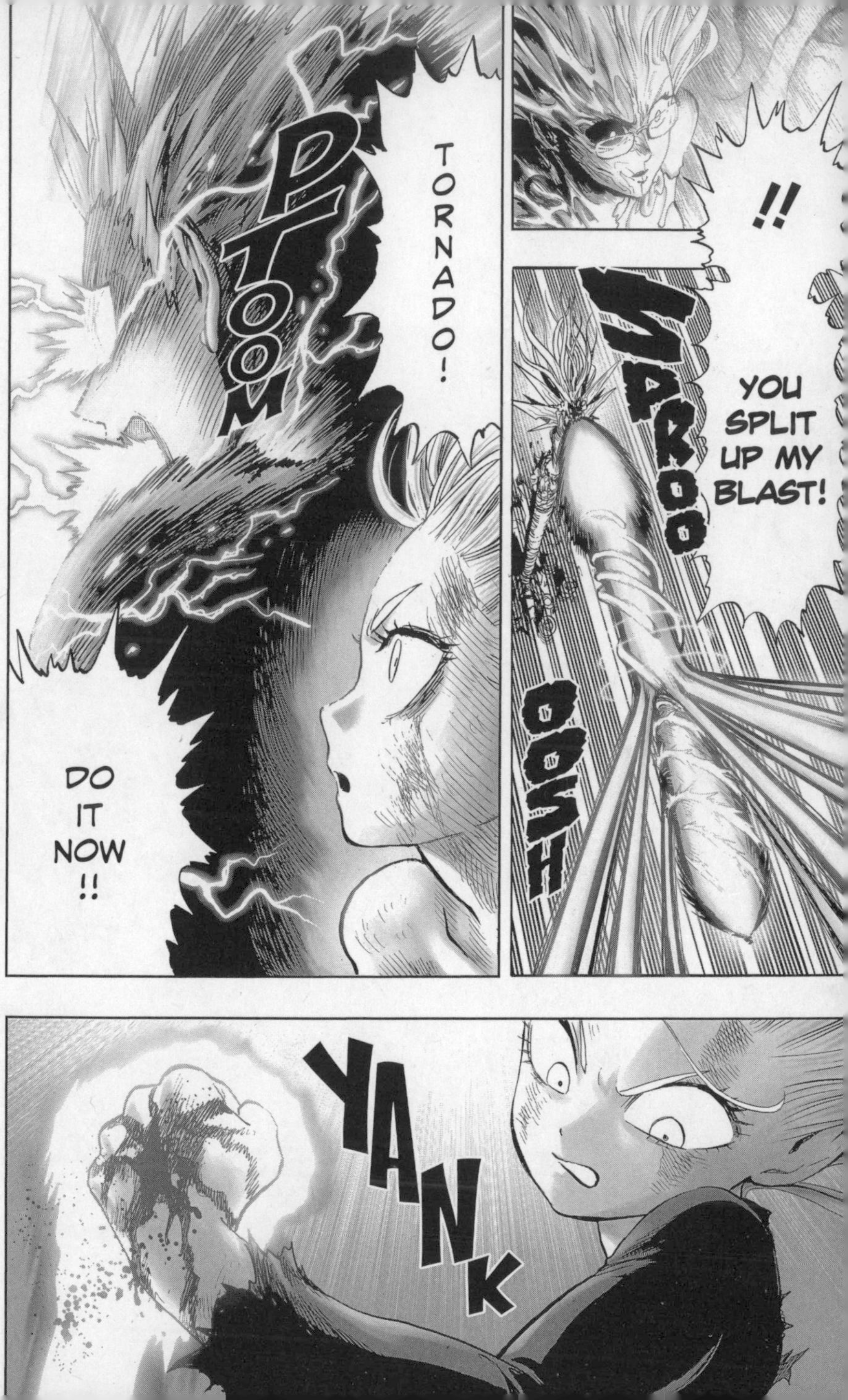
!!
SPROOOOSH
YOU SPLIT UP MY BLAST!
PTOOM
TORNADO!
DO IT NOW !!
YANK

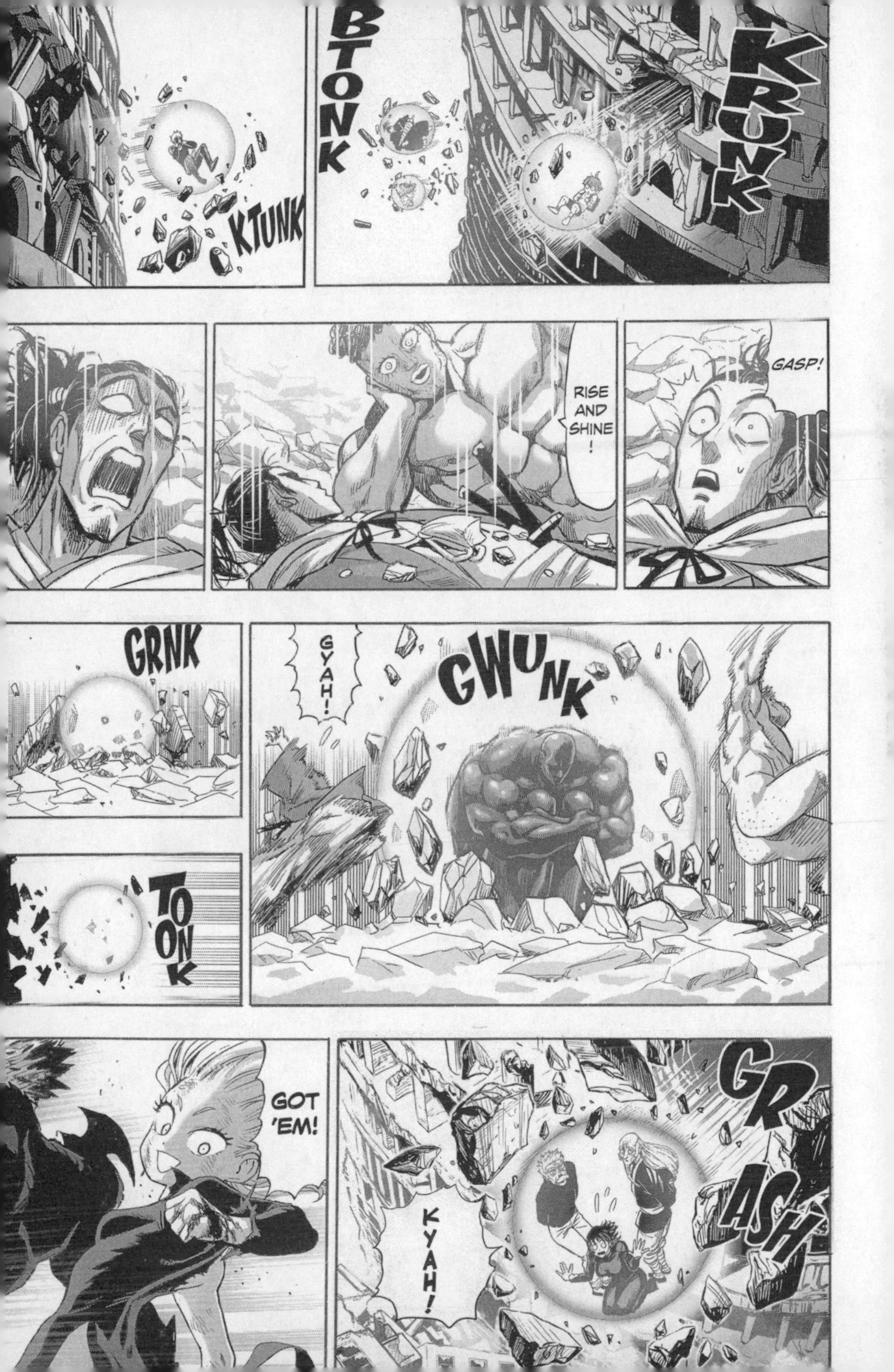
KRUNK
BTONK
KTUNK
GASP!
RISE AND SHINE!
GYAH!
GWUNK
GRNK
TOONK
GRASH
KYAH!
GOT 'EM!

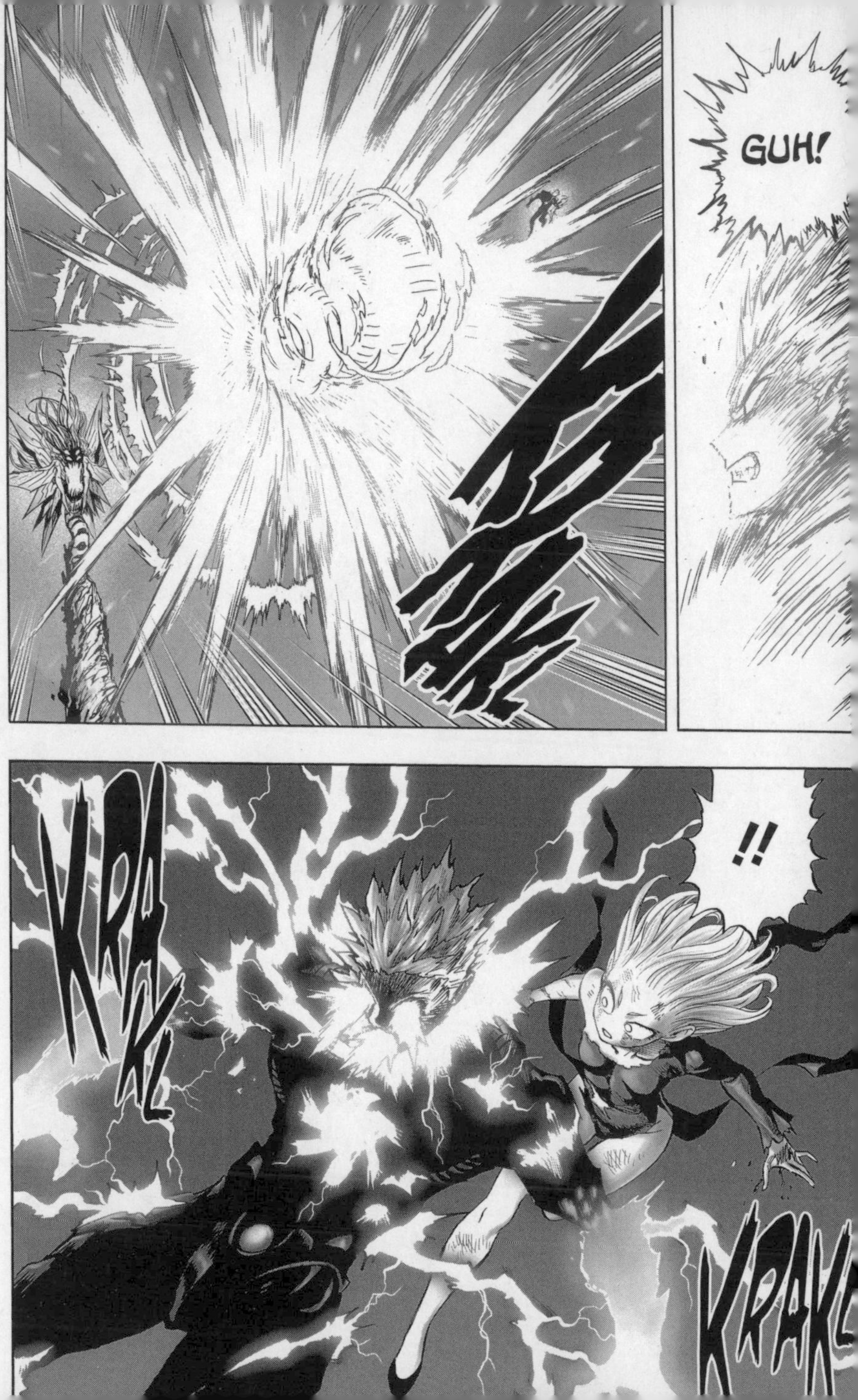
GUH!
!!
KRAKL
KRAKL

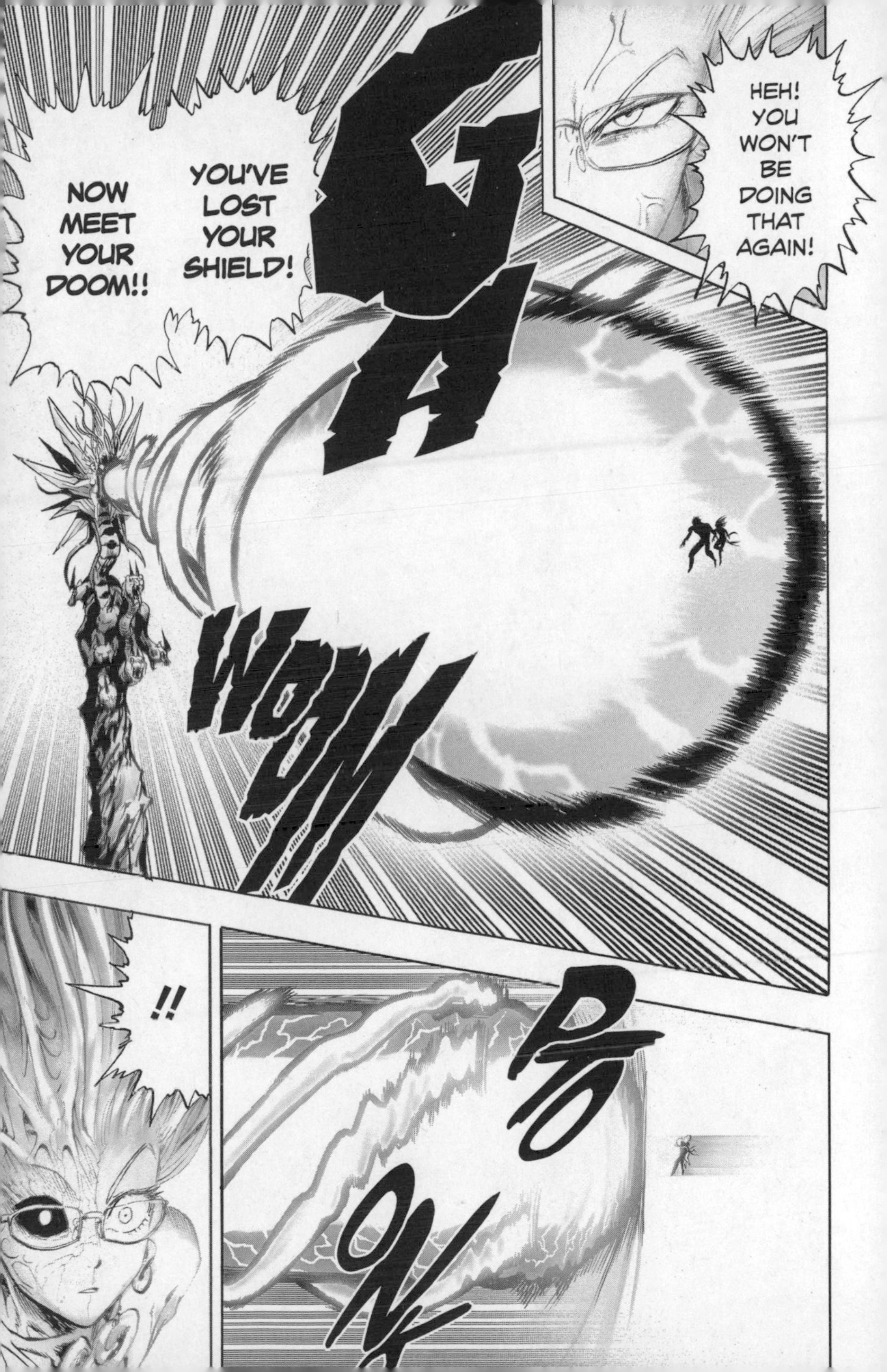
HEH! YOU WON'T BE DOING THAT AGAIN!
YOU'VE LOST YOUR SHIELD!
NOW MEET YOUR DOOM!!
WOOM
!!

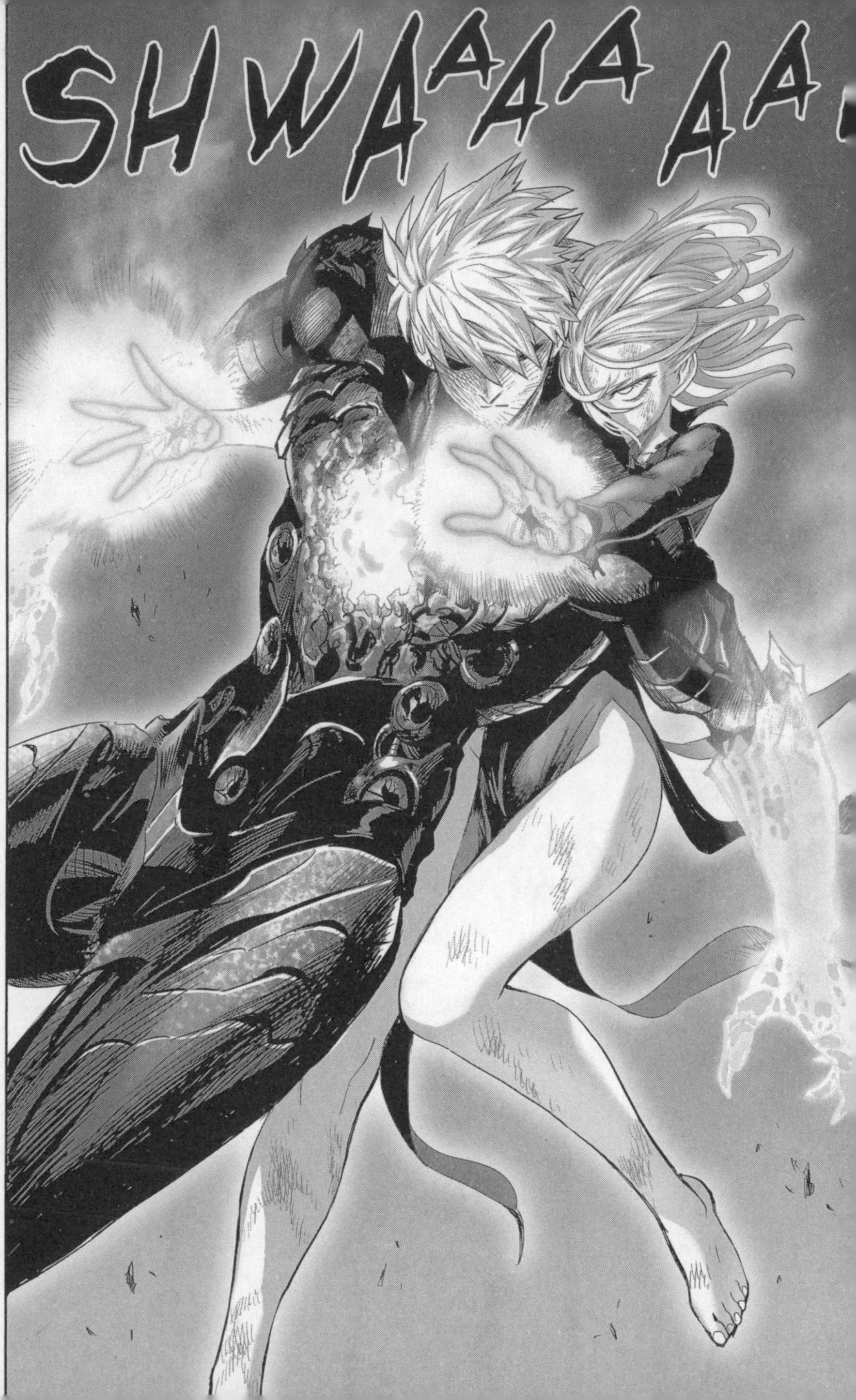
SHWAAAAAA

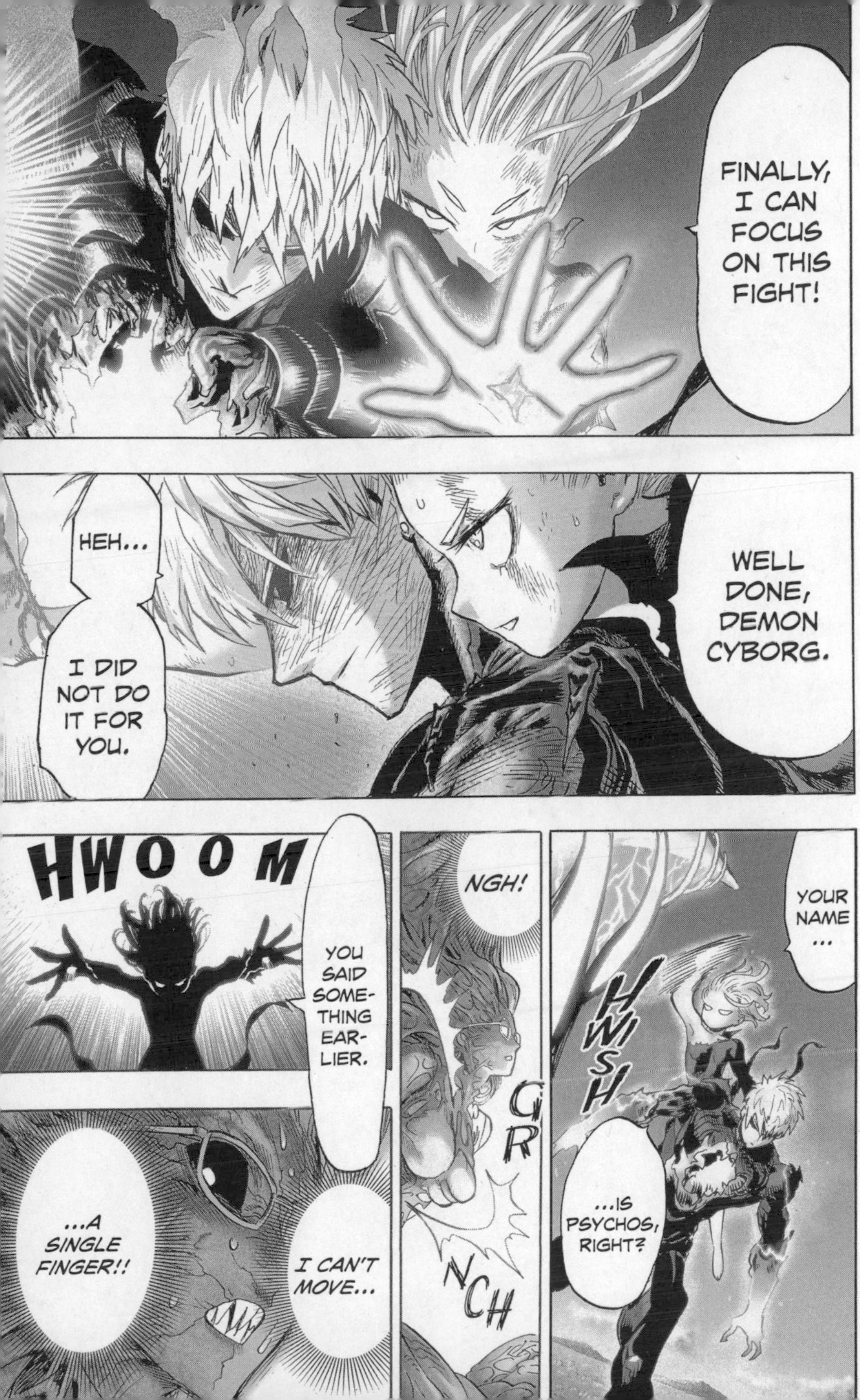
FINALLY, I CAN FOCUS ON THIS FIGHT!
WELL DONE, DEMON CYBORG.
HEH...
I DID NOT DO IT FOR YOU.
YOUR NAME ...
HWISH
...IS PSYCHOS, RIGHT?
NGH!
GR
NCH
HWOOM
YOU SAID SOME-THING EAR-LIER.
I CAN'T MOVE...
...A SINGLE FINGER!!

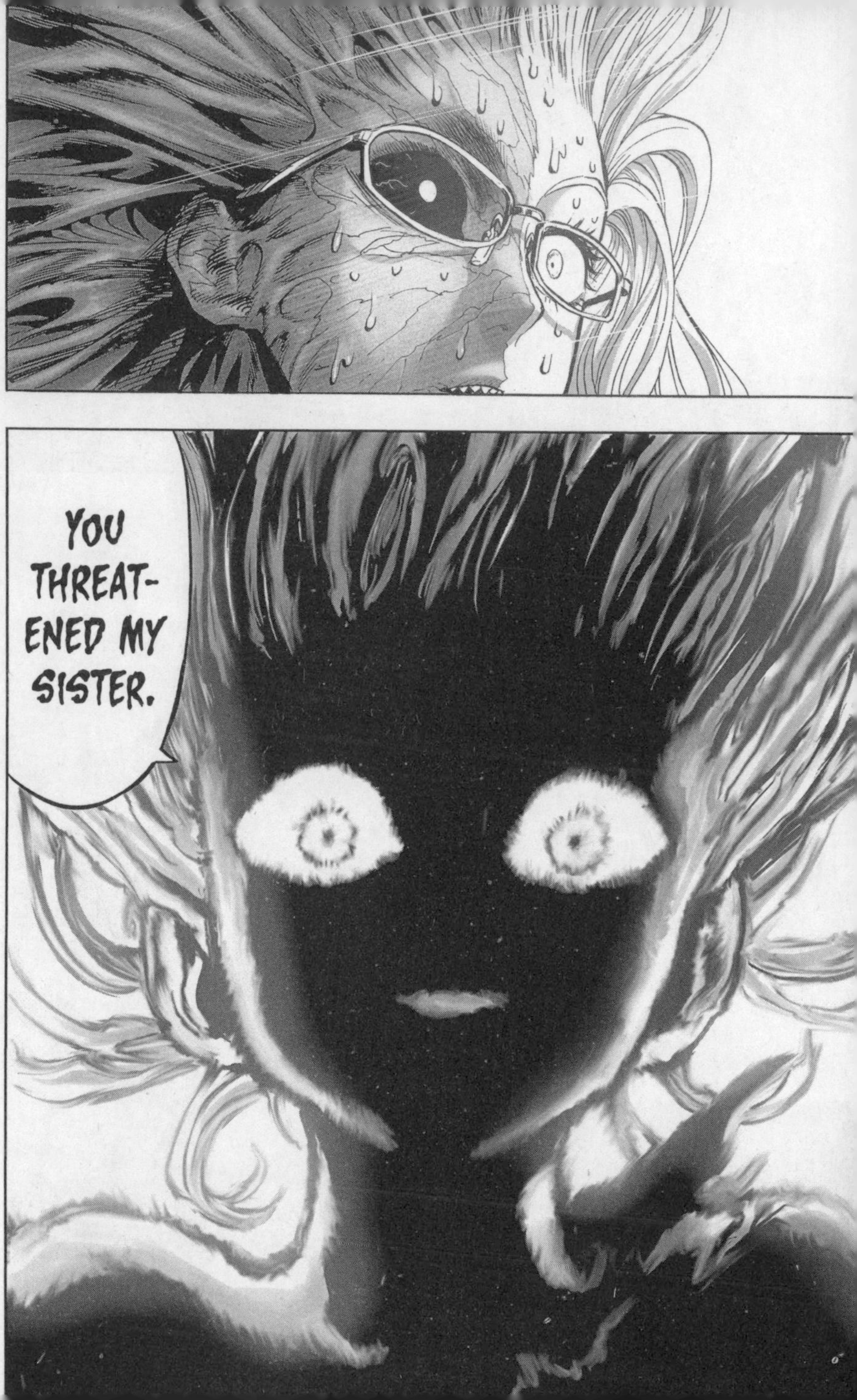
YOU THREAT-ENED MY SISTER.

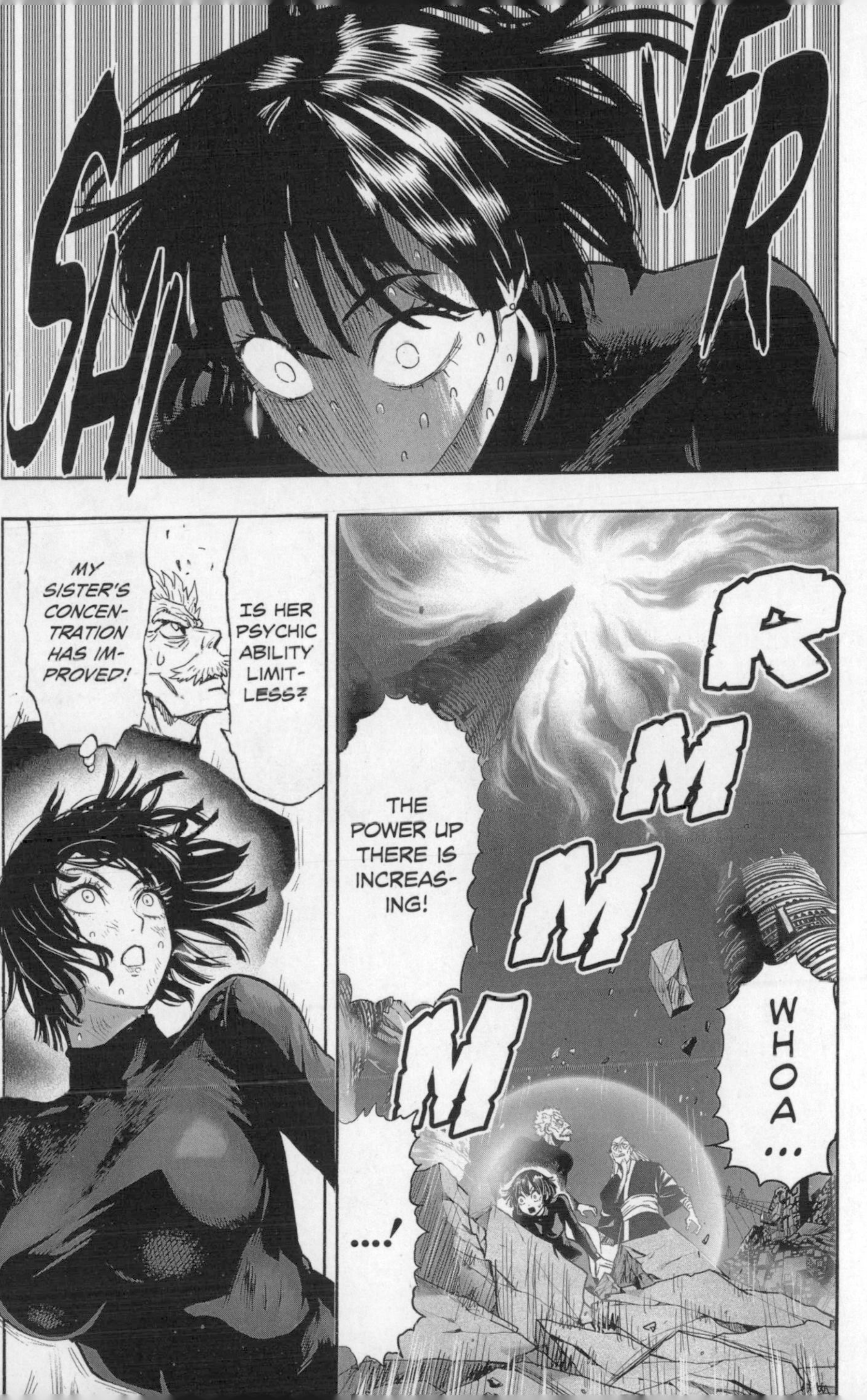
SHIVER
RMMMM
THE POWER UP THERE IS INCREAS-ING!
WHOA...
...!
IS HER PSYCHIC ABILITY LIMIT-LESS?
MY SISTER'S CONCEN-TRATION HAS IM-PROVED!

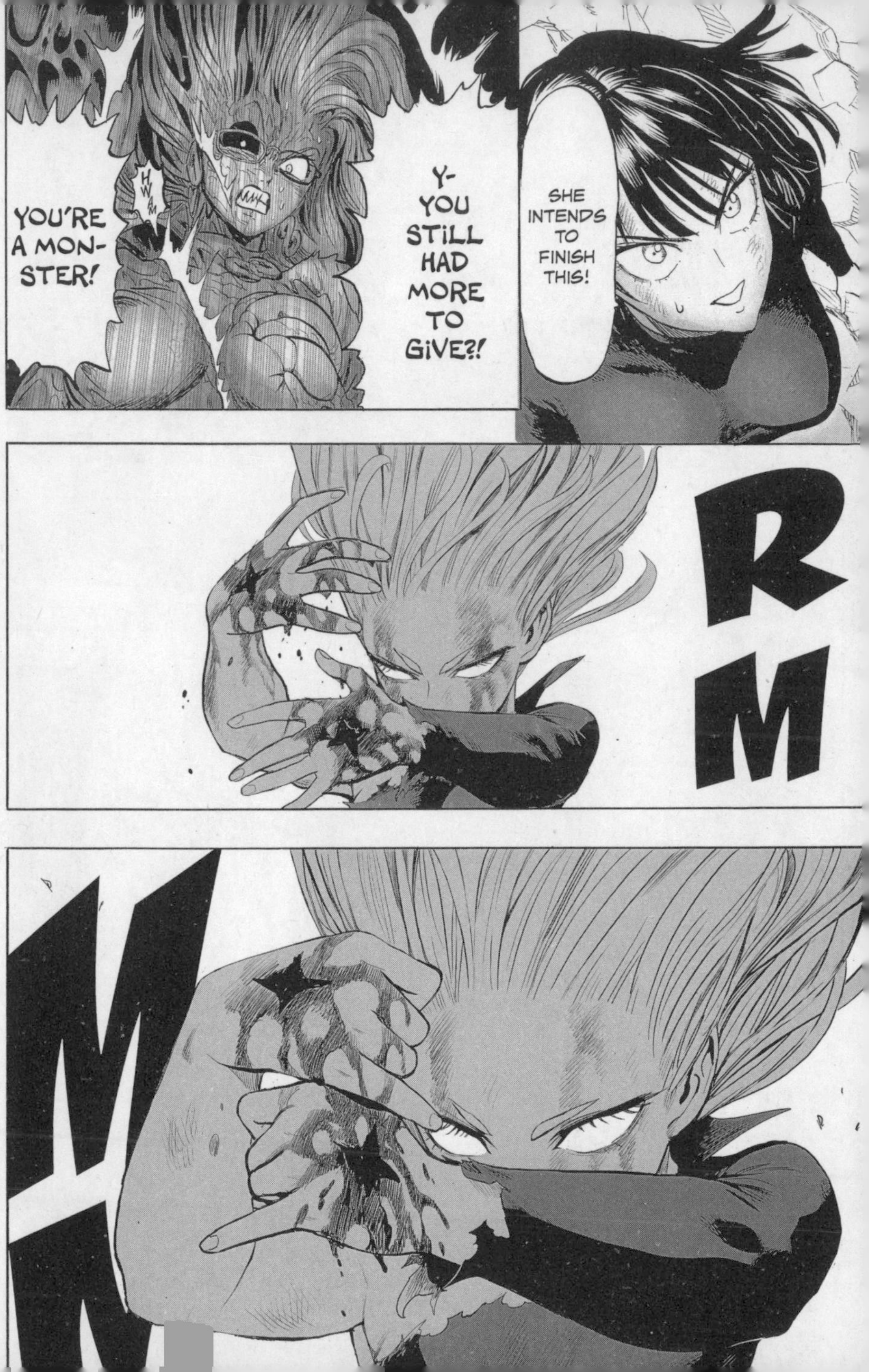
SHE INTENDS TO FINISH THIS!
Y- YOU STILL HAD MORE TO GIVE?!
HWAM
YOU'RE A MONSTER!
RM
M

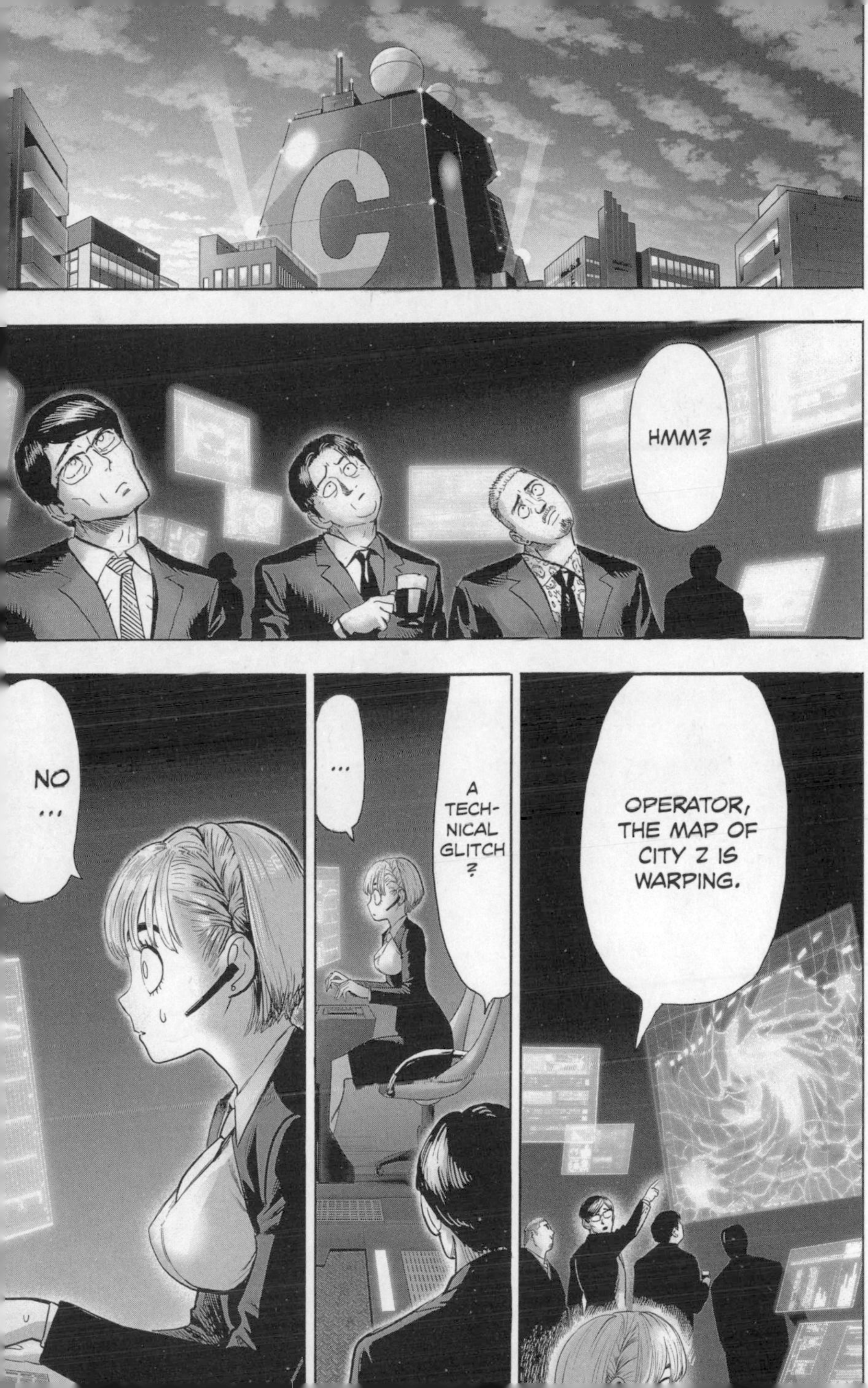
HMM?
OPERATOR, THE MAP OF CITY Z IS WARPING.
A TECH-NICAL GLITCH?
...
NO ...

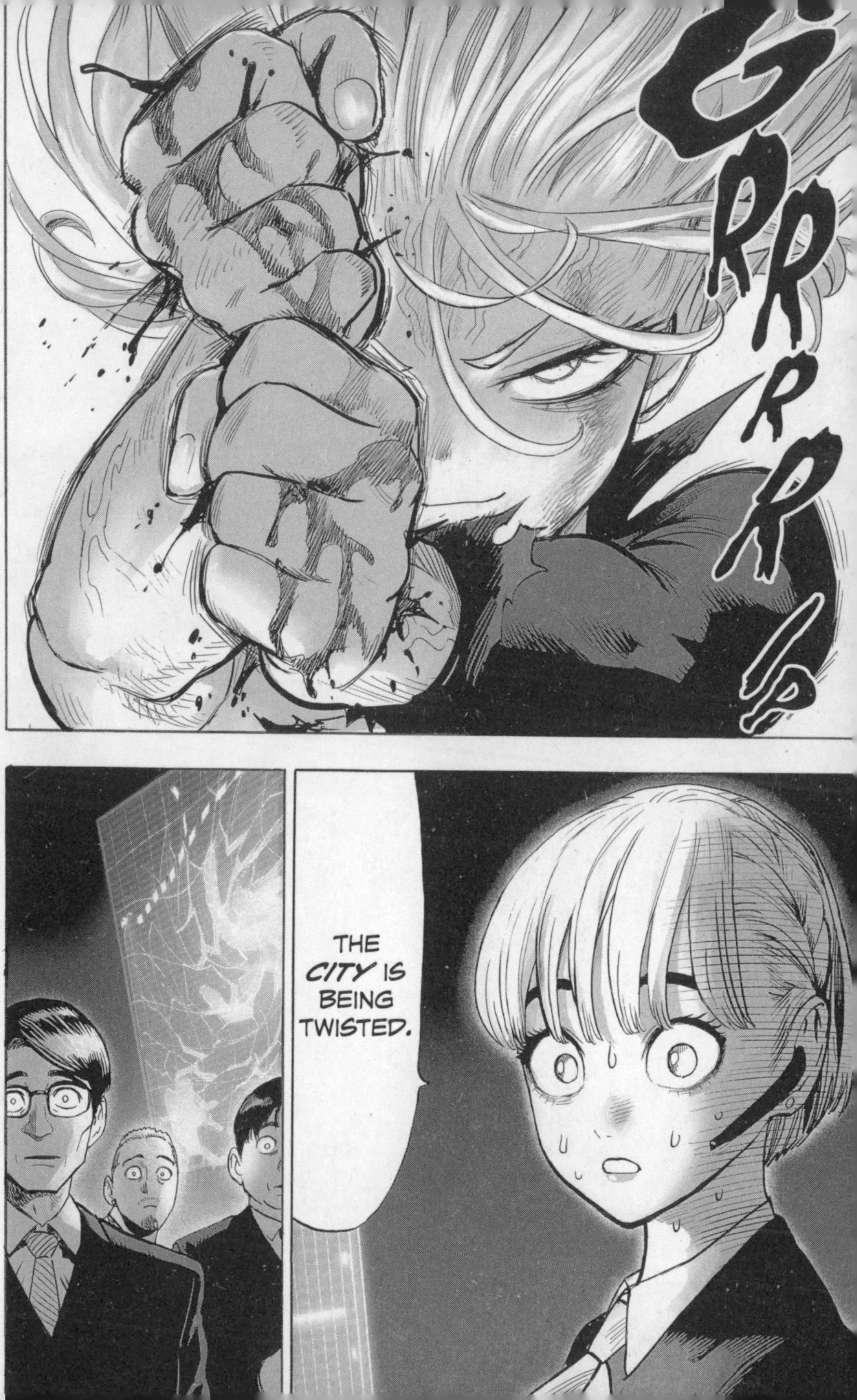
GRRRRRIP
THE CITY IS BEING TWISTED.

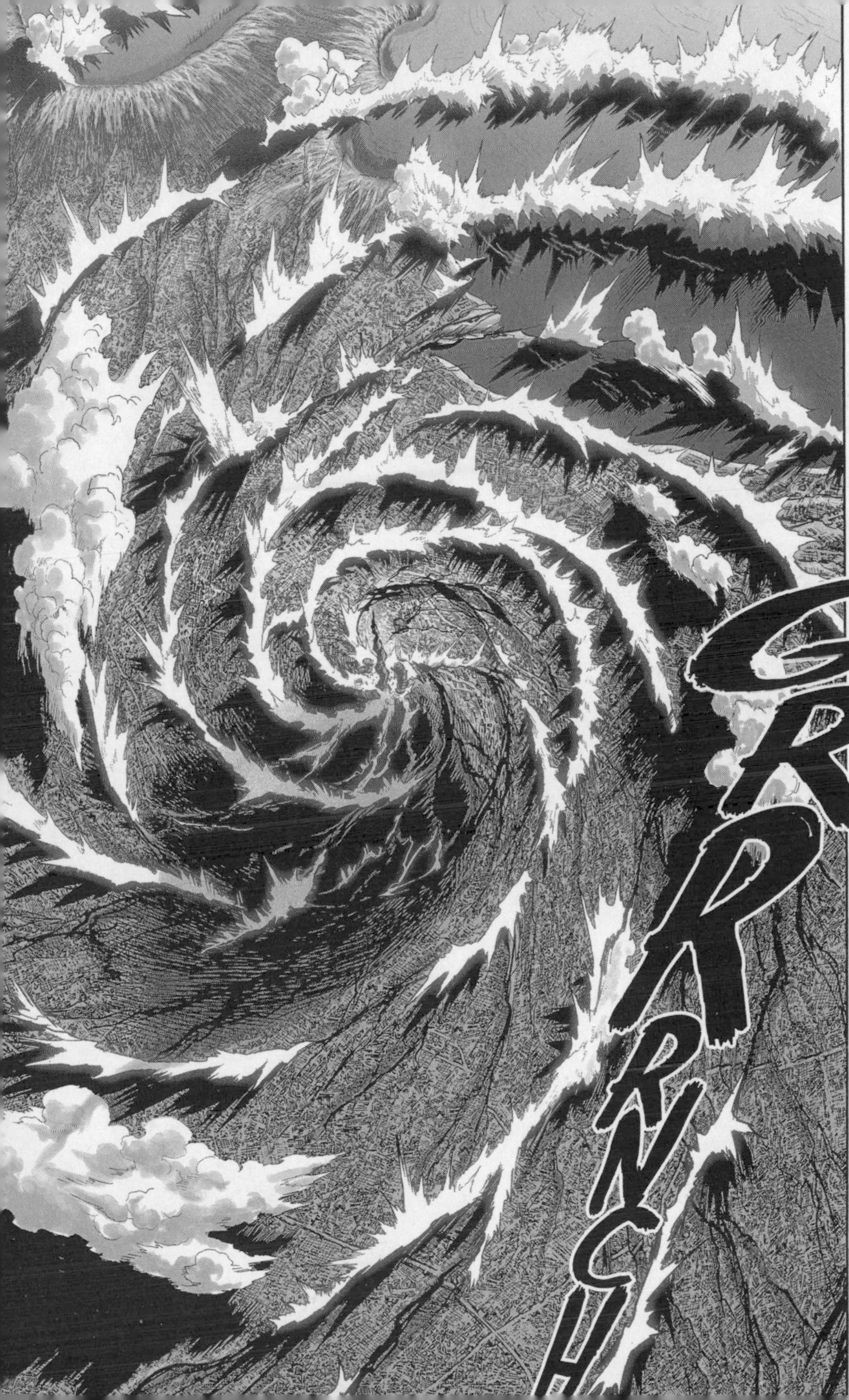
GRRRNCH

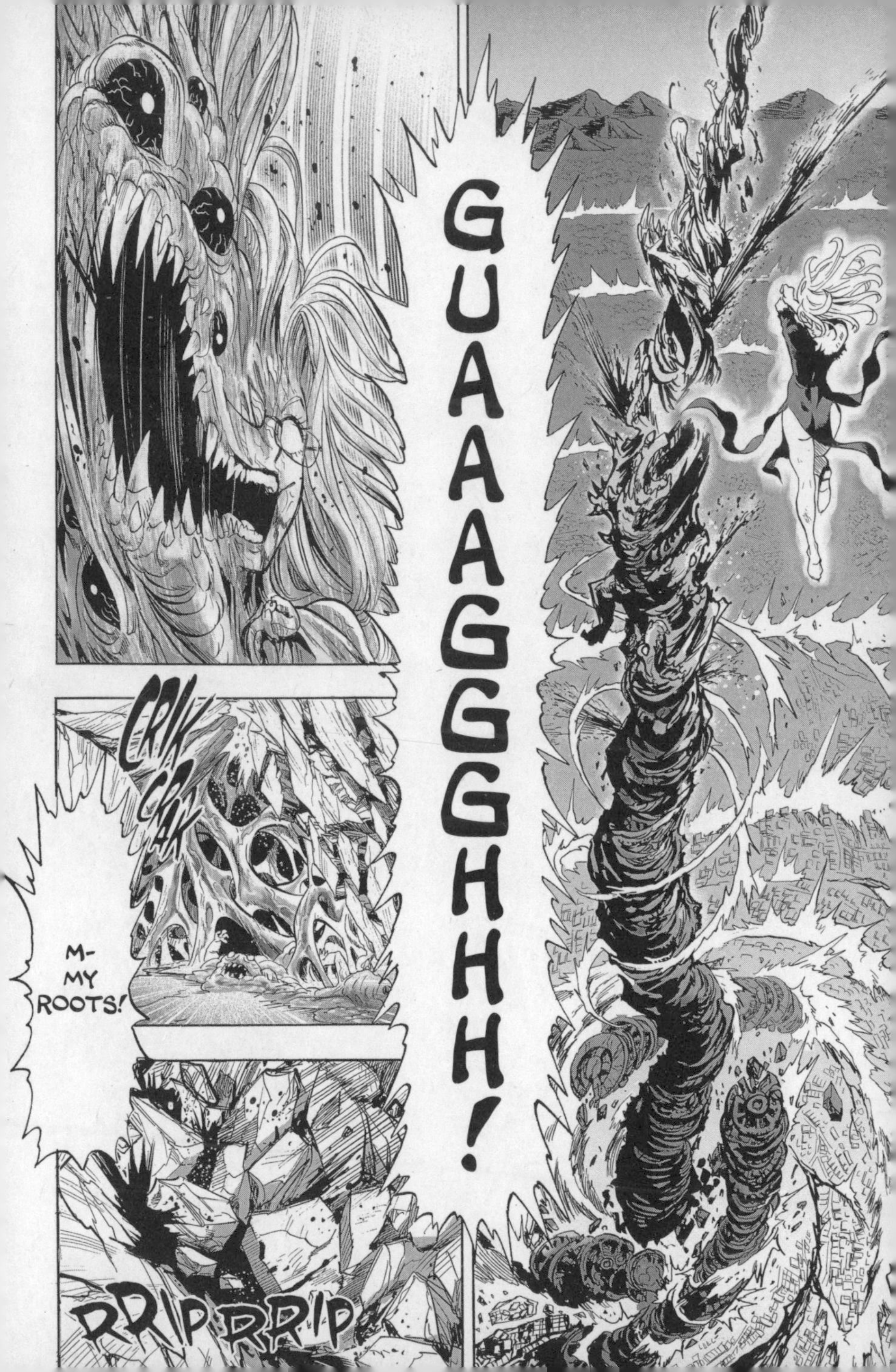
GUAAGGGH!
CRIK CRAK
M- MY ROOTS!
RRIP RRIP

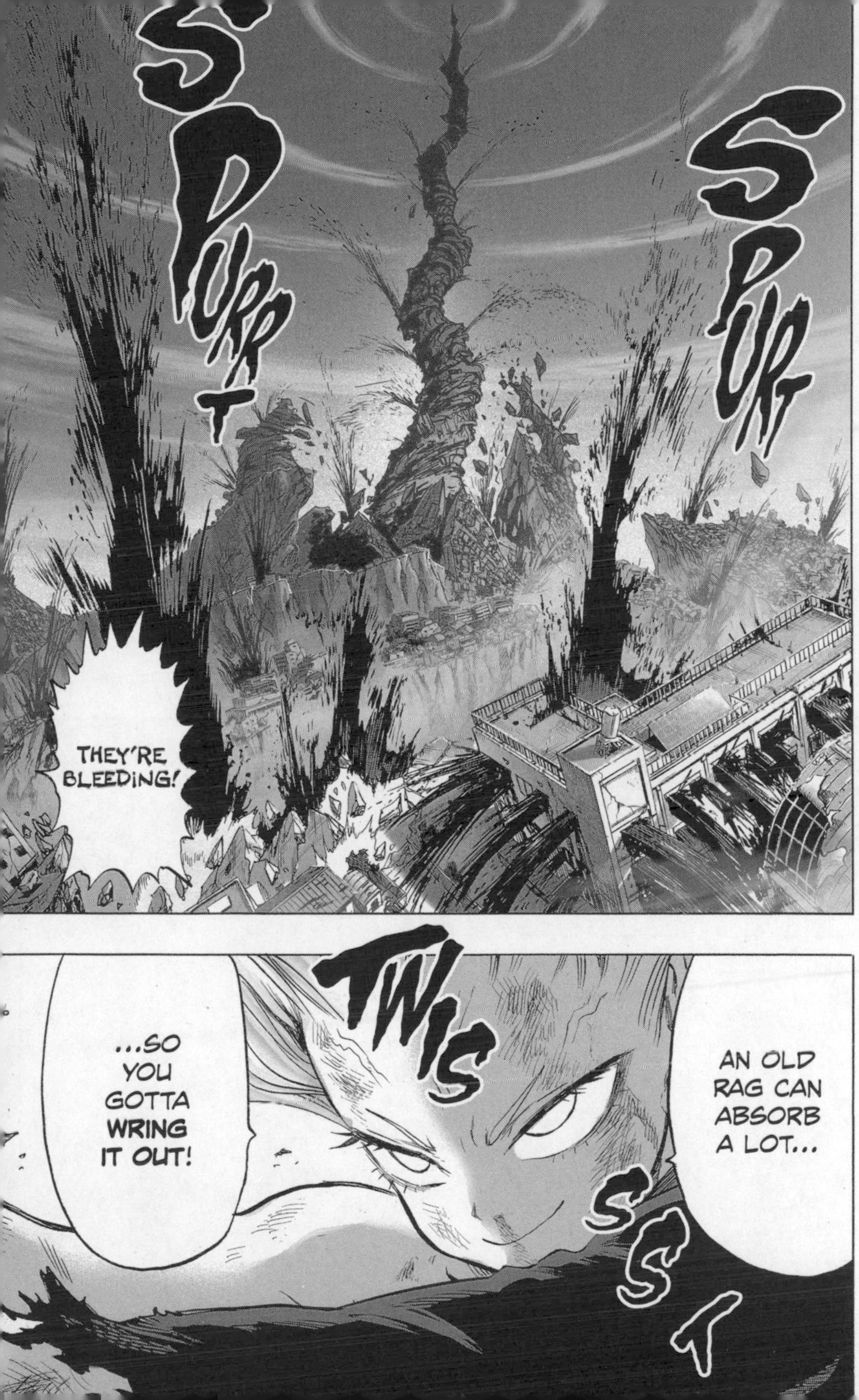
SPURT
SPURRT
THEY'RE BLEEDING!
AN OLD RAG CAN ABSORB A LOT...
TWISSSST
...SO YOU GOTTA WRING IT OUT!

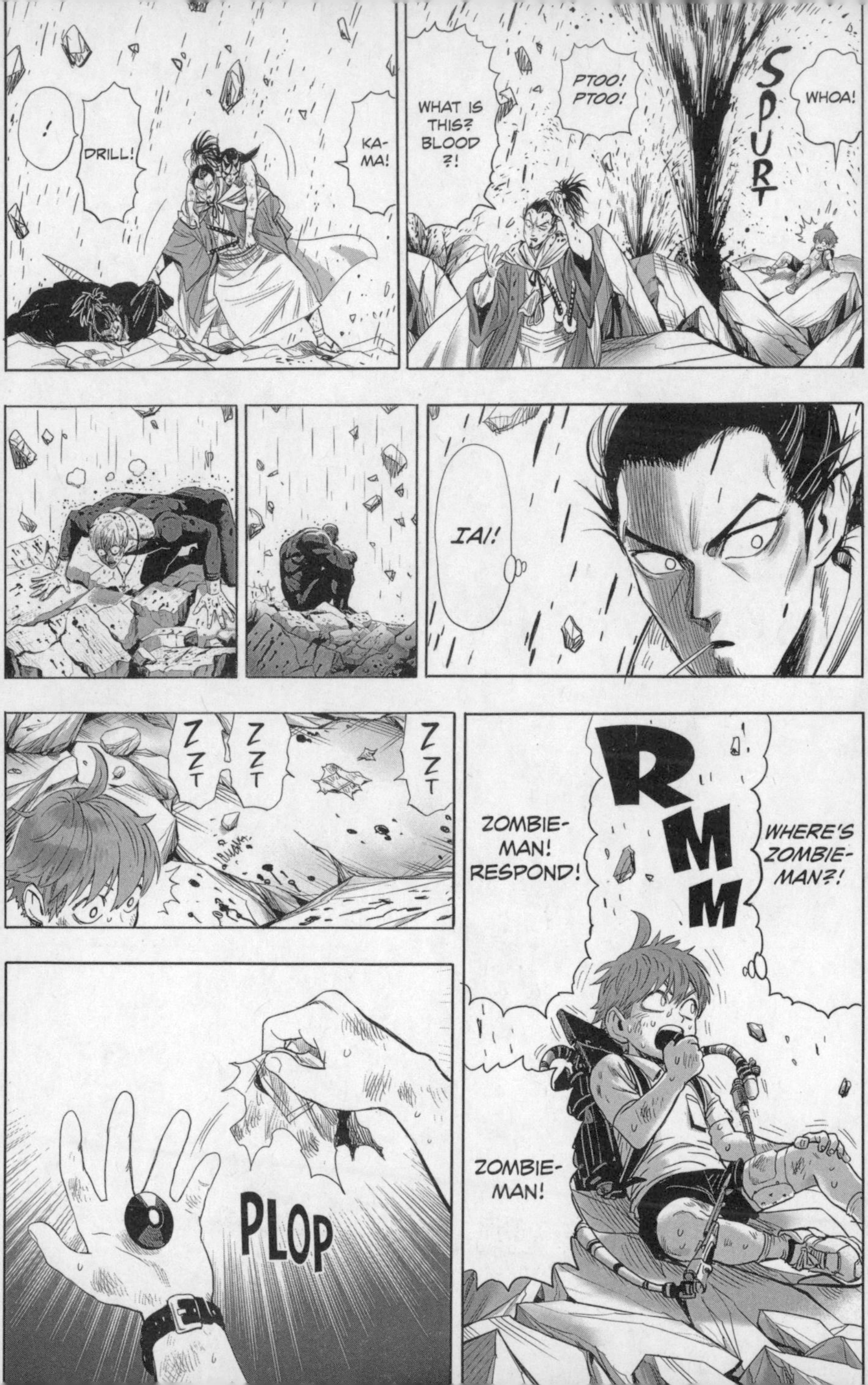
WHOA!
SPURT
PTOO! PTOO!
WHAT IS THIS? BLOOD?!
KAMA!
DRILL!
!
IAI!
RMM
WHERE'S ZOMBIE-MAN?!
ZOMBIE-MAN! RESPOND!
ZOMBIE-MAN!
ZZT
ZZT
ZZT
PLOP

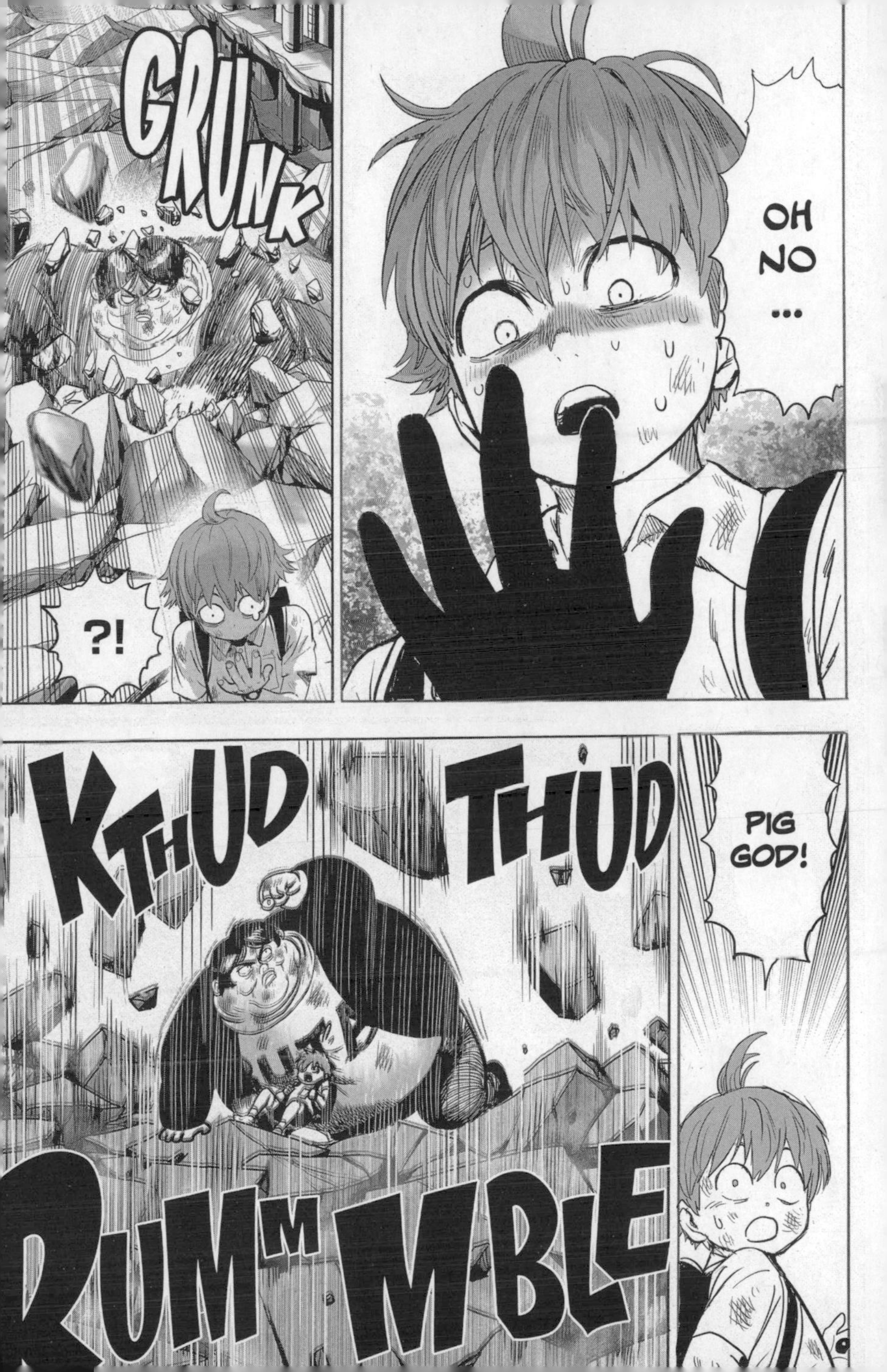
OH NO ...
GRUNK
?!
PIG GOD!
KTHUD
THUD
RUMMMBLE

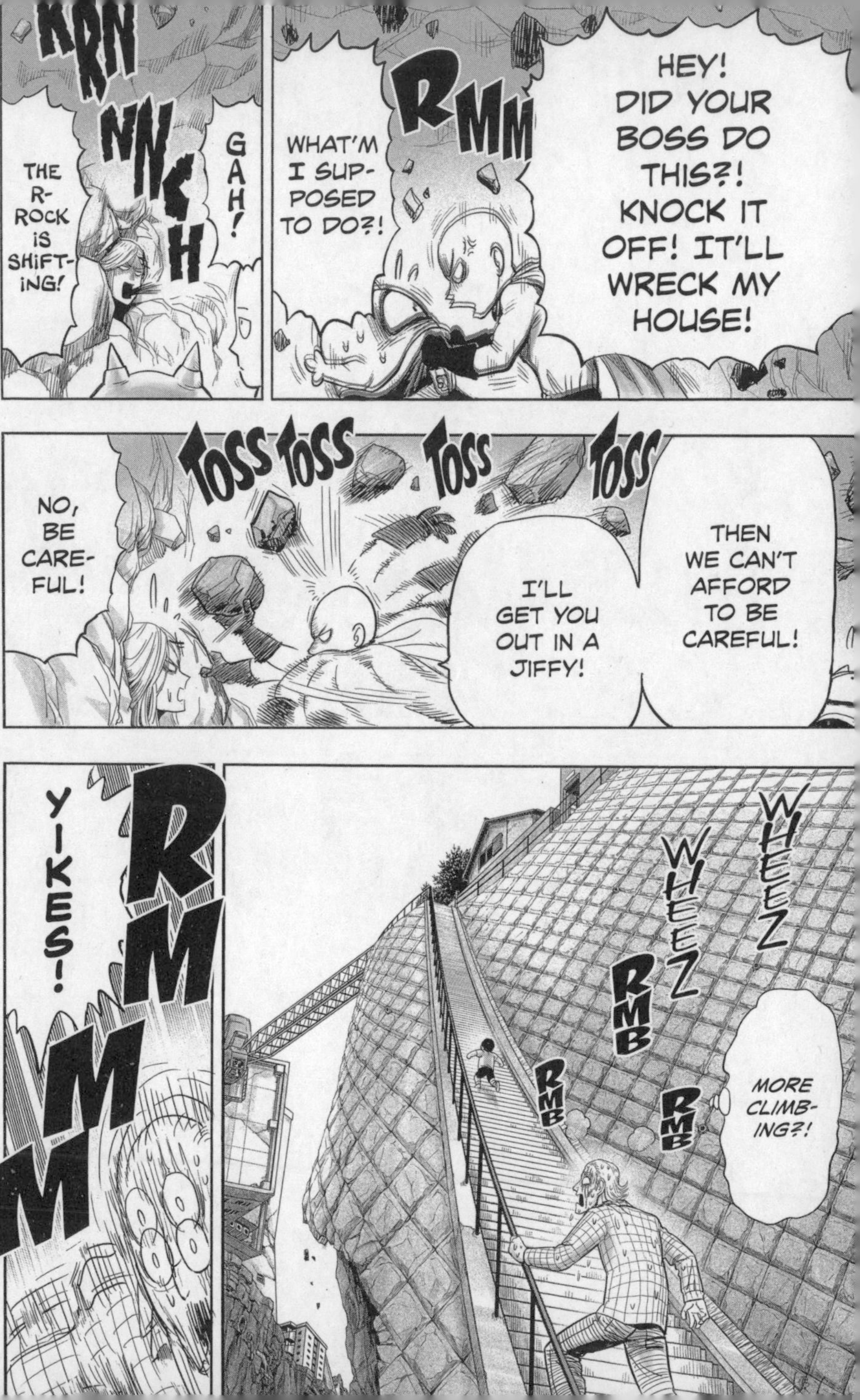
RMM
HEY! DID YOUR BOSS DO THIS?! KNOCK IT OFF! IT'LL WRECK MY HOUSE!
WHAT'M I SUP-POSED TO DO?!
KRNNNKH
GAH!
THE R-ROCK IS SHIFT-ING!
TOSS TOSS TOSS TOSS
THEN WE CAN'T AFFORD TO BE CAREFUL!
I'LL GET YOU OUT IN A JIFFY!
NO, BE CARE-FUL!
WHEEZ
WHEEZ
RMB
RMB
RMB
MORE CLIMB-ING?!
RMMMM
YIKES!

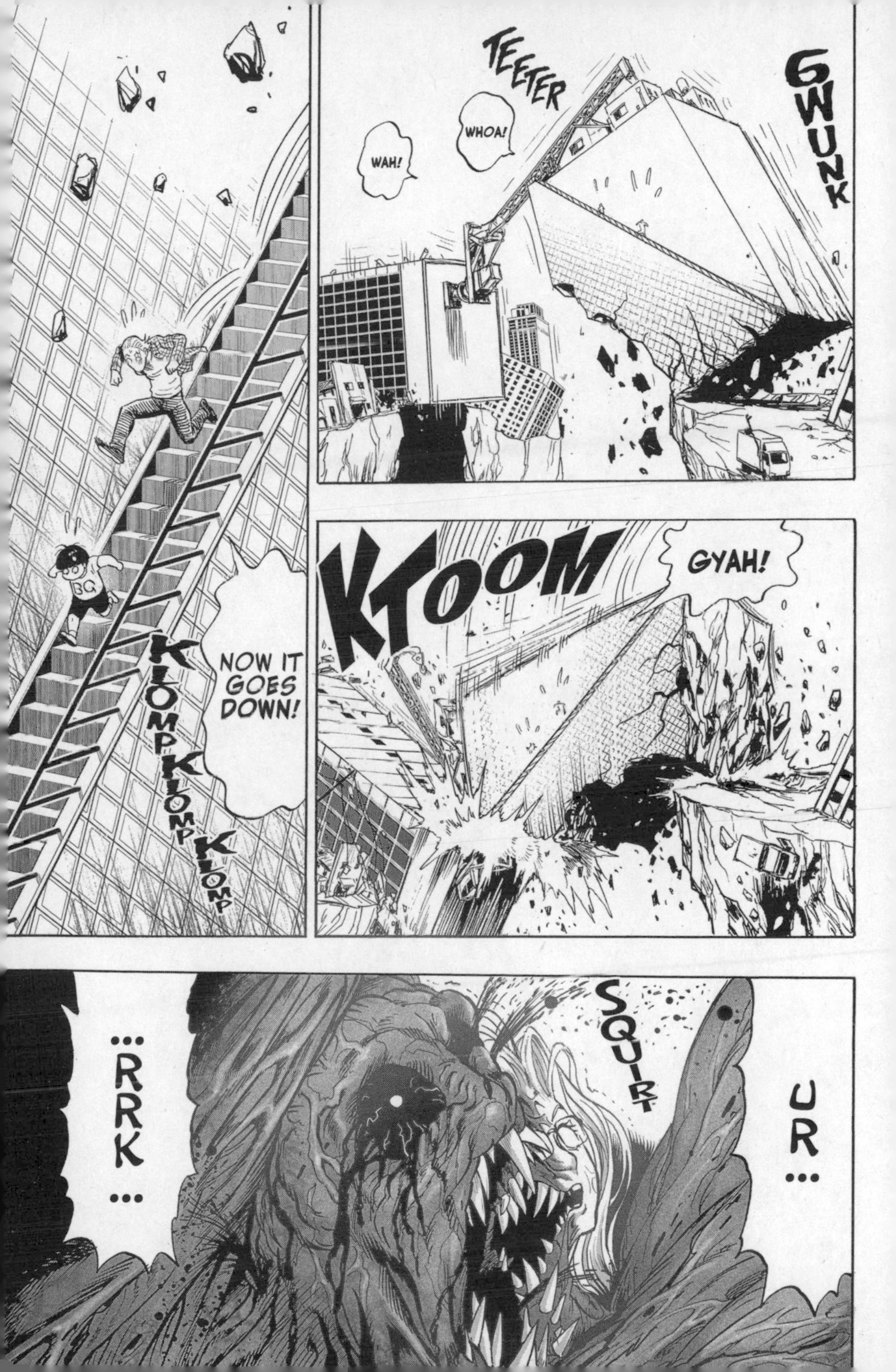
GWUNK
TEETER
WHOA!
WAH!
GYAH!
KTOOM
NOW IT GOES DOWN!
KLOMP KLOMP KLOMP
UR...
SQUIRT
...RRK...

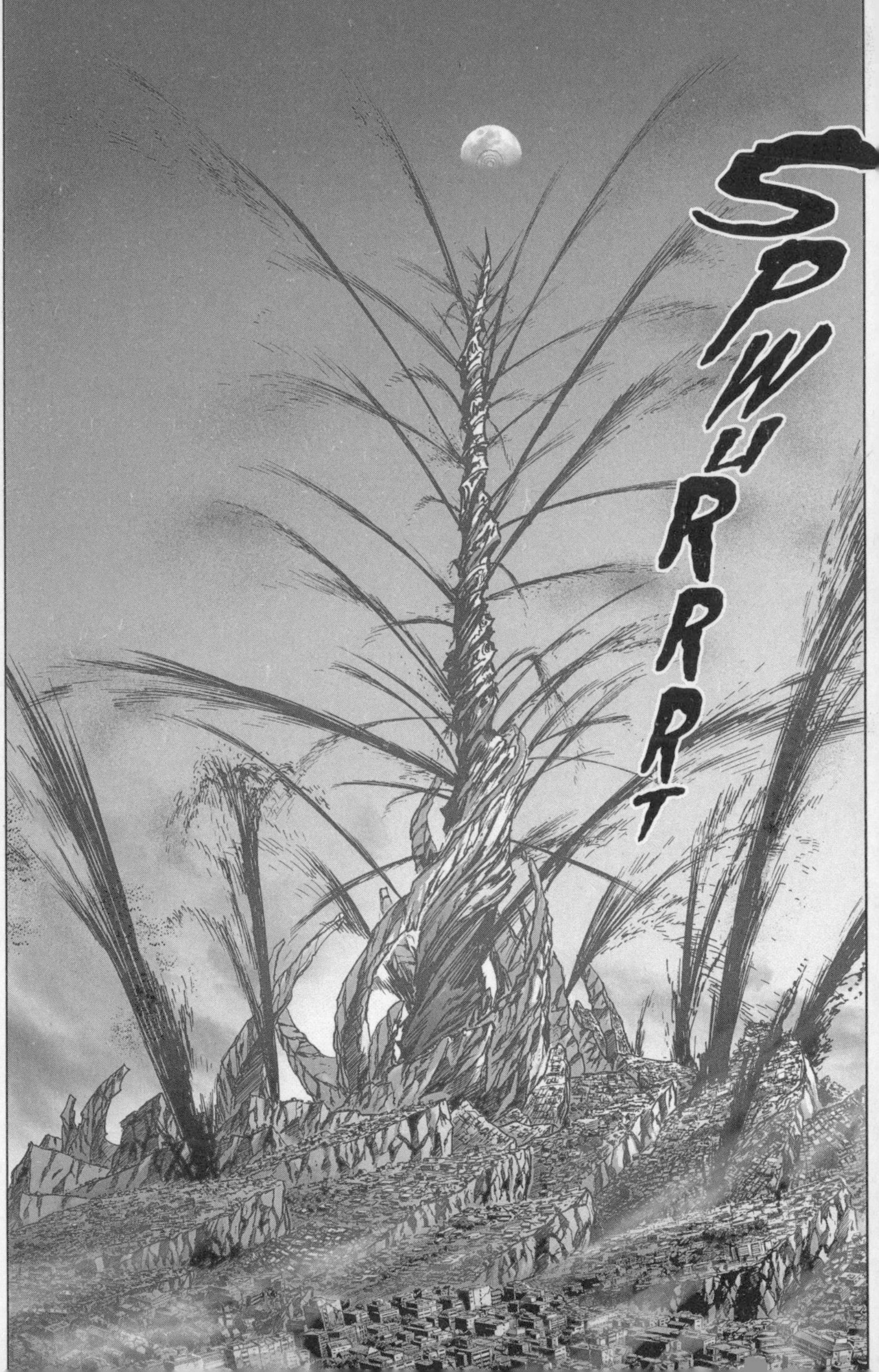
SPWURRRT

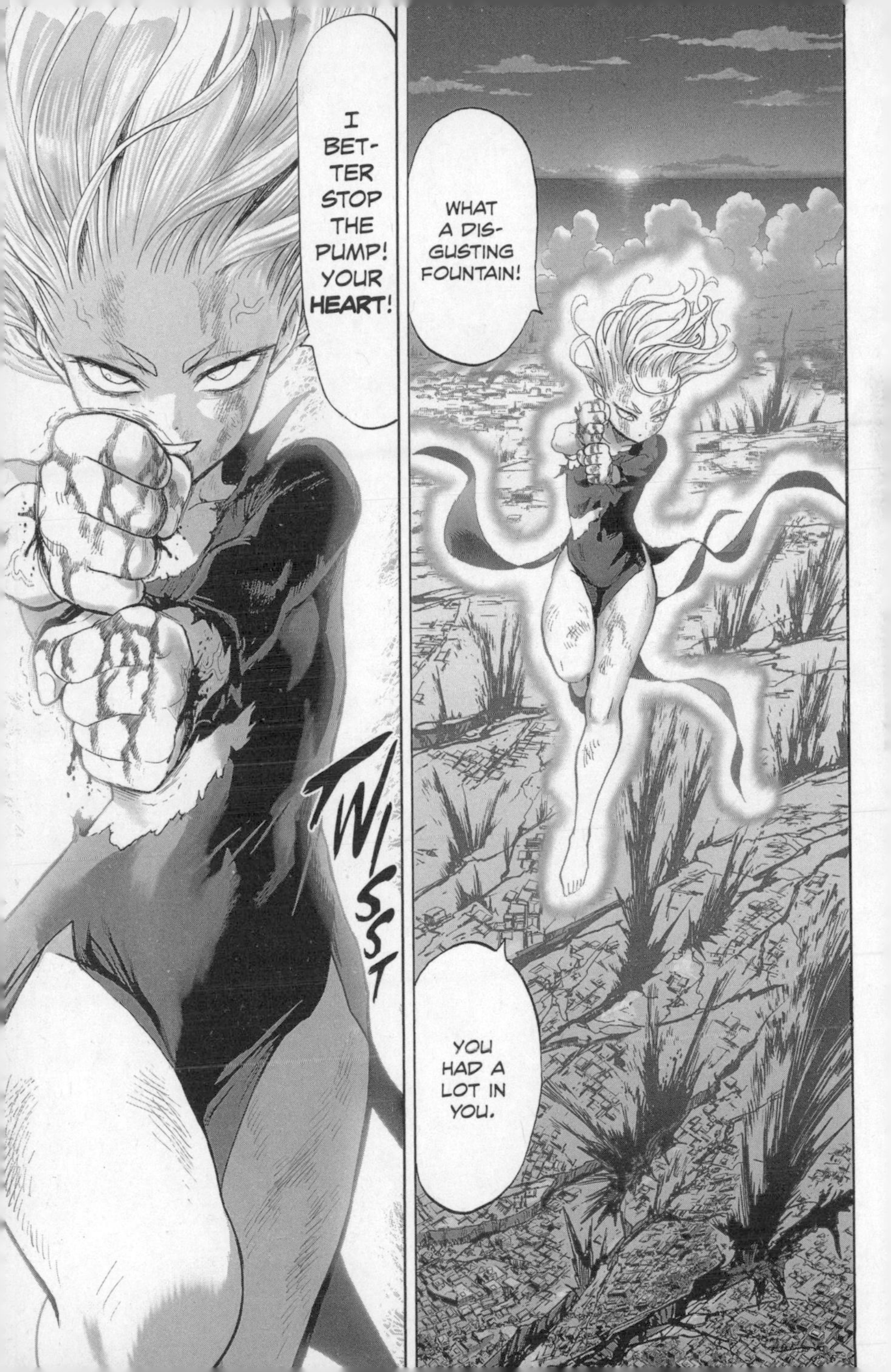
WHAT A DISGUSTING FOUNTAIN!
YOU HAD A LOT IN YOU.
I BETTER STOP THE PUMP! YOUR HEART!
TWISSST

PUNCH 139: GIANT BARRIER

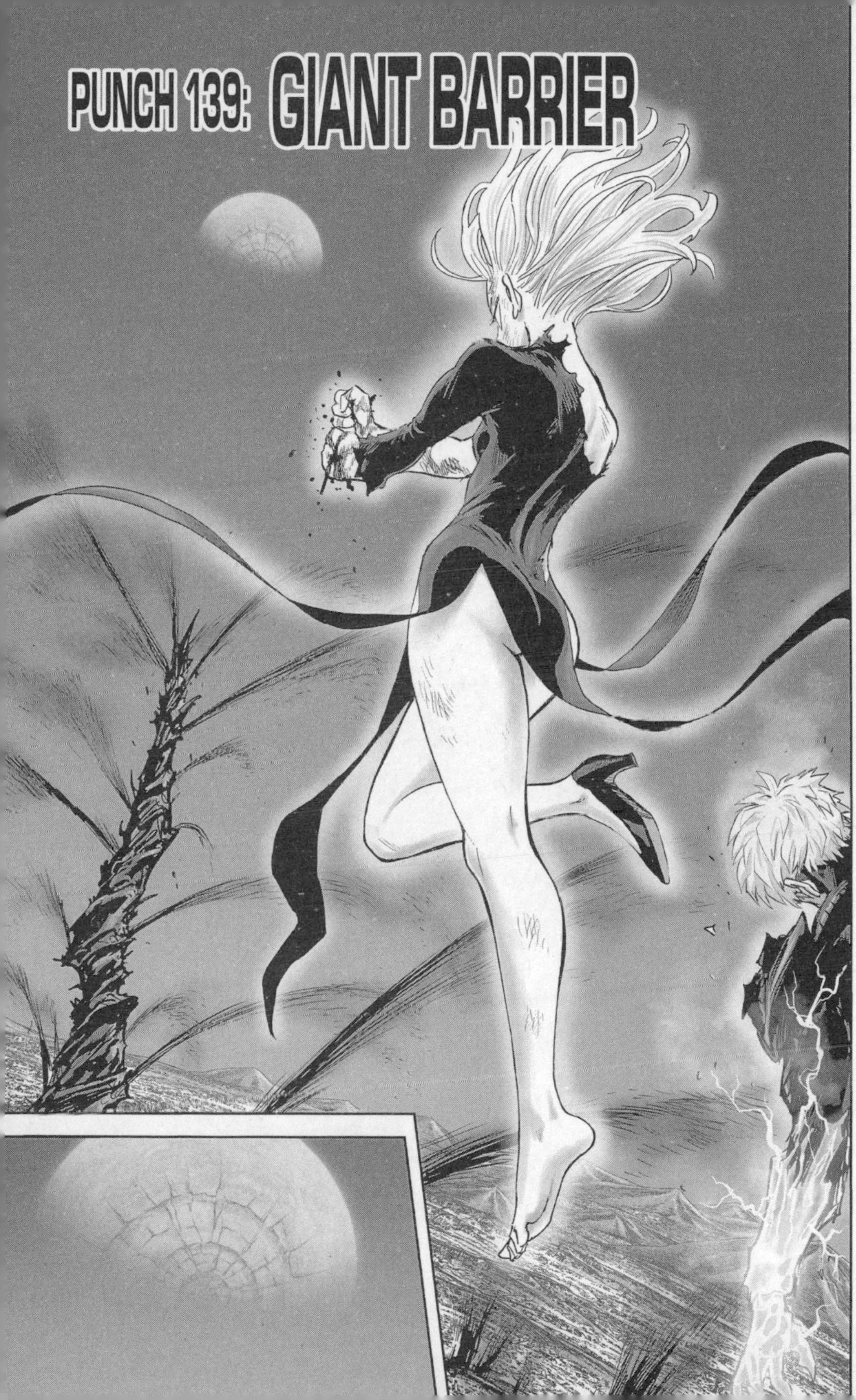

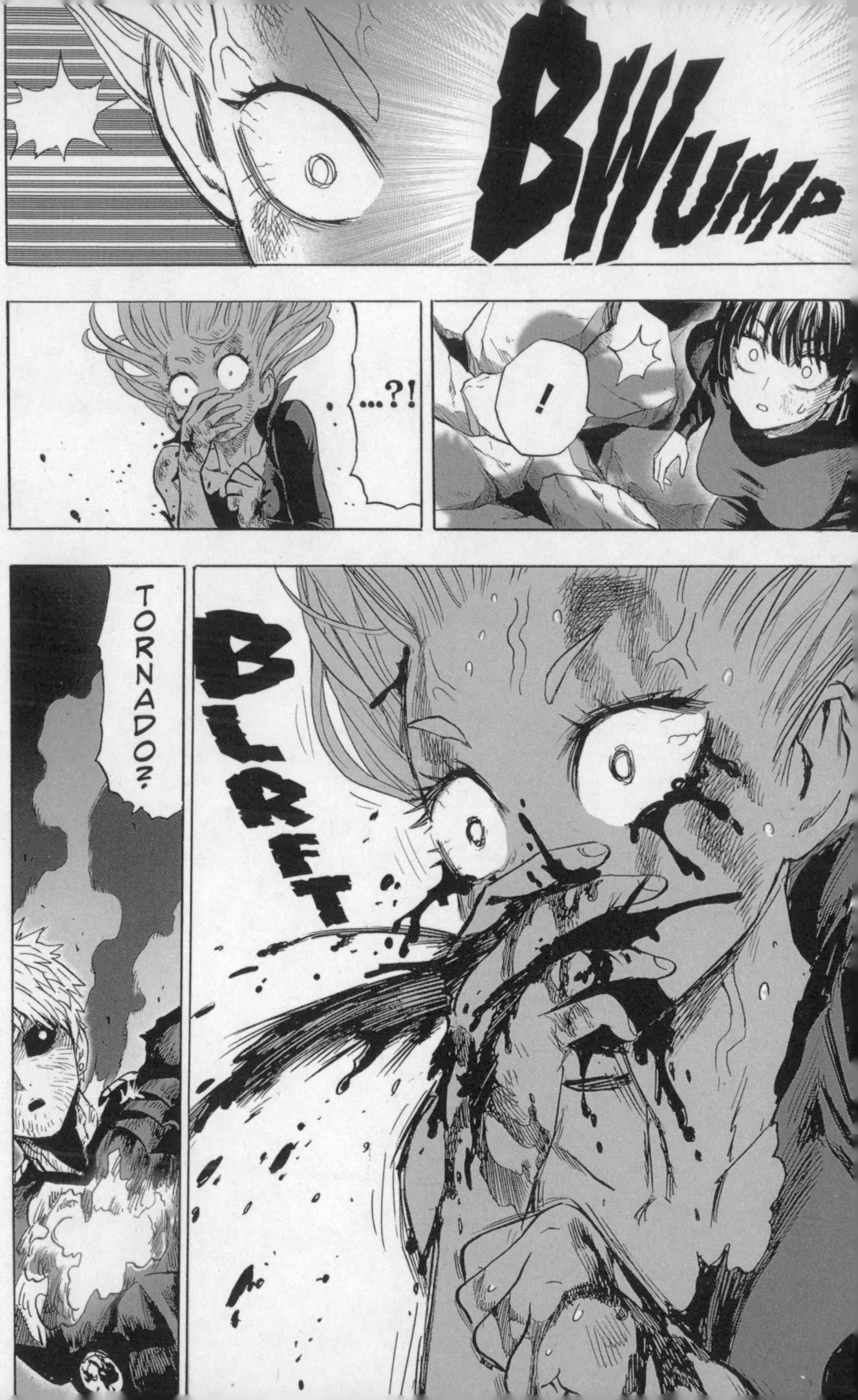
BWUMP
!
...?!
BLRFT
TORNADO?

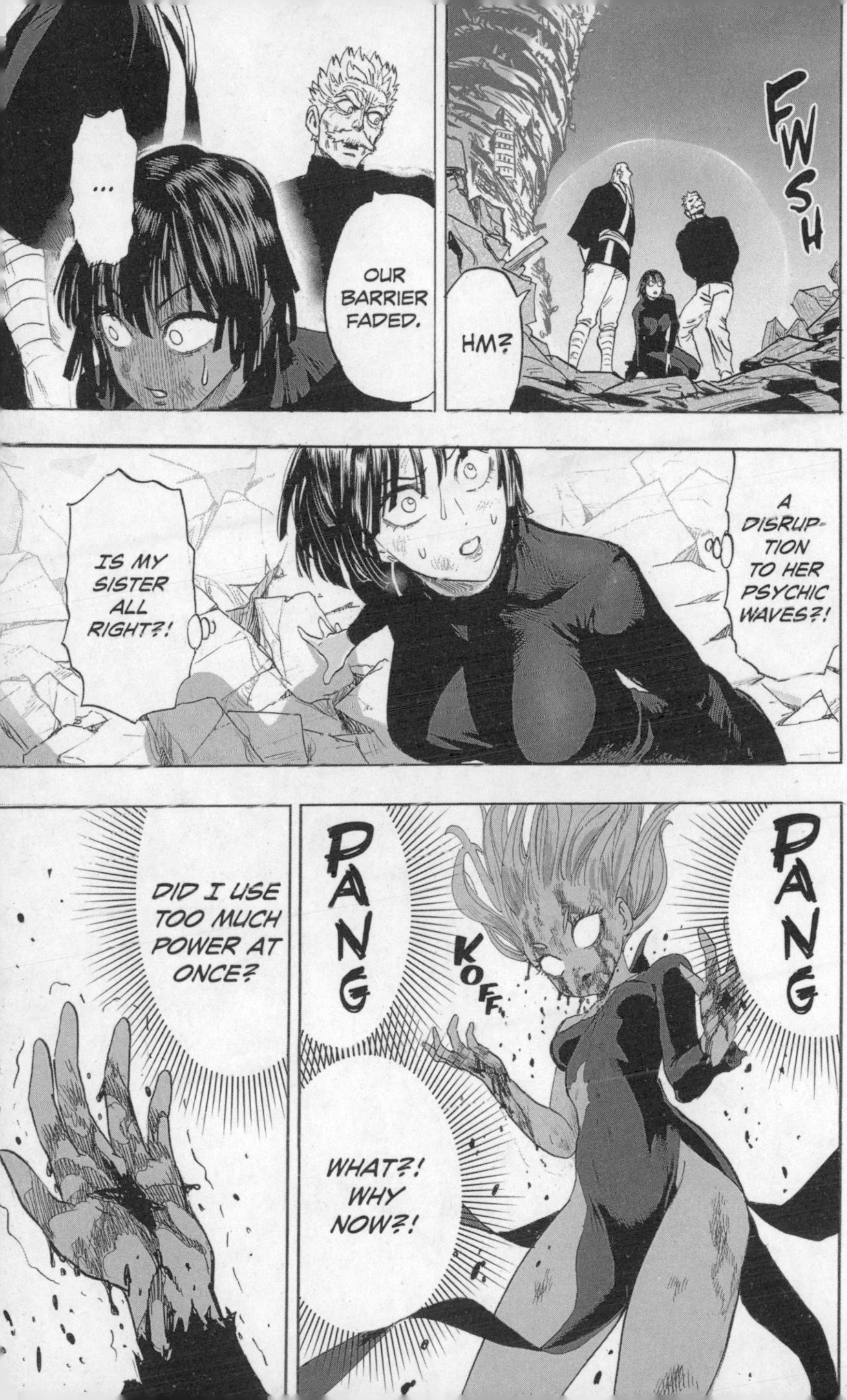
FWSH
HM?
OUR BARRIER FADED.
...
A DISRUPTION TO HER PSYCHIC WAVES?!
IS MY SISTER ALL RIGHT?!
PANG
PANG
KOFF
WHAT?! WHY NOW?!
DID I USE TOO MUCH POWER AT ONCE?

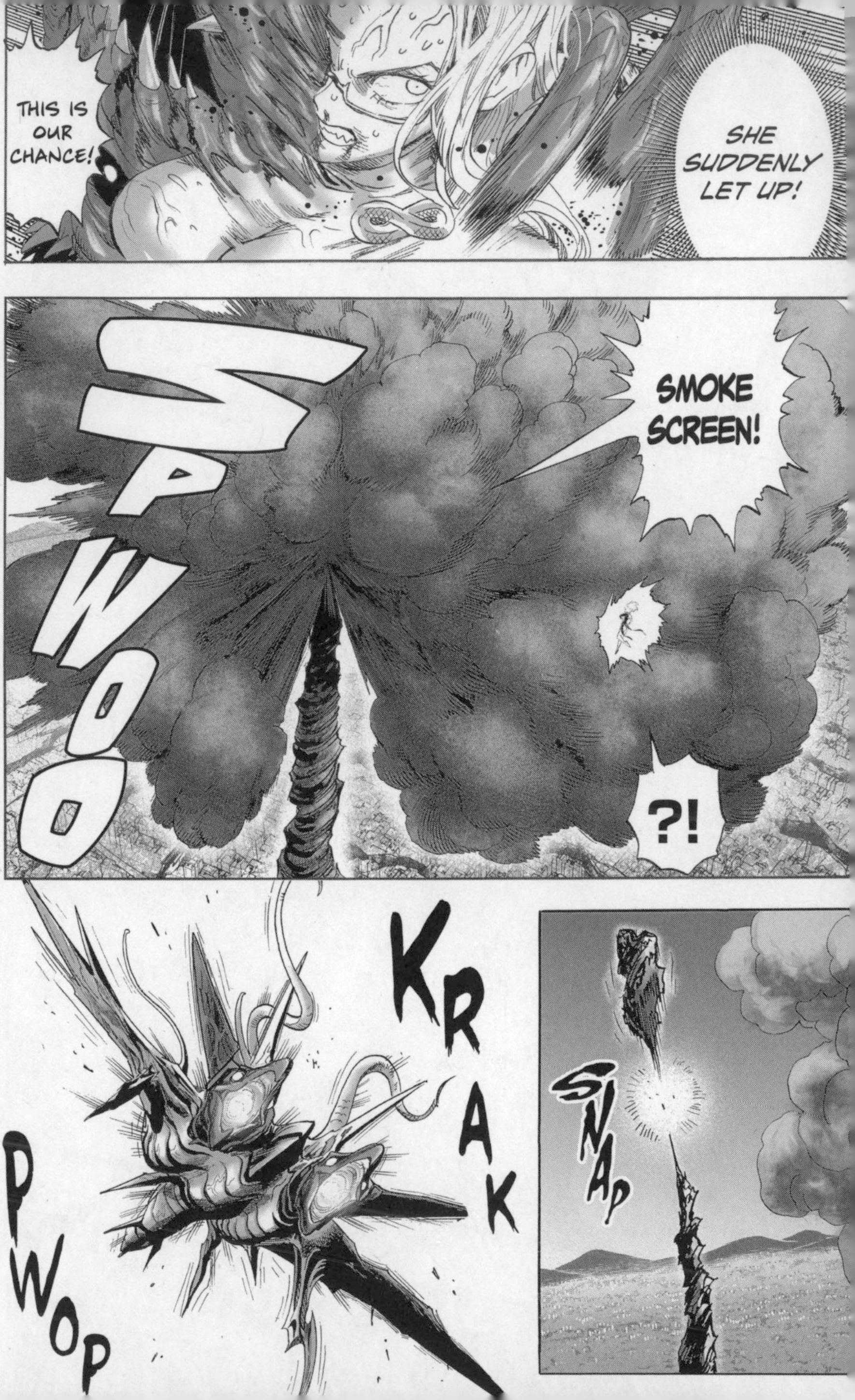
SHE SUDDENLY LET UP!
THIS IS OUR CHANCE!
SMOKE SCREEN!
SPWOO
?!
SNAP
KRAK
PWOP

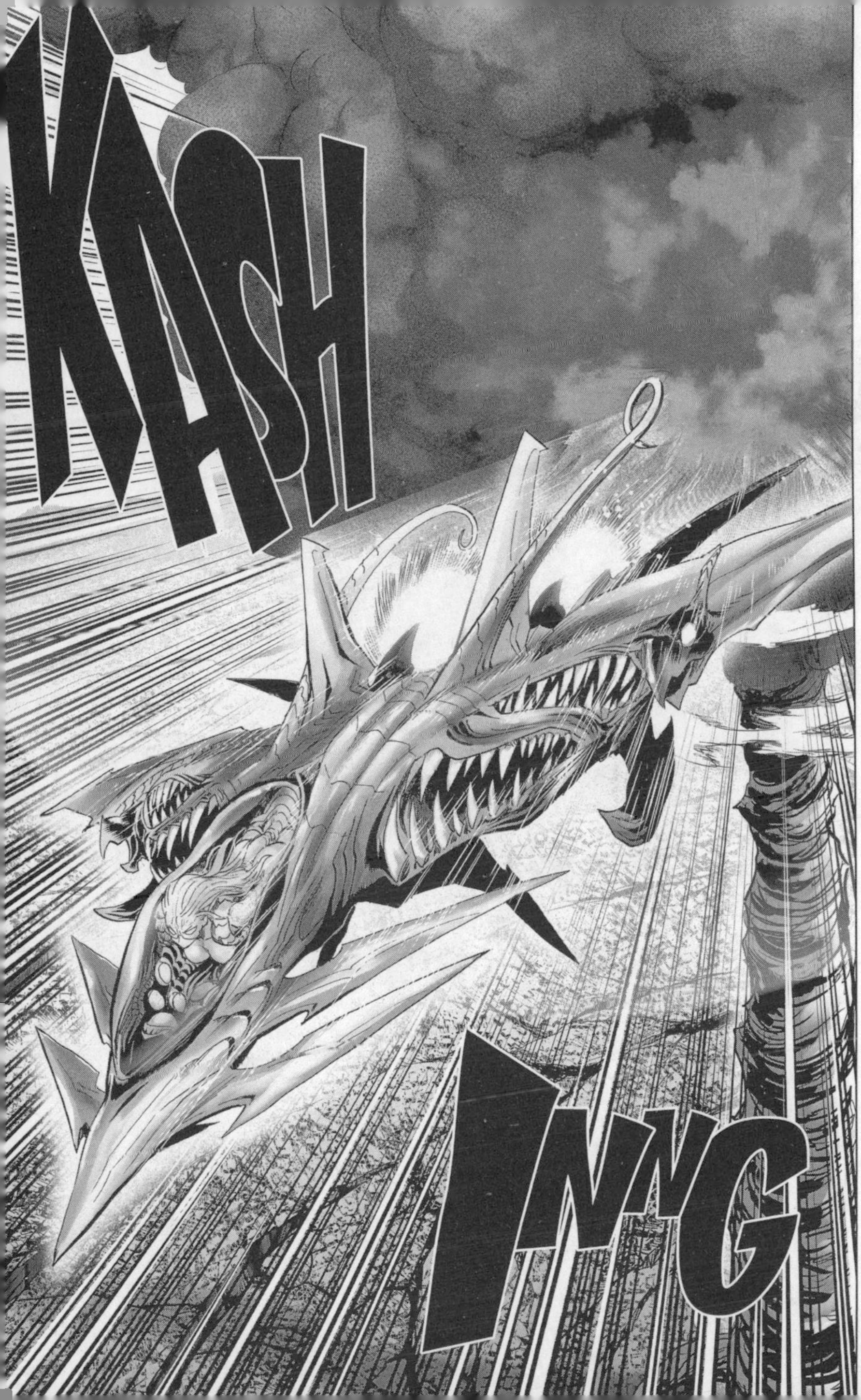
KASH
INNG

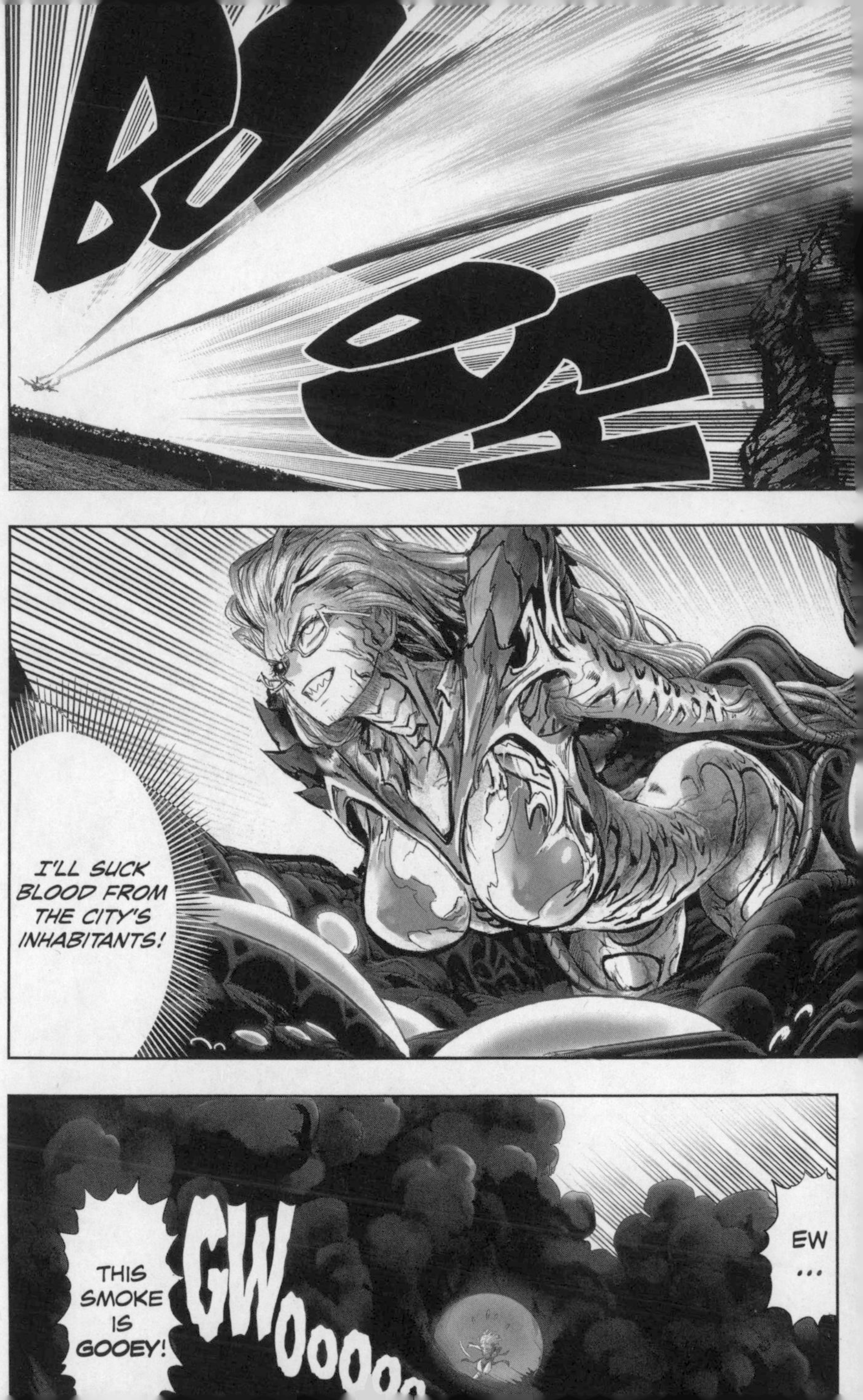
I'LL SUCK BLOOD FROM THE CITY'S INHABITANTS!
EW ...
GWOOOO
THIS SMOKE IS GOOEY!

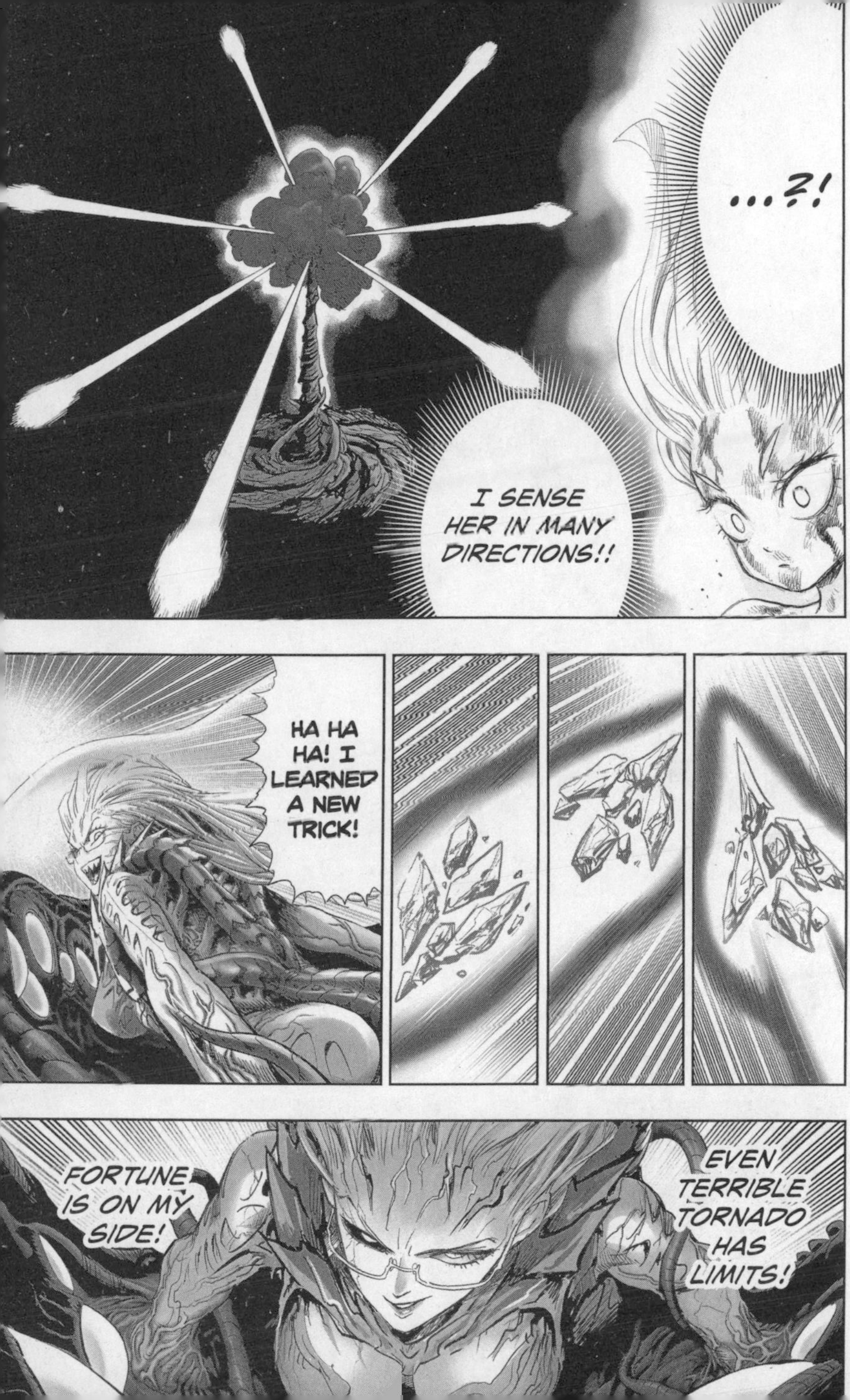
...?!
I SENSE HER IN MANY DIRECTIONS!!
HA HA HA! I LEARNED A NEW TRICK!
EVEN TERRIBLE TORNADO HAS LIMITS!
FORTUNE IS ON MY SIDE!

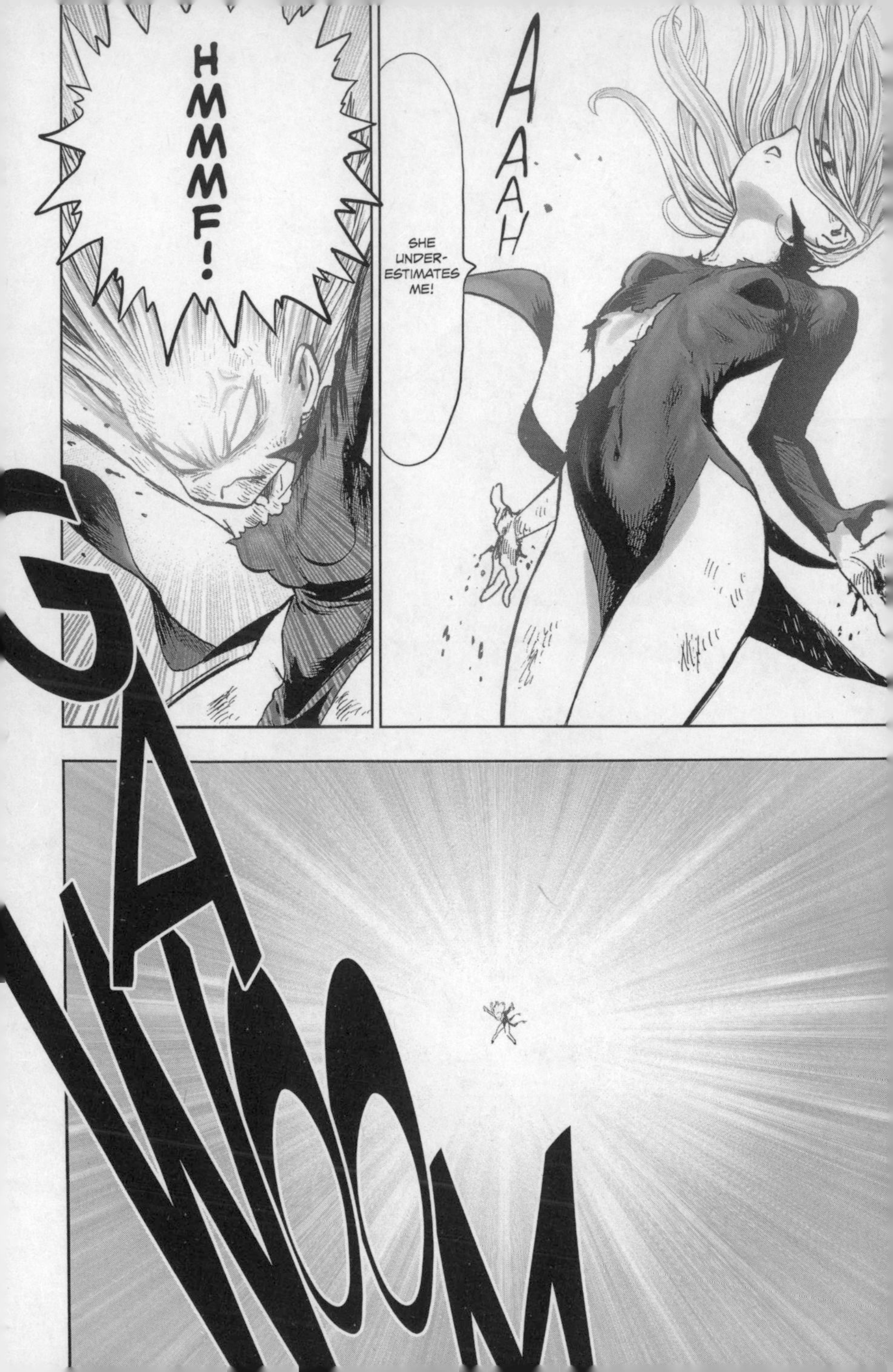
AAAH
SHE UNDER-ESTIMATES ME!
HMMMF!
GAWOOM

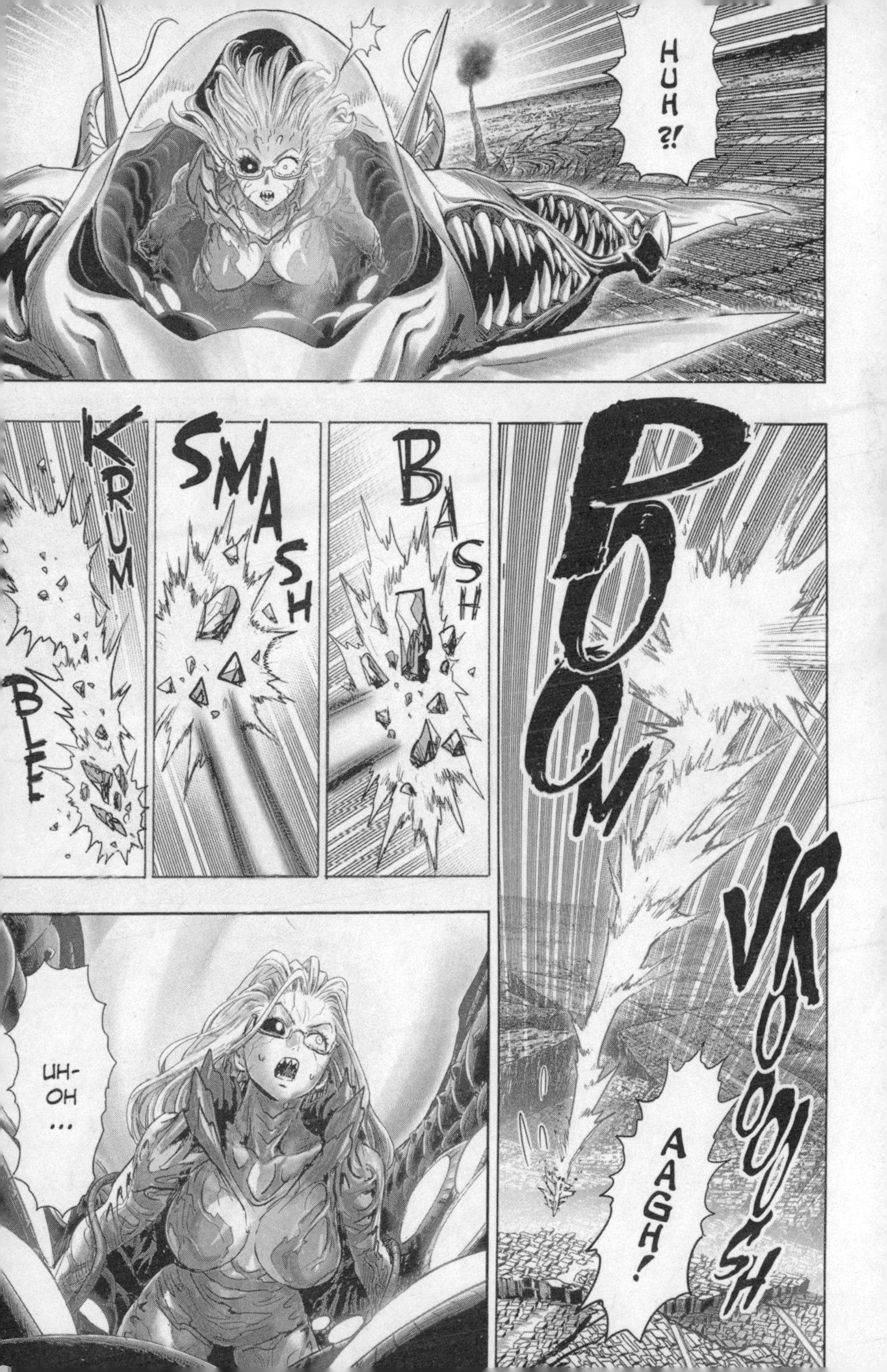
HUH?!
DOOM
VROOOOSH
AAGH!
BASH
SMASH
KRUMBLE
UH-OH...

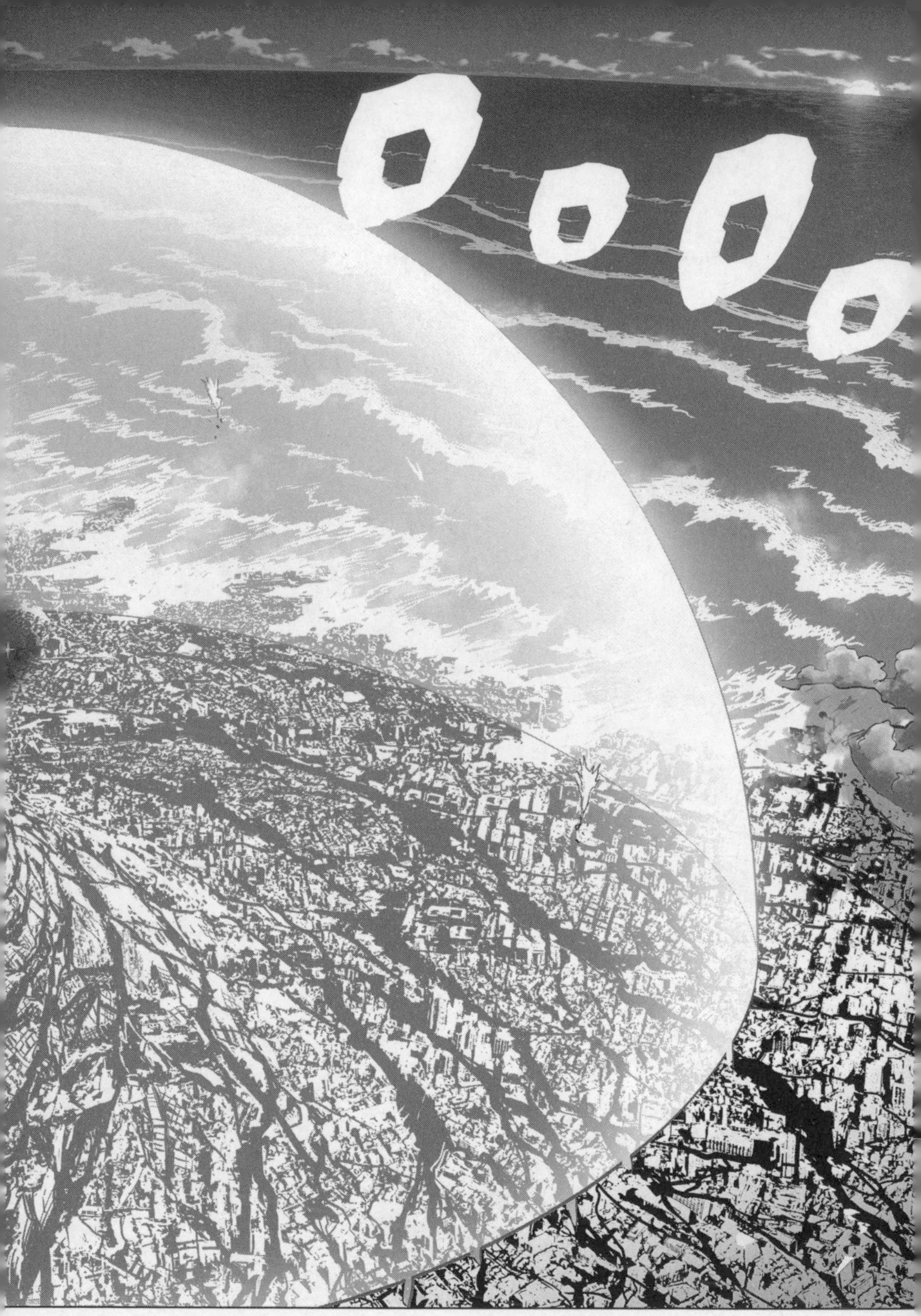
OOOO

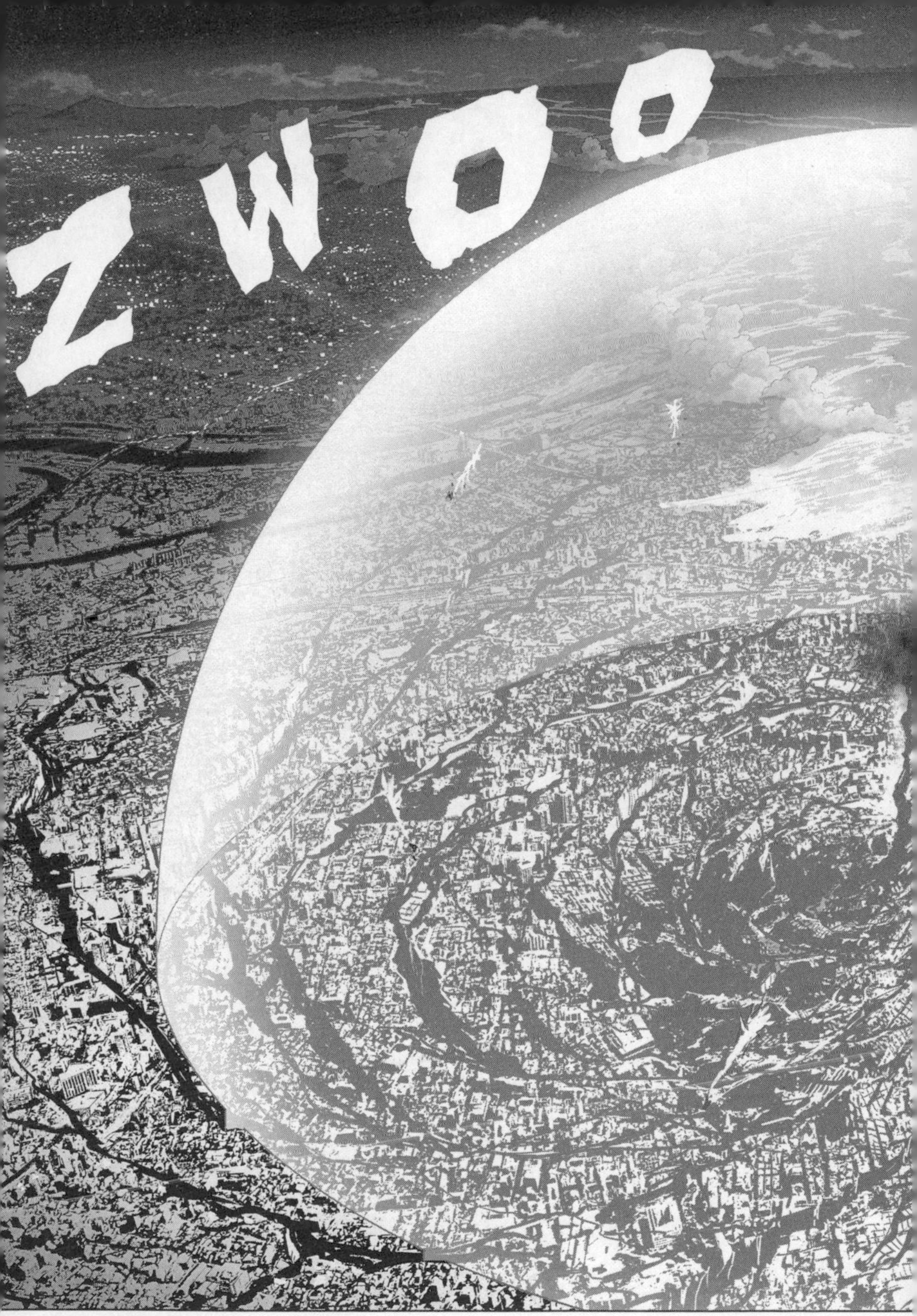
ZWOO

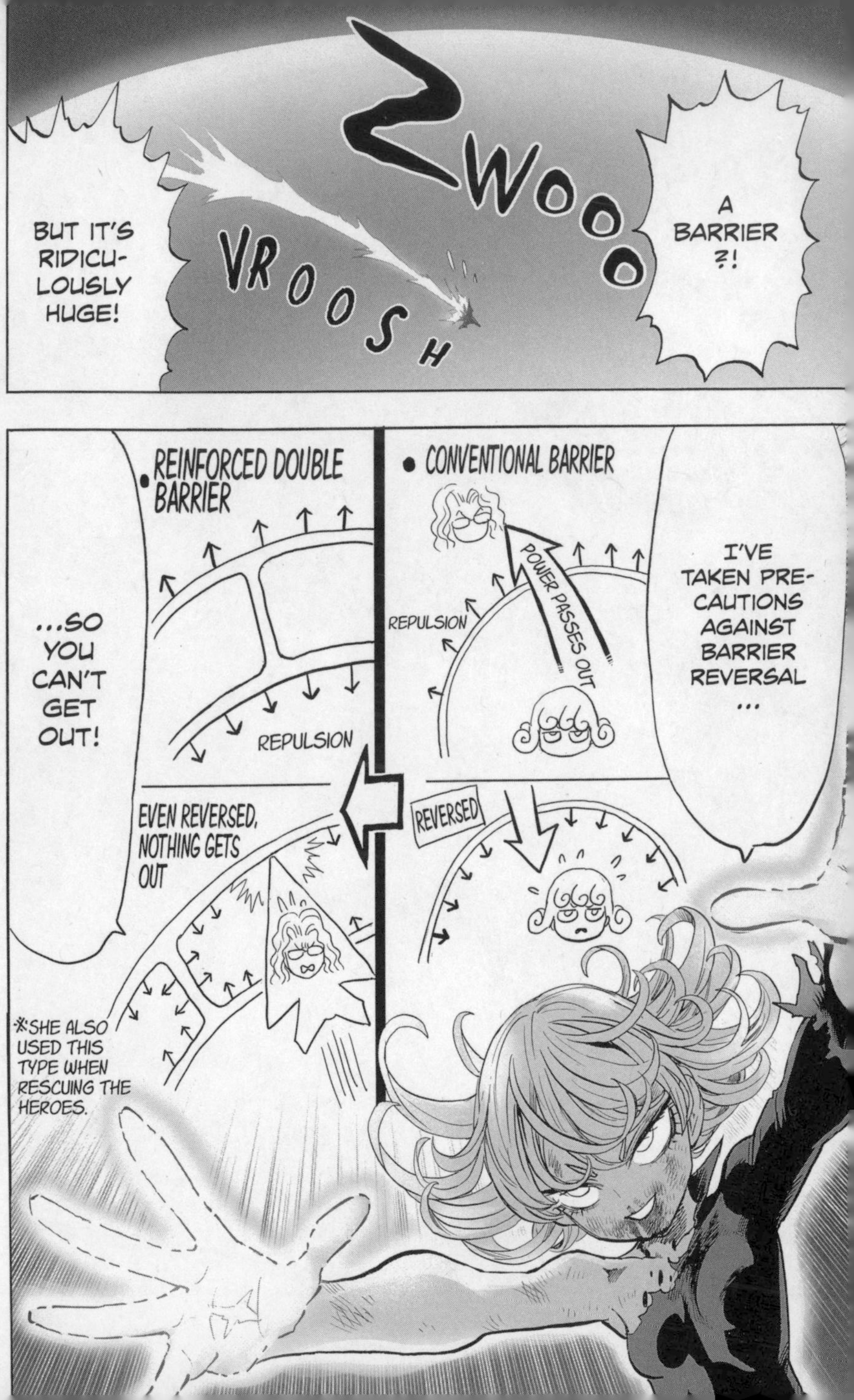
A BARRIER ?!
ZWOOO
VROOSH
BUT IT'S RIDICU-LOUSLY HUGE!
I'VE TAKEN PRE-CAUTIONS AGAINST BARRIER REVERSAL ...
• CONVENTIONAL BARRIER
POWER PASSES OUT
REPULSION
REVERSED
• REINFORCED DOUBLE BARRIER
REPULSION
EVEN REVERSED, NOTHING GETS OUT
...SO YOU CAN'T GET OUT!
※SHE ALSO USED THIS TYPE WHEN RESCUING THE HEROES.

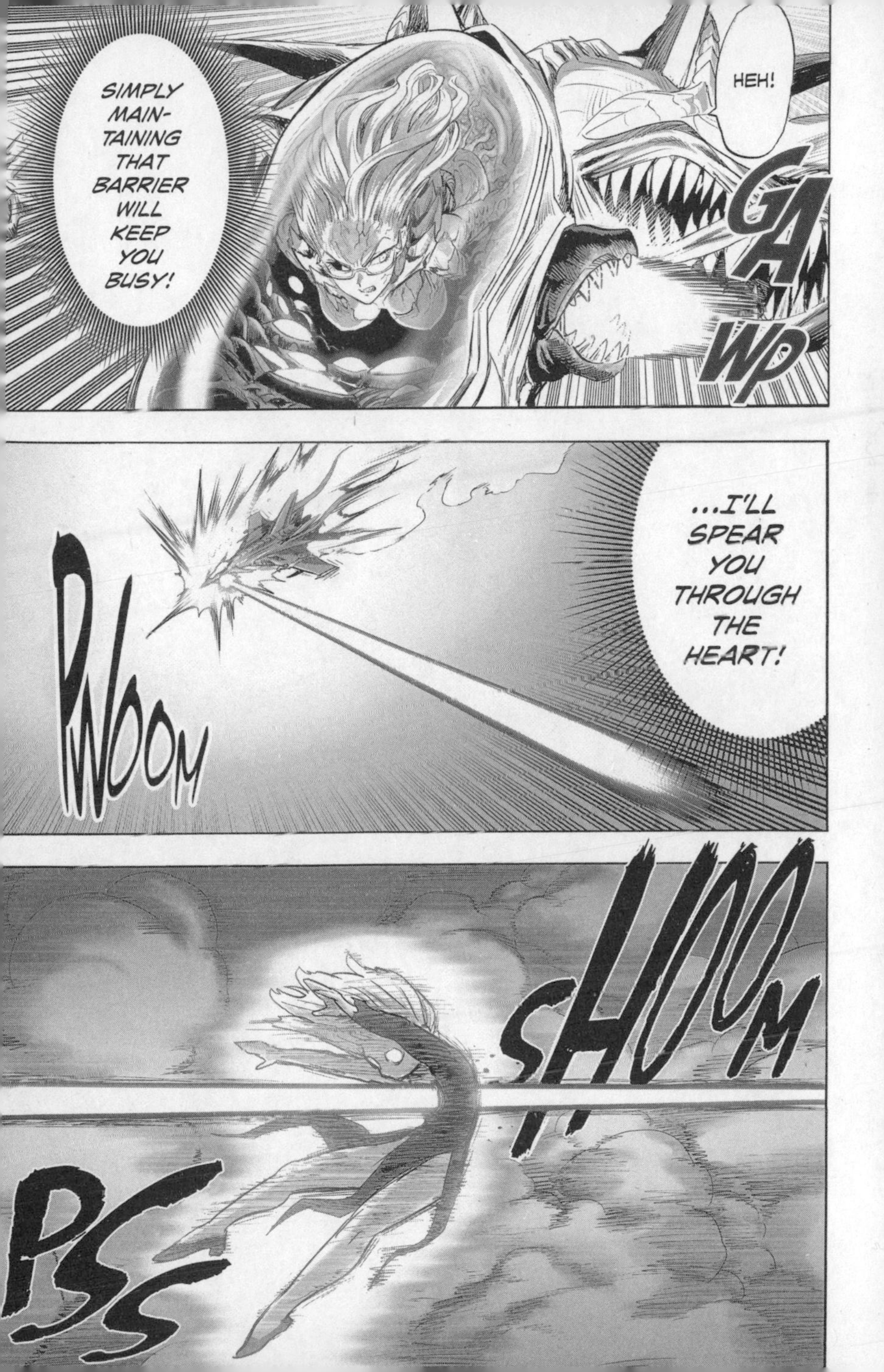
HEH!
GAWP
SIMPLY MAIN-TAINING THAT BARRIER WILL KEEP YOU BUSY!
...I'LL SPEAR YOU THROUGH THE HEART!
PWOOM
SHOOM
PSS

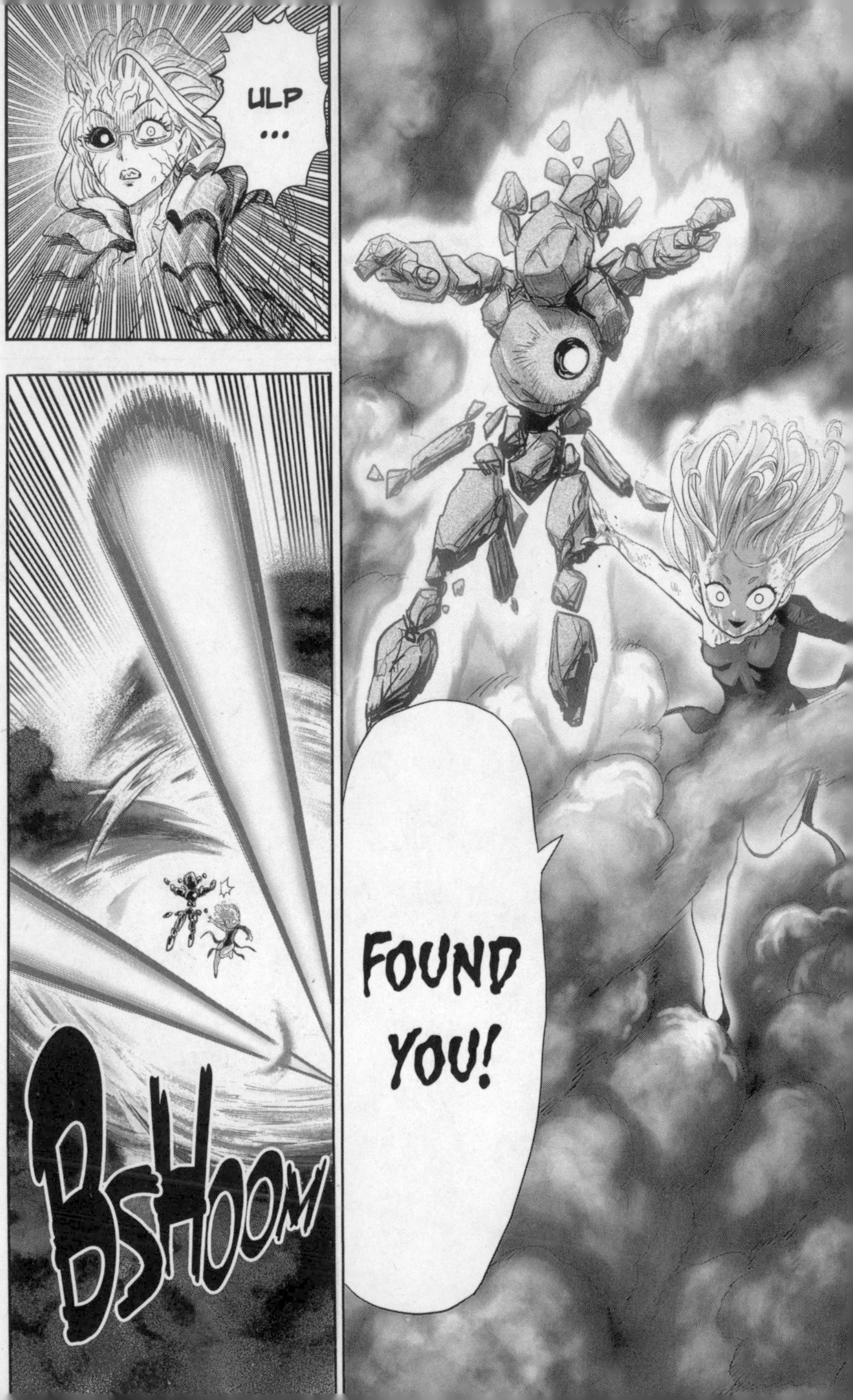
FOUND YOU!
ULP ...
BSHOOM

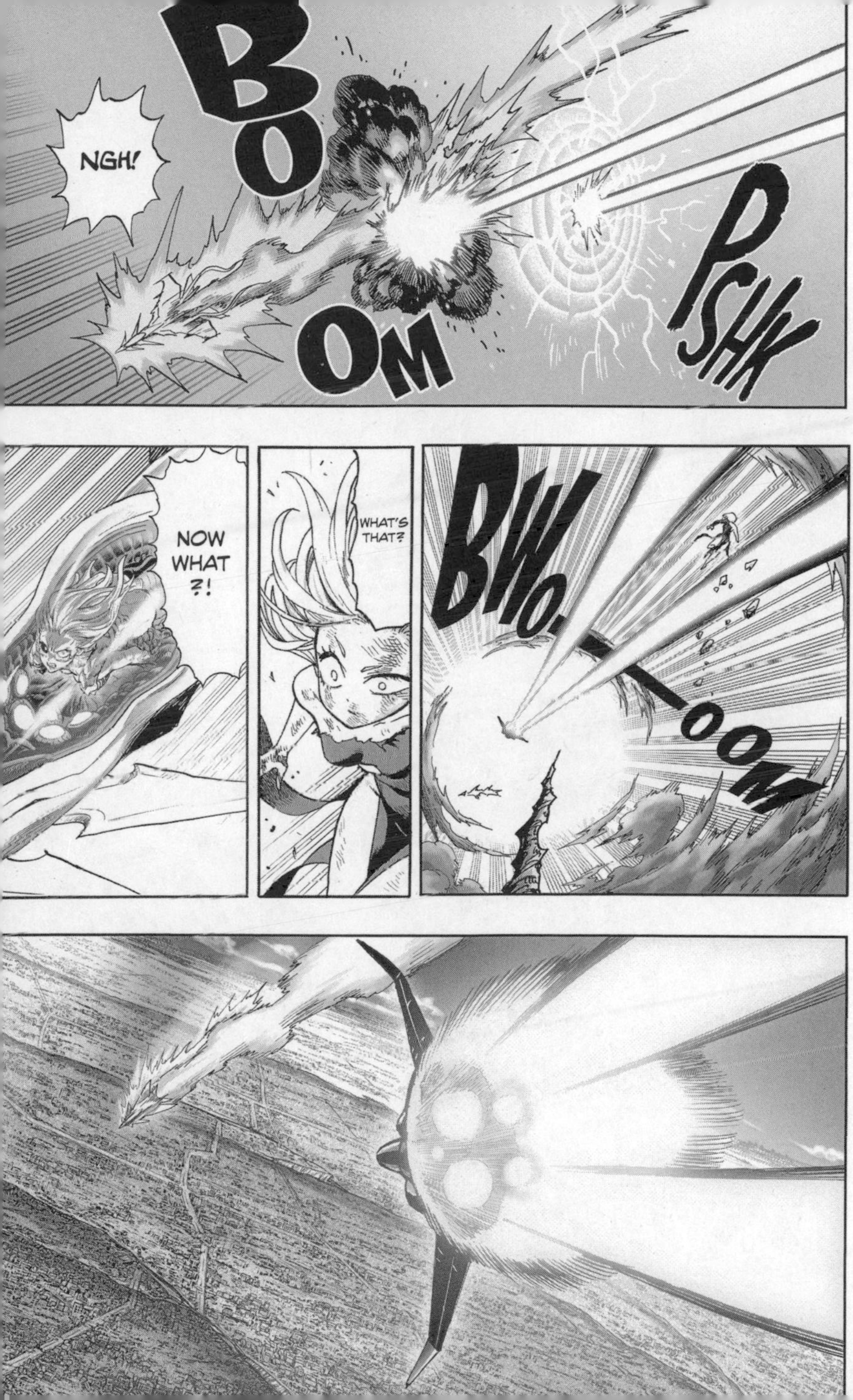
PSHK
BOOOM
NGH!
BWOOOM
WHAT'S THAT?
NOW WHAT?!

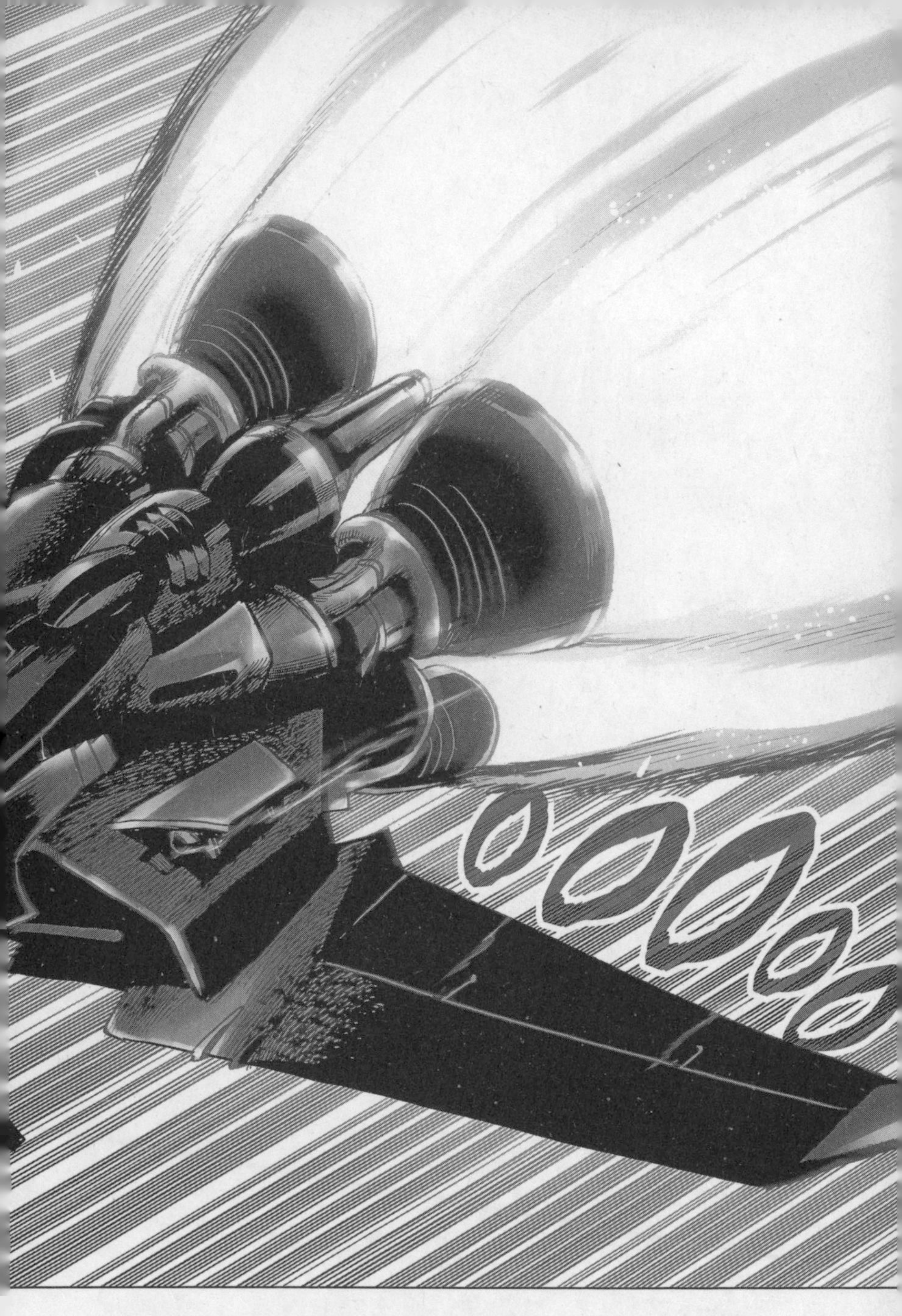

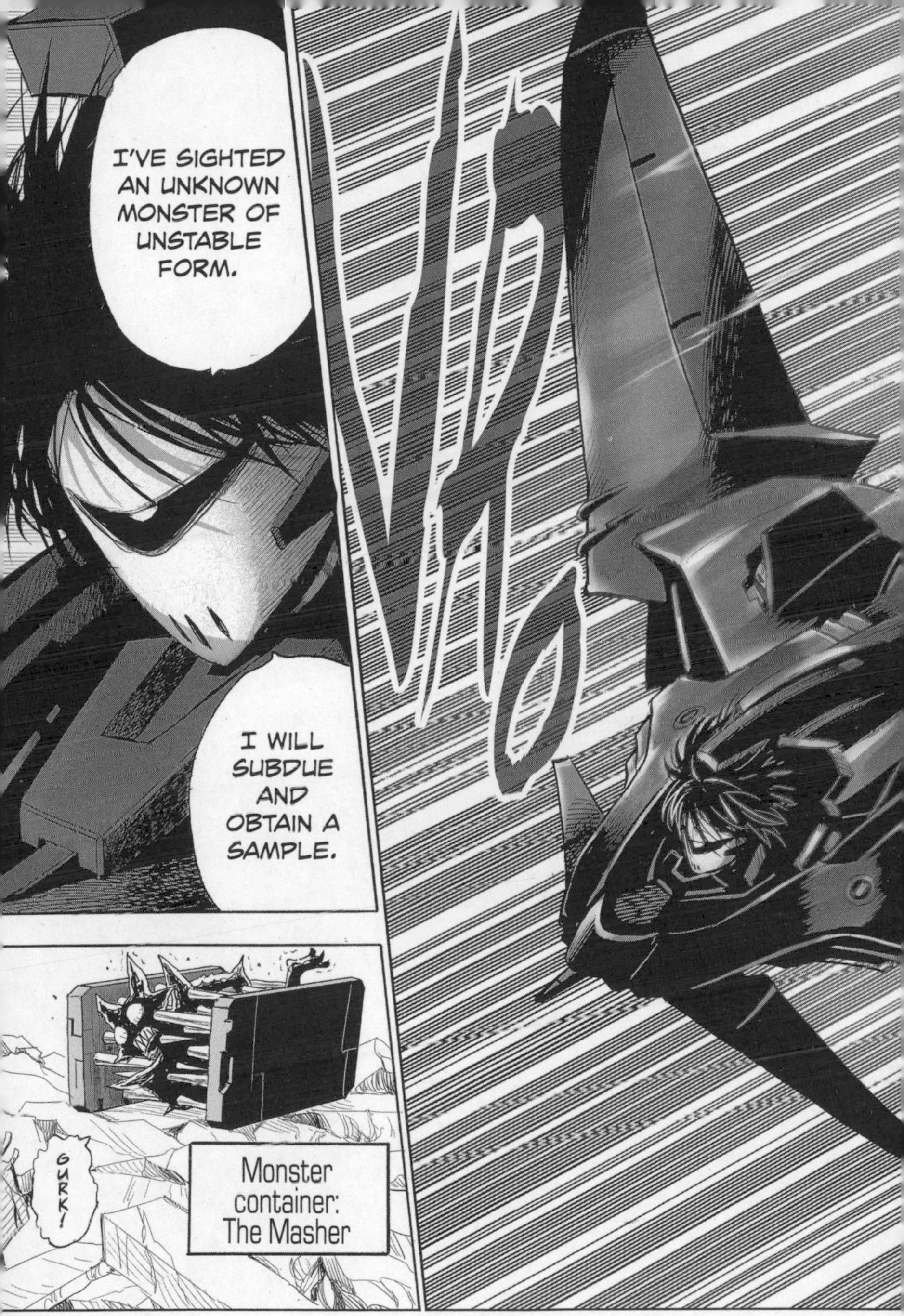
I'VE SIGHTED AN UNKNOWN MONSTER OF UNSTABLE FORM.
I WILL SUBDUE AND OBTAIN A SAMPLE.
Monster container: The Masher
GURK!

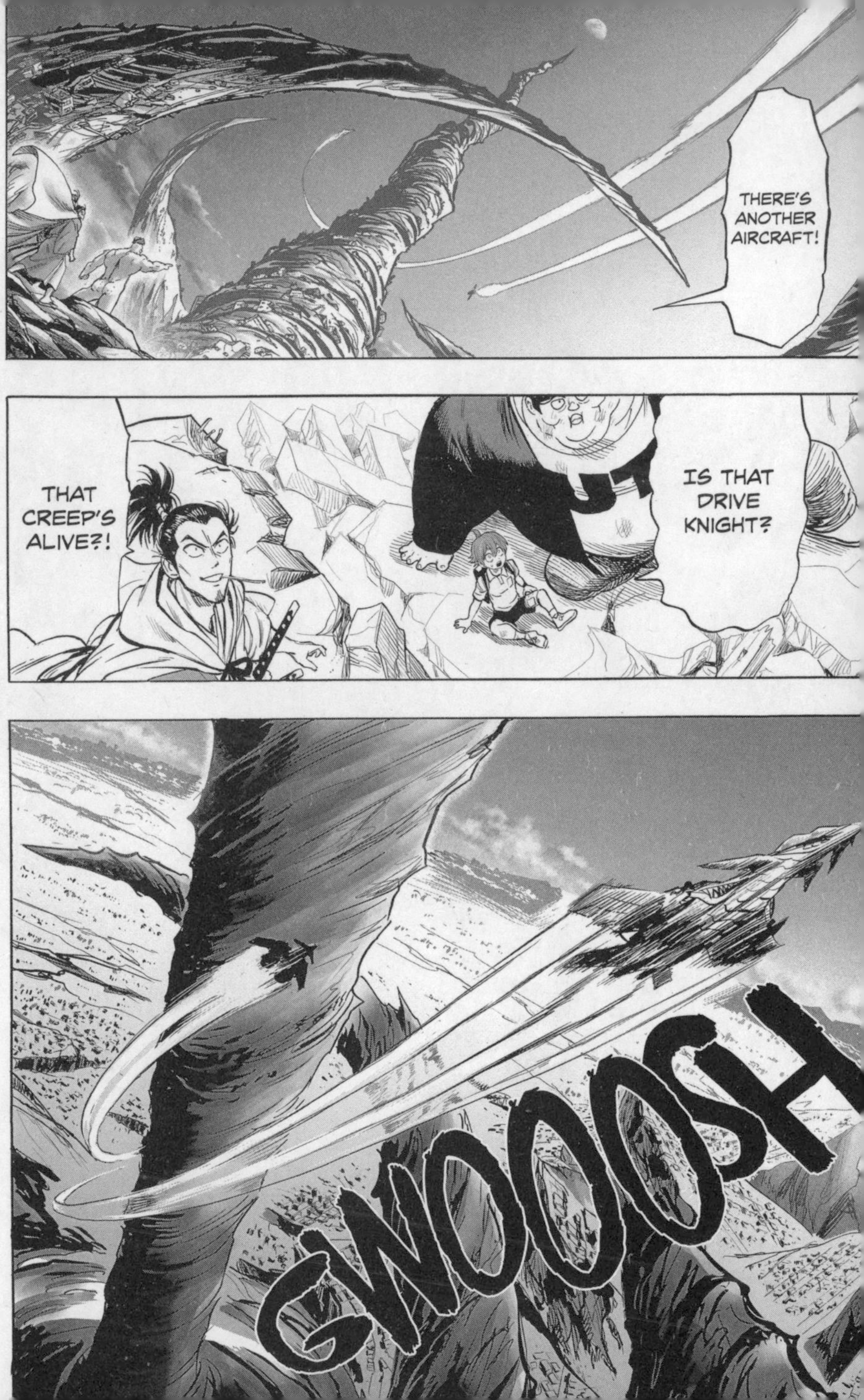
THERE'S ANOTHER AIRCRAFT!
IS THAT DRIVE KNIGHT?
THAT CREEP'S ALIVE?!
GWOOOSH

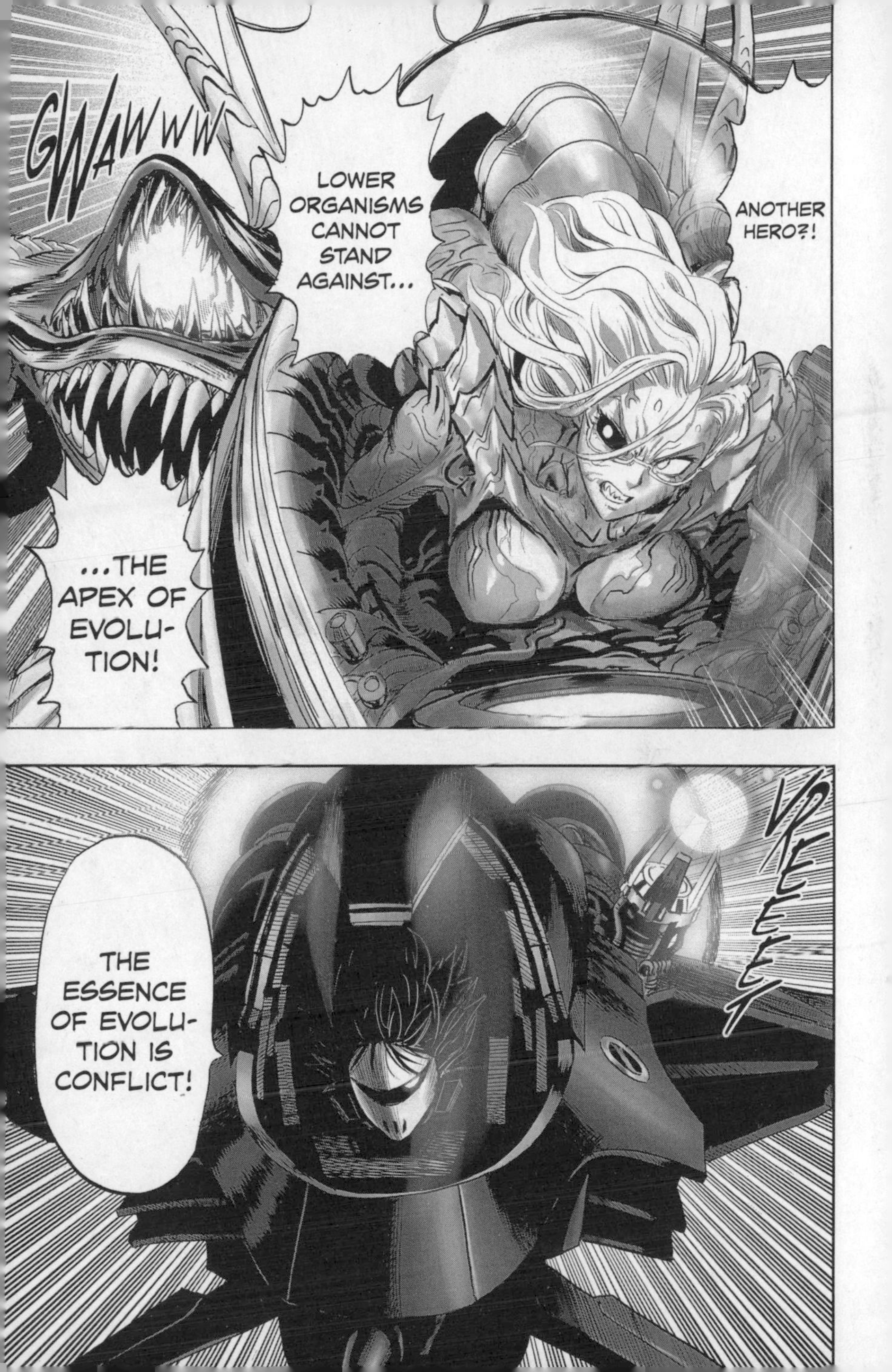
ANOTHER HERO?!
LOWER ORGANISMS CANNOT STAND AGAINST...
GWAWWW
...THE APEX OF EVOLU-TION!
VREEEEEK
THE ESSENCE OF EVOLU-TION IS CONFLICT!

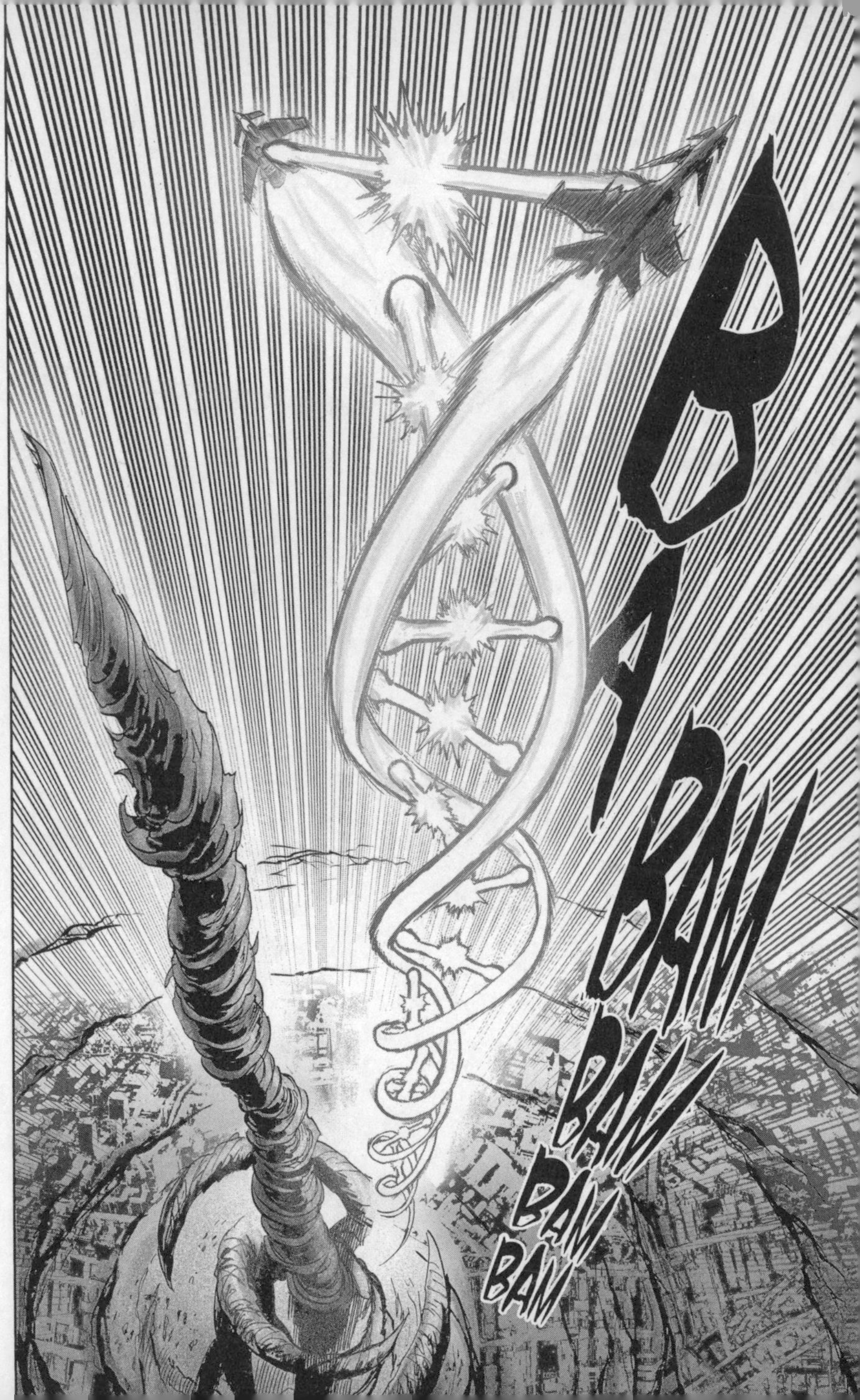
BABAM
BAM
BAM
BAM

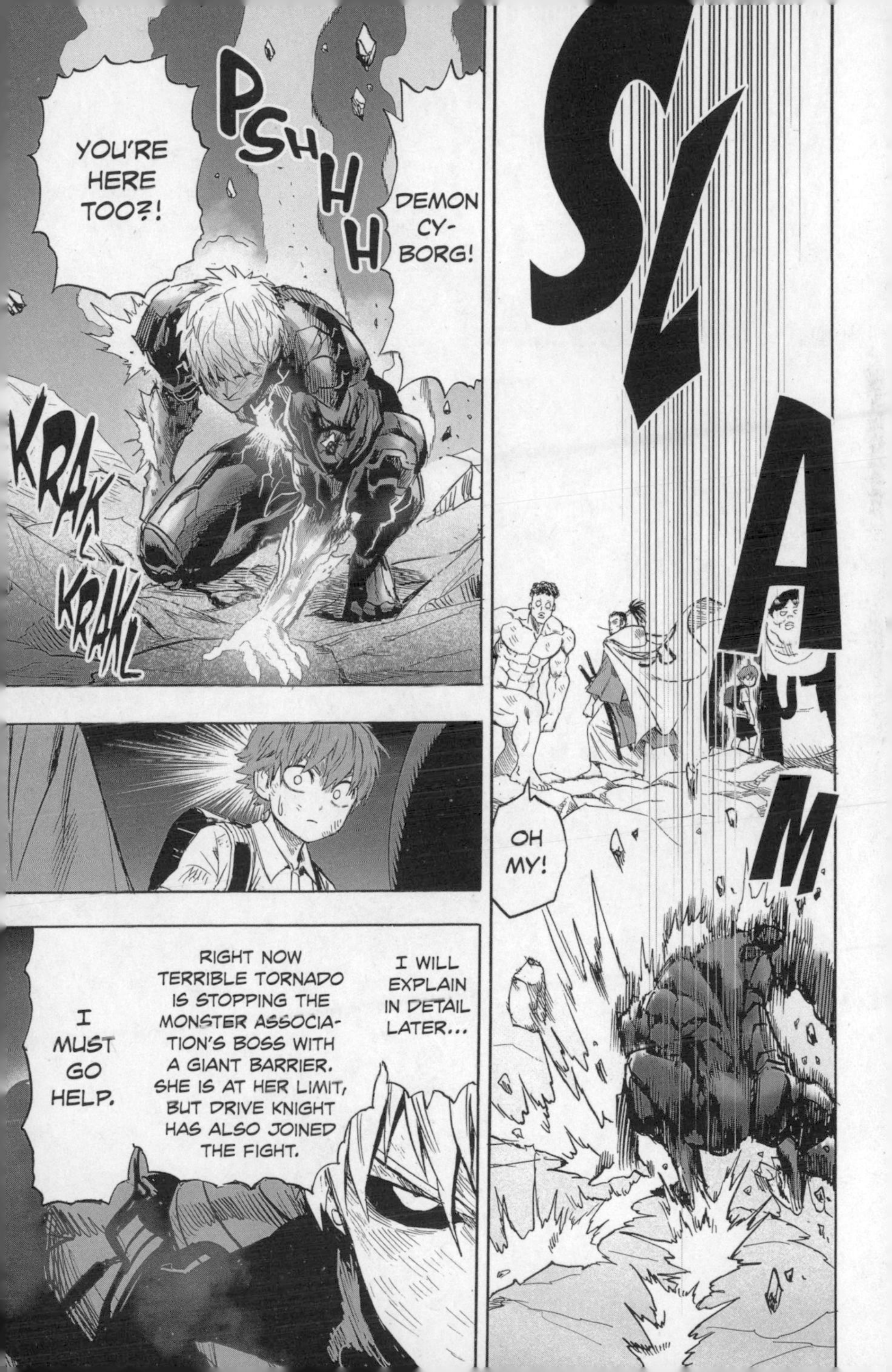
SLAM
OH MY!
DEMON CY-BORG!
PSHHH
YOU'RE HERE TOO?!
KRAKL KRAKL
I WILL EXPLAIN IN DETAIL LATER...
RIGHT NOW TERRIBLE TORNADO IS STOPPING THE MONSTER ASSOCIA-TION'S BOSS WITH A GIANT BARRIER. SHE IS AT HER LIMIT, BUT DRIVE KNIGHT HAS ALSO JOINED THE FIGHT.
I MUST GO HELP.

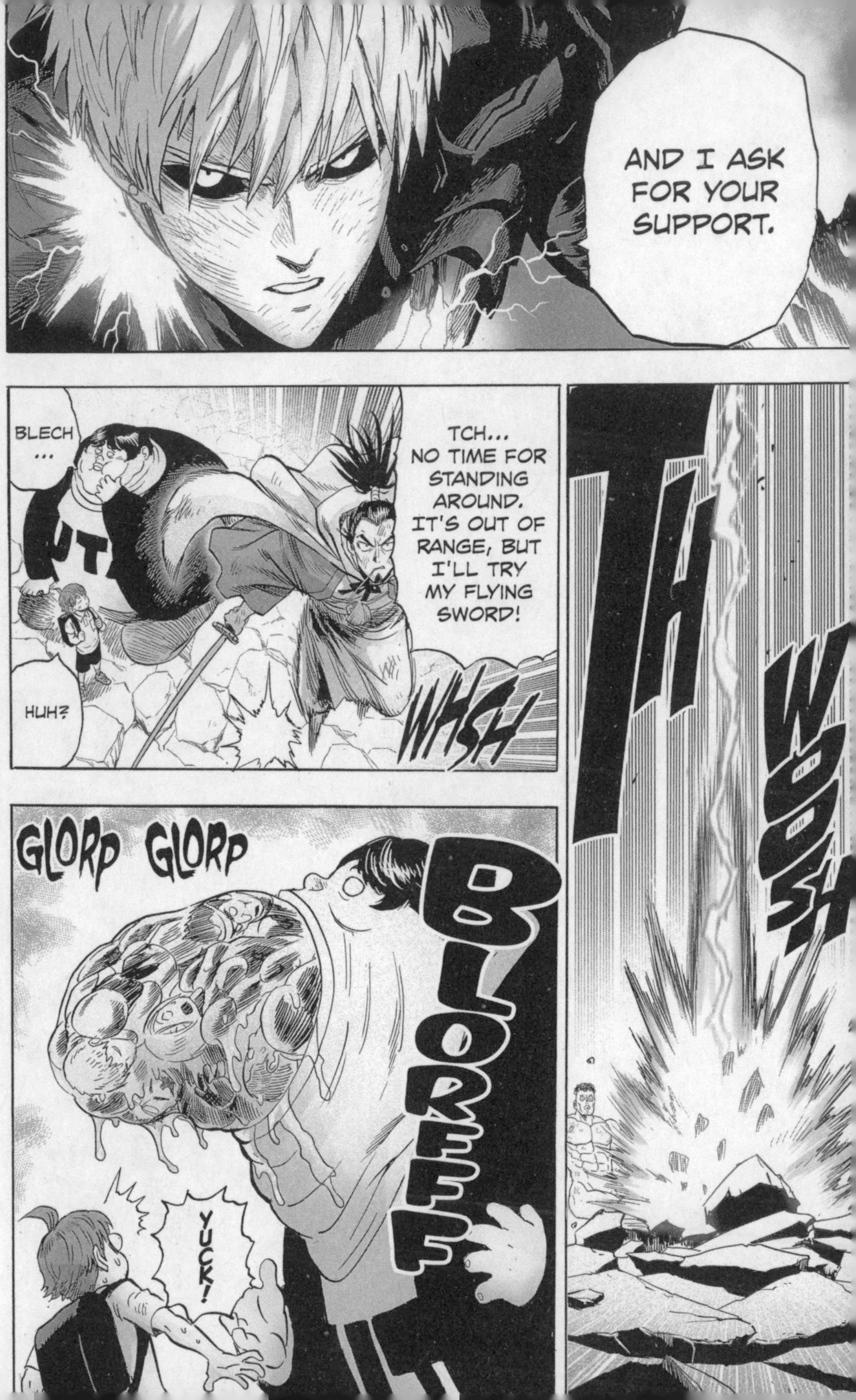
AND I ASK FOR YOUR SUPPORT.
WHOOSH
TCH... NO TIME FOR STANDING AROUND. IT'S OUT OF RANGE, BUT I'LL TRY MY FLYING SWORD!
BLECH ...
WHSH
HUH?
GLORP GLORP
BLORFFF
YUCK!

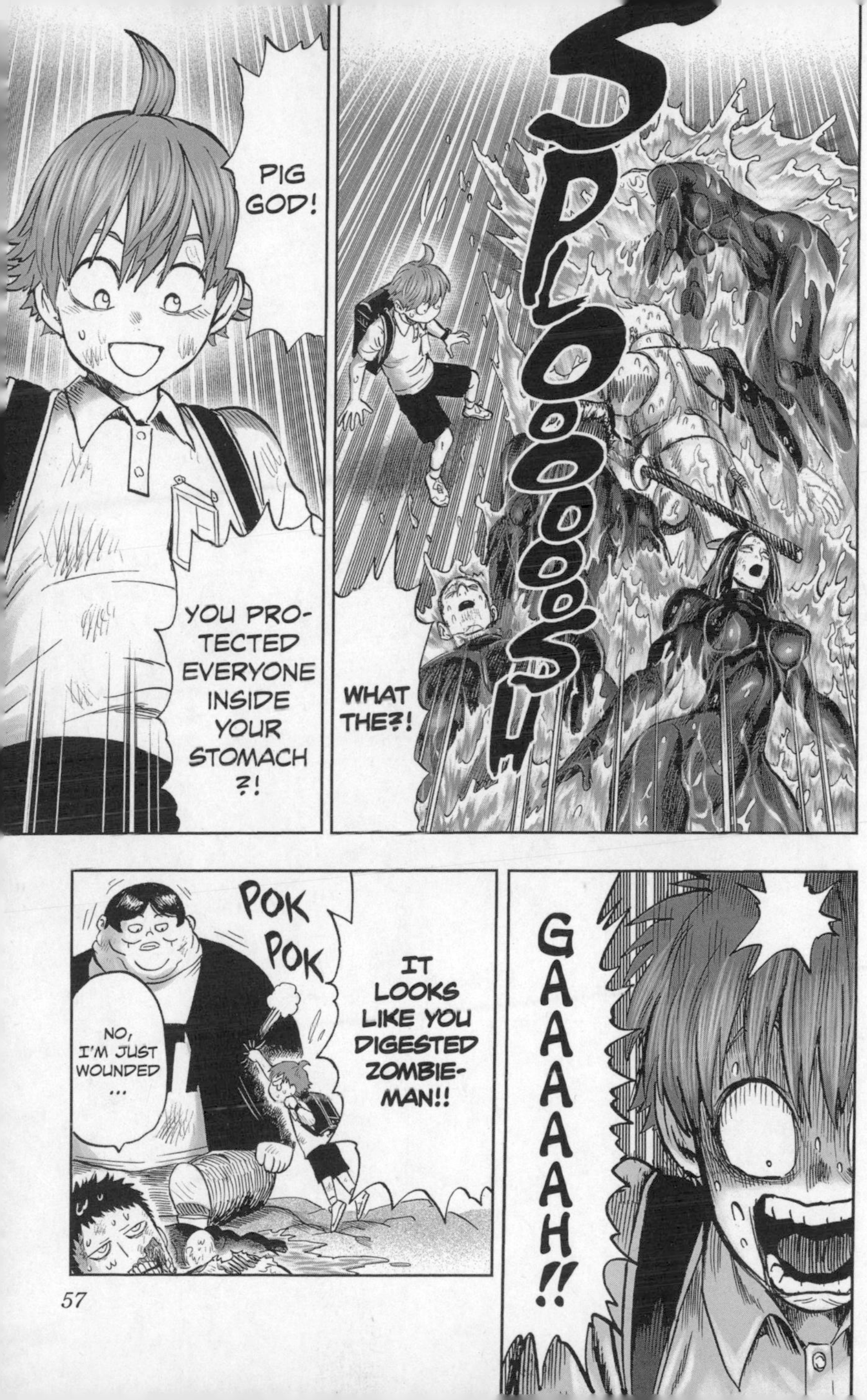
SPLOOOOOOSH
WHAT THE?!
PIG GOD!
YOU PRO-TECTED EVERYONE INSIDE YOUR STOMACH?!
GAAAAAH!!
POK POK
IT LOOKS LIKE YOU DIGESTED ZOMBIE-MAN!!
NO, I'M JUST WOUNDED...

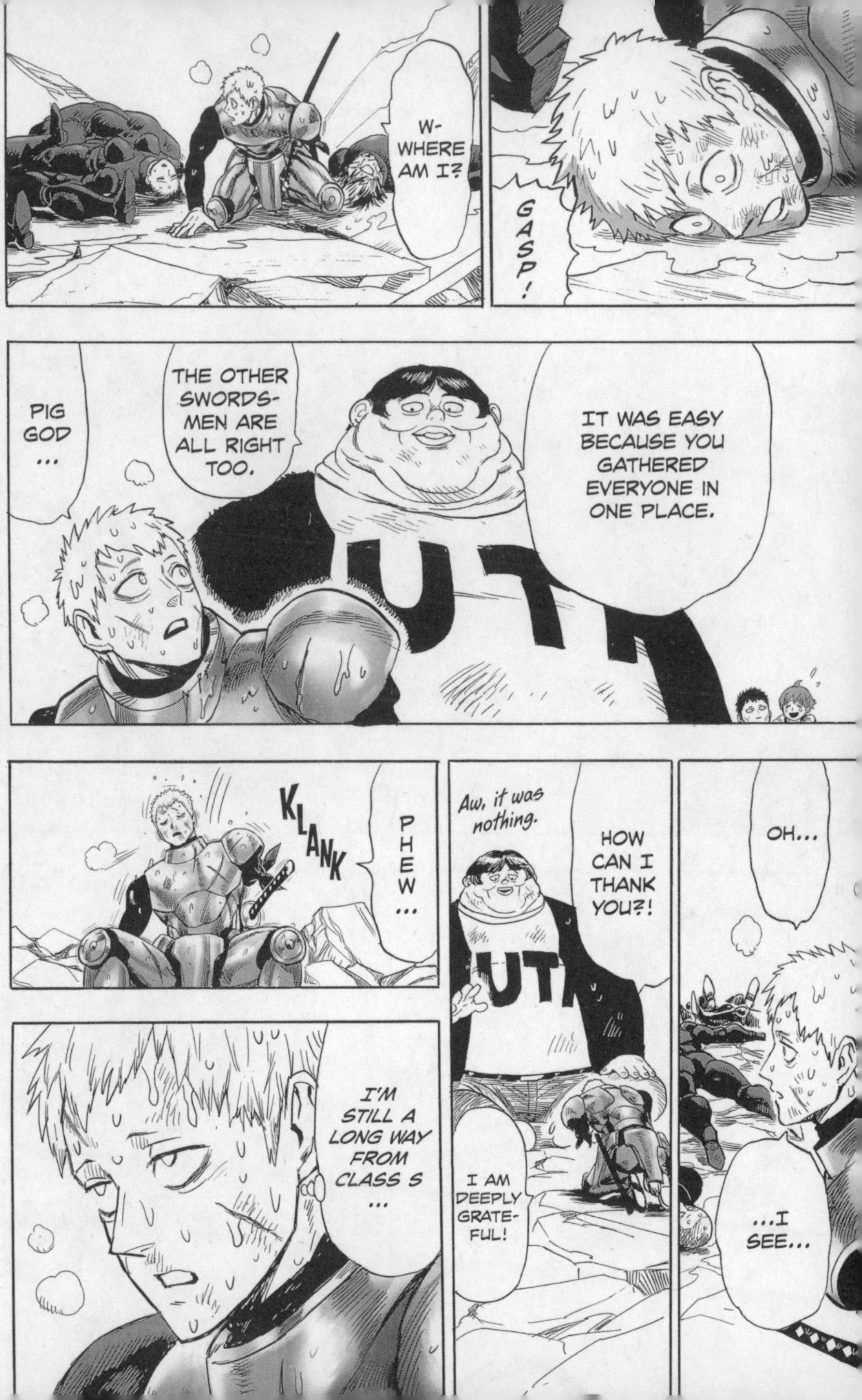
GASP!
W- WHERE AM I?
IT WAS EASY BECAUSE YOU GATHERED EVERYONE IN ONE PLACE.
THE OTHER SWORDSMEN ARE ALL RIGHT TOO.
PIG GOD ...
OH...
...I SEE...
HOW CAN I THANK YOU?!
Aw, it was nothing.
I AM DEEPLY GRATEFUL!
PHEW ...
KLANK
I'M STILL A LONG WAY FROM CLASS S ...

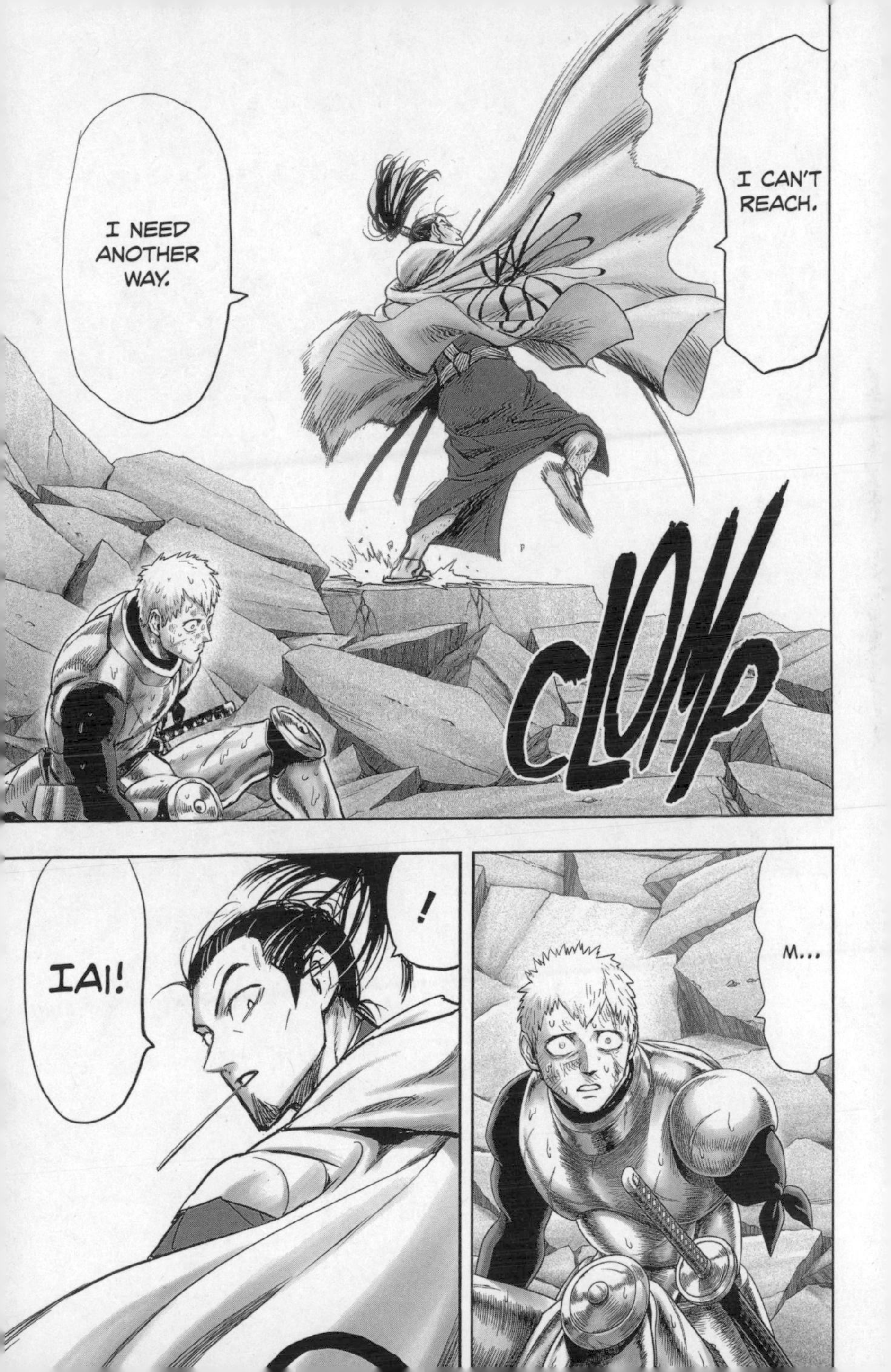
I CAN'T REACH.
I NEED ANOTHER WAY.
CLOMP
M...
!
IAI!

MASTER!

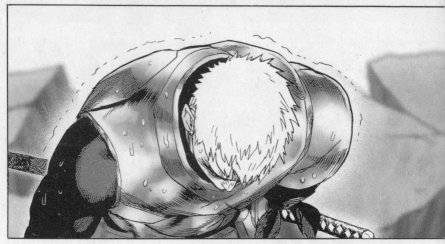

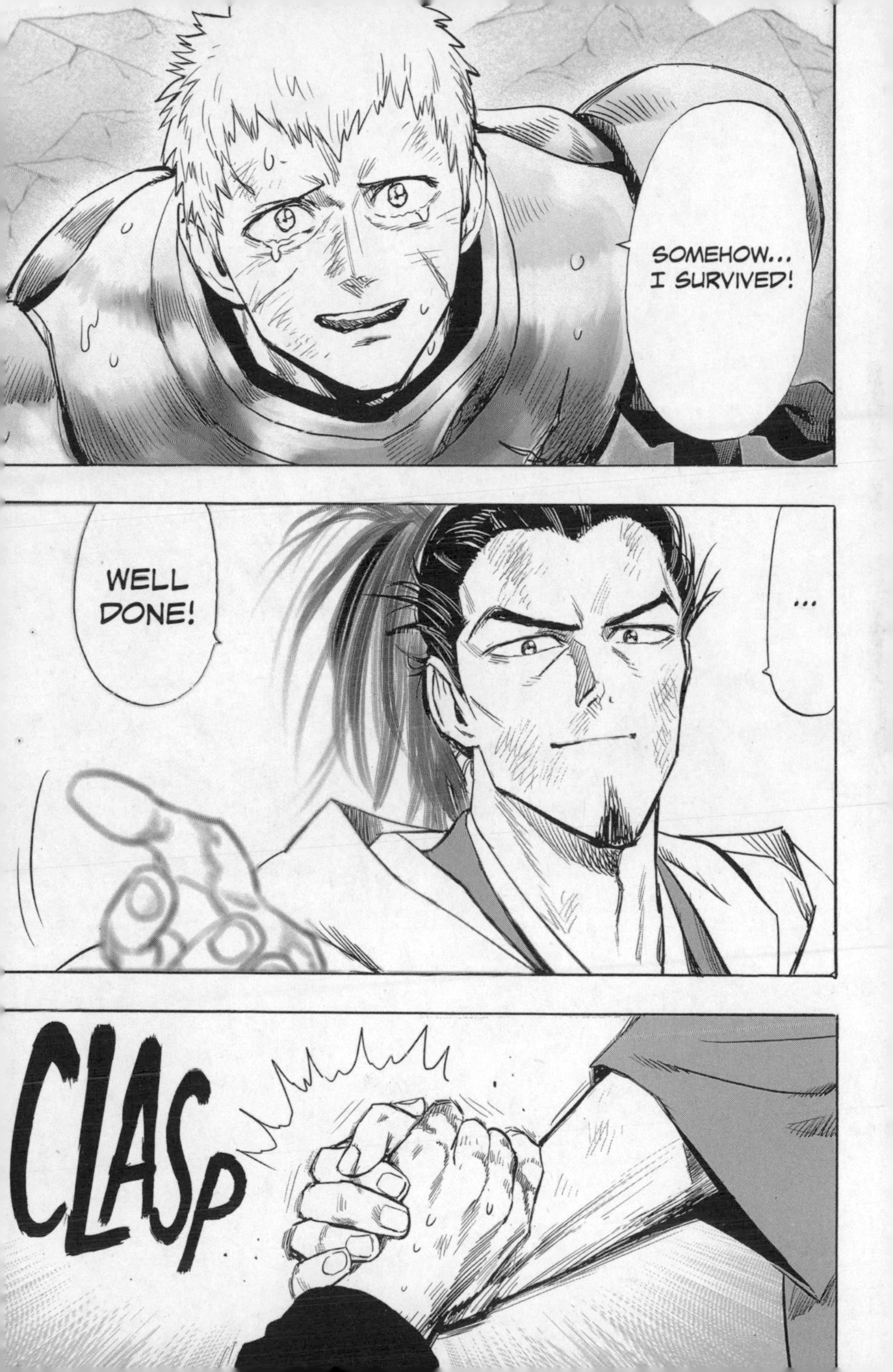
SOMEHOW...
I SURVIVED!
...
WELL
DONE!
CLASP

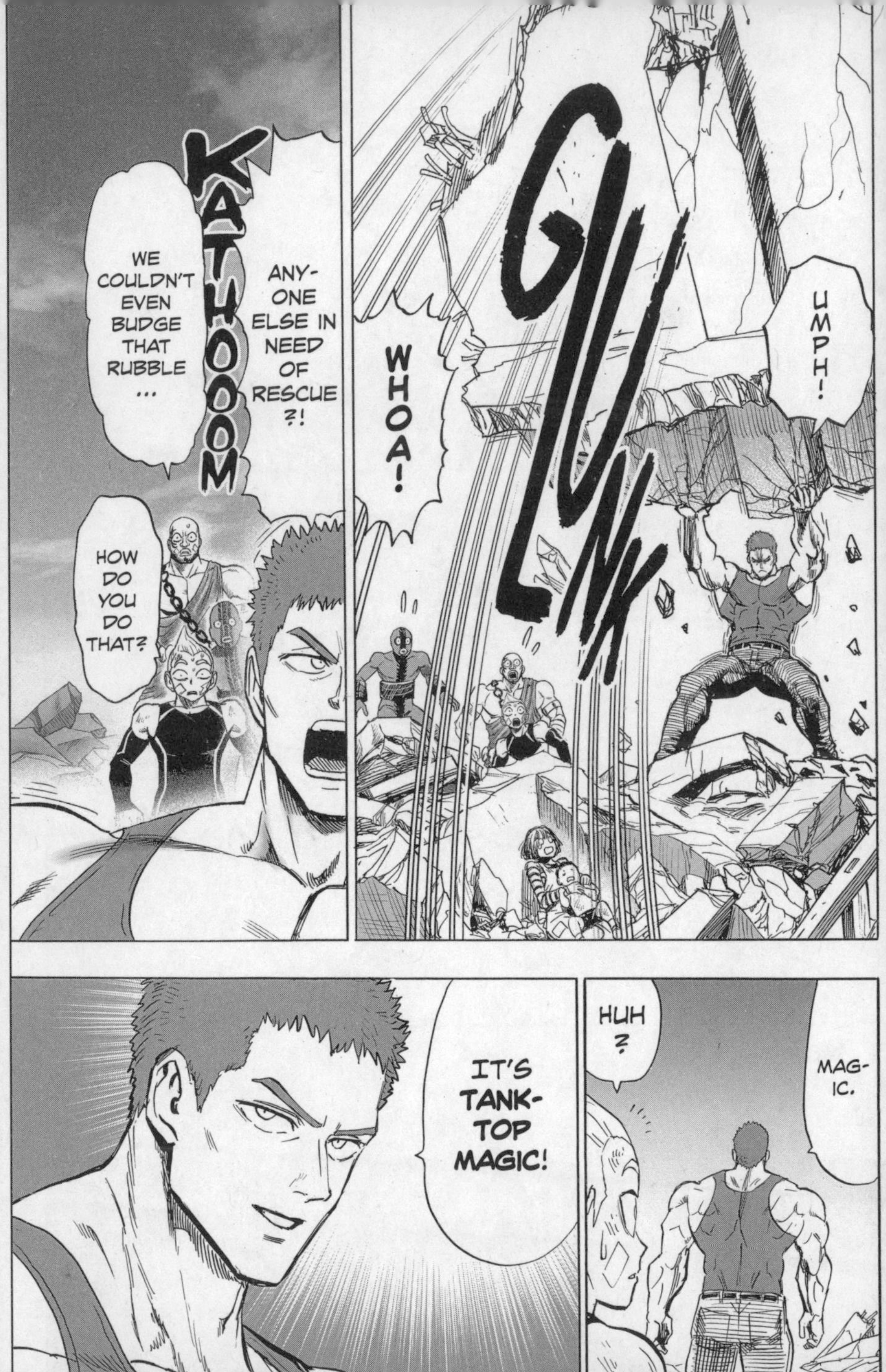
UMPH!
WHOA!
KATHOOOM
ANY-ONE ELSE IN NEED OF RESCUE ?!
WE COULDN'T EVEN BUDGE THAT RUBBLE ...
HOW DO YOU DO THAT?
MAG-IC.
HUH ?
IT'S TANK-TOP MAGIC!

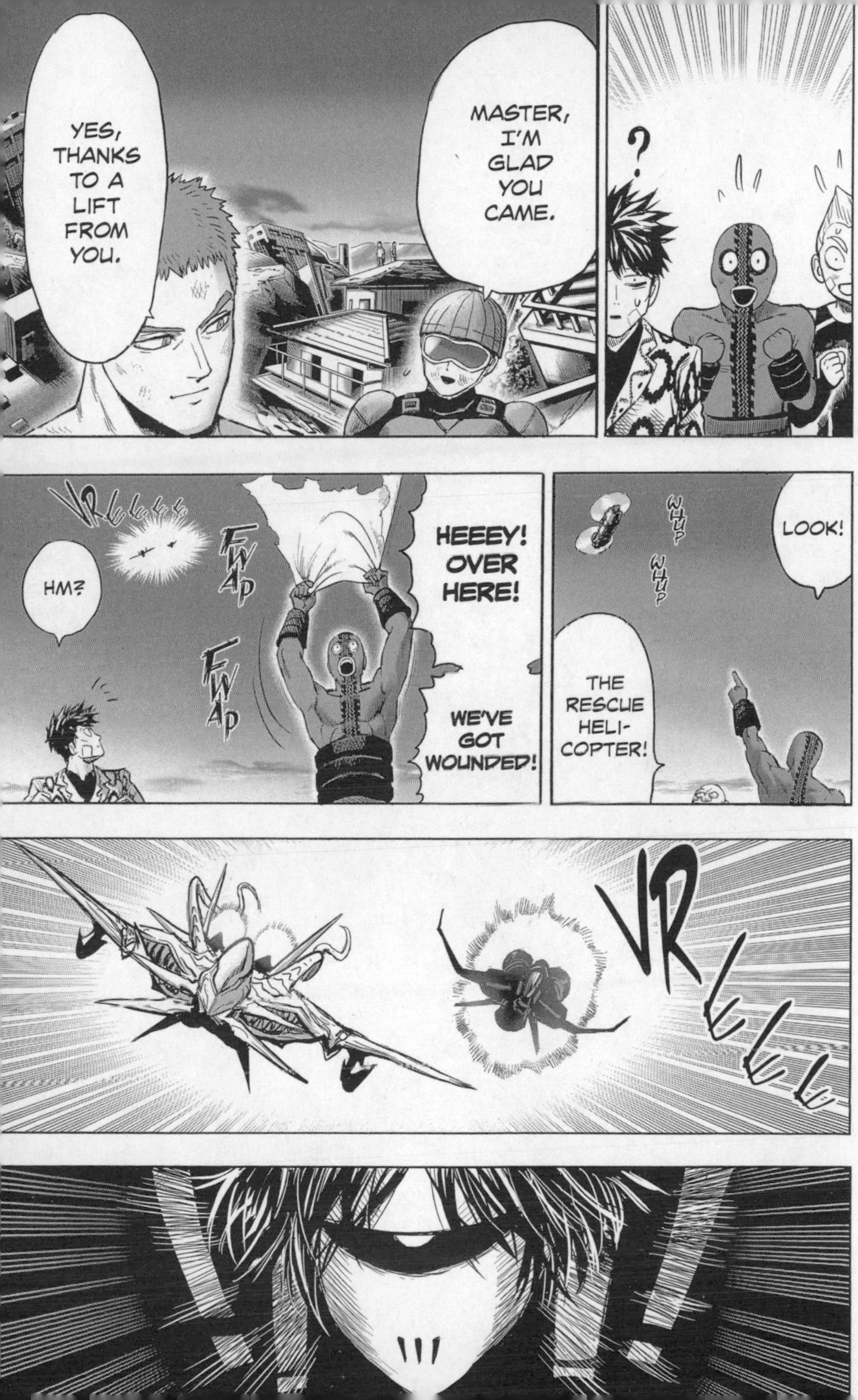
MASTER, I'M GLAD YOU CAME.
YES, THANKS TO A LIFT FROM YOU.
LOOK!
WHUP
WHUP
THE RESCUE HELI-COPTER!
HEEEY! OVER HERE!
WE'VE GOT WOUNDED!
FWAP
FWAP
VREEEE
HM?
VREEEE

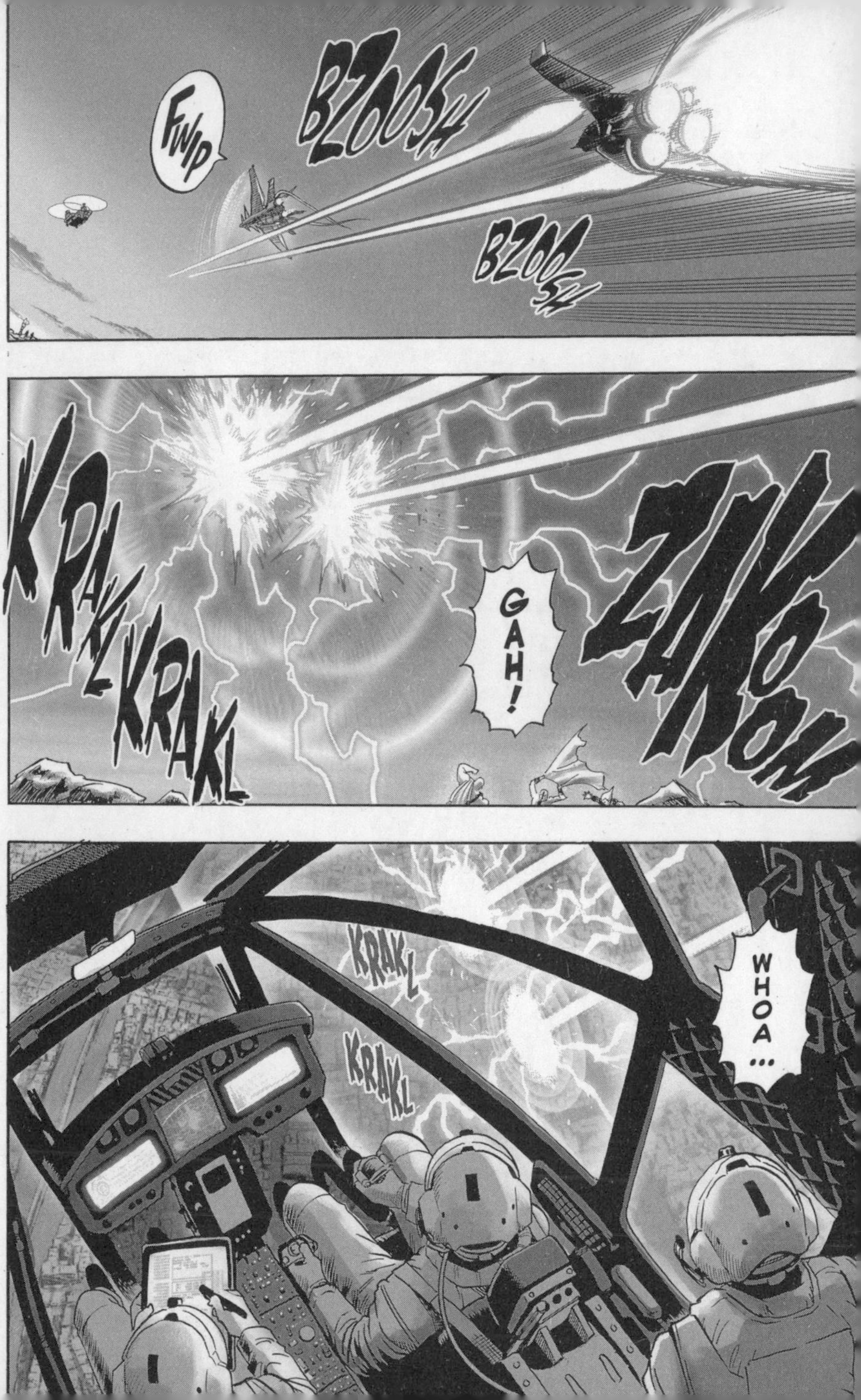
BZOOSH
FWIP
BZOOSH
ZAKOOM
GAH!
KRAKL
KRAKL
WHOA...
KRAKL
KRAKL

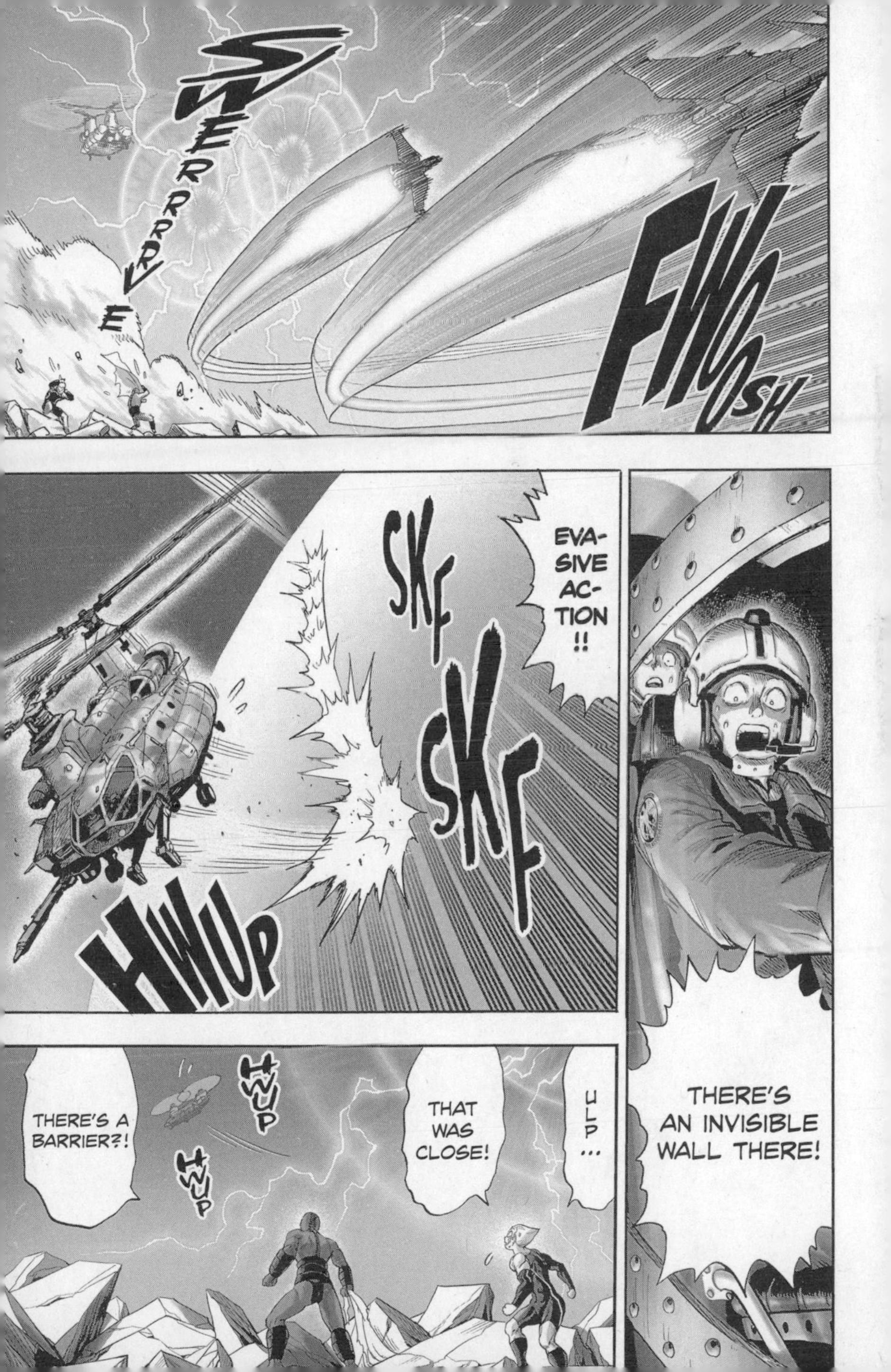
SWERRRRVE
FWOOSH
THERE'S AN INVISIBLE WALL THERE!
EVA-SIVE AC-TION!!
SKF SKF
HWUP
ULP...
THAT WAS CLOSE!
HWUP
HWUP
THERE'S A BARRIER?!

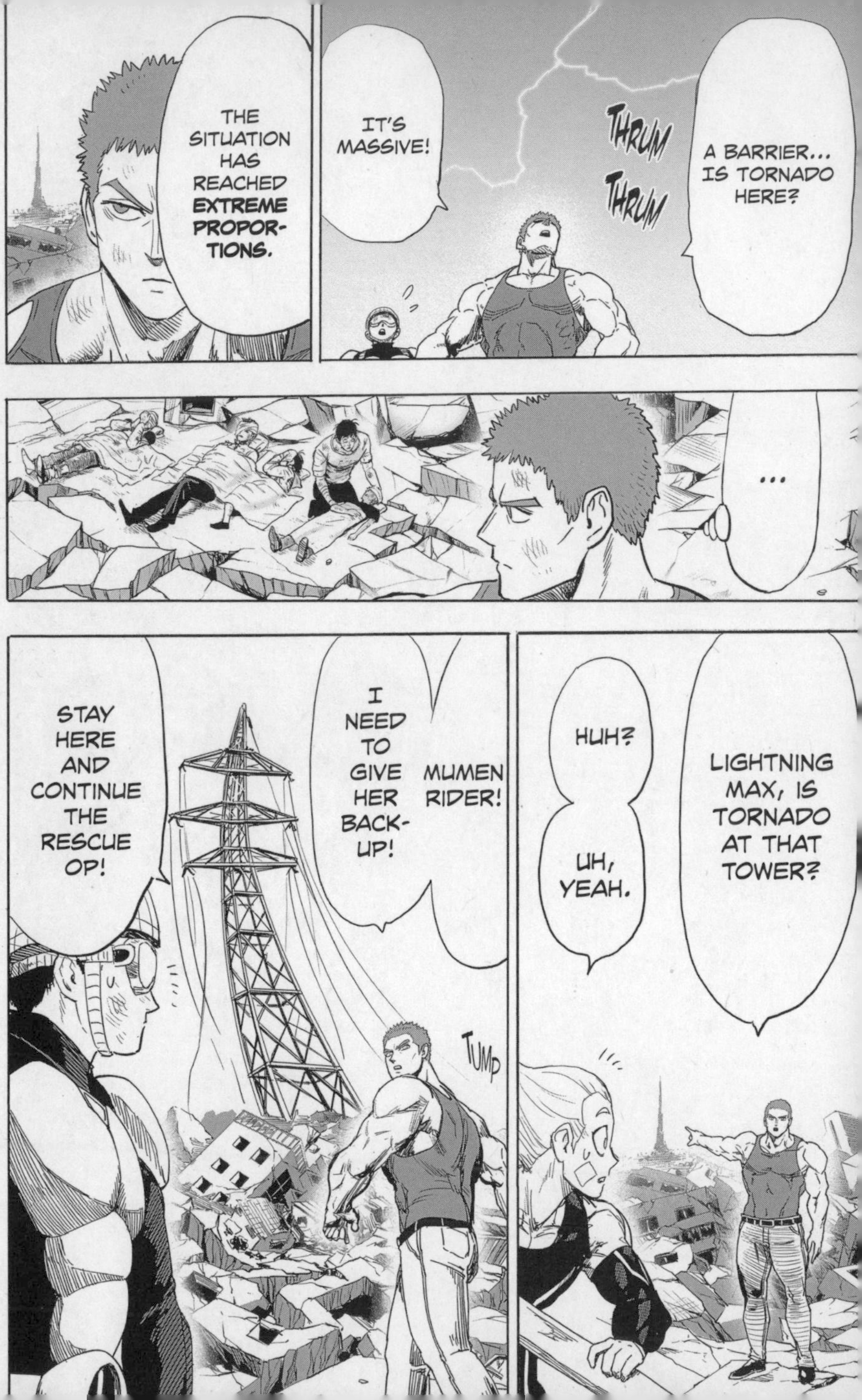
A BARRIER... IS TORNADO HERE?
THRUM THRUM
IT'S MASSIVE!
THE SITUATION HAS REACHED EXTREME PROPORTIONS.
...
LIGHTNING MAX, IS TORNADO AT THAT TOWER?
HUH?
UH, YEAH.
MUMEN RIDER!
I NEED TO GIVE HER BACK-UP!
TUMP
STAY HERE AND CONTINUE THE RESCUE OP!

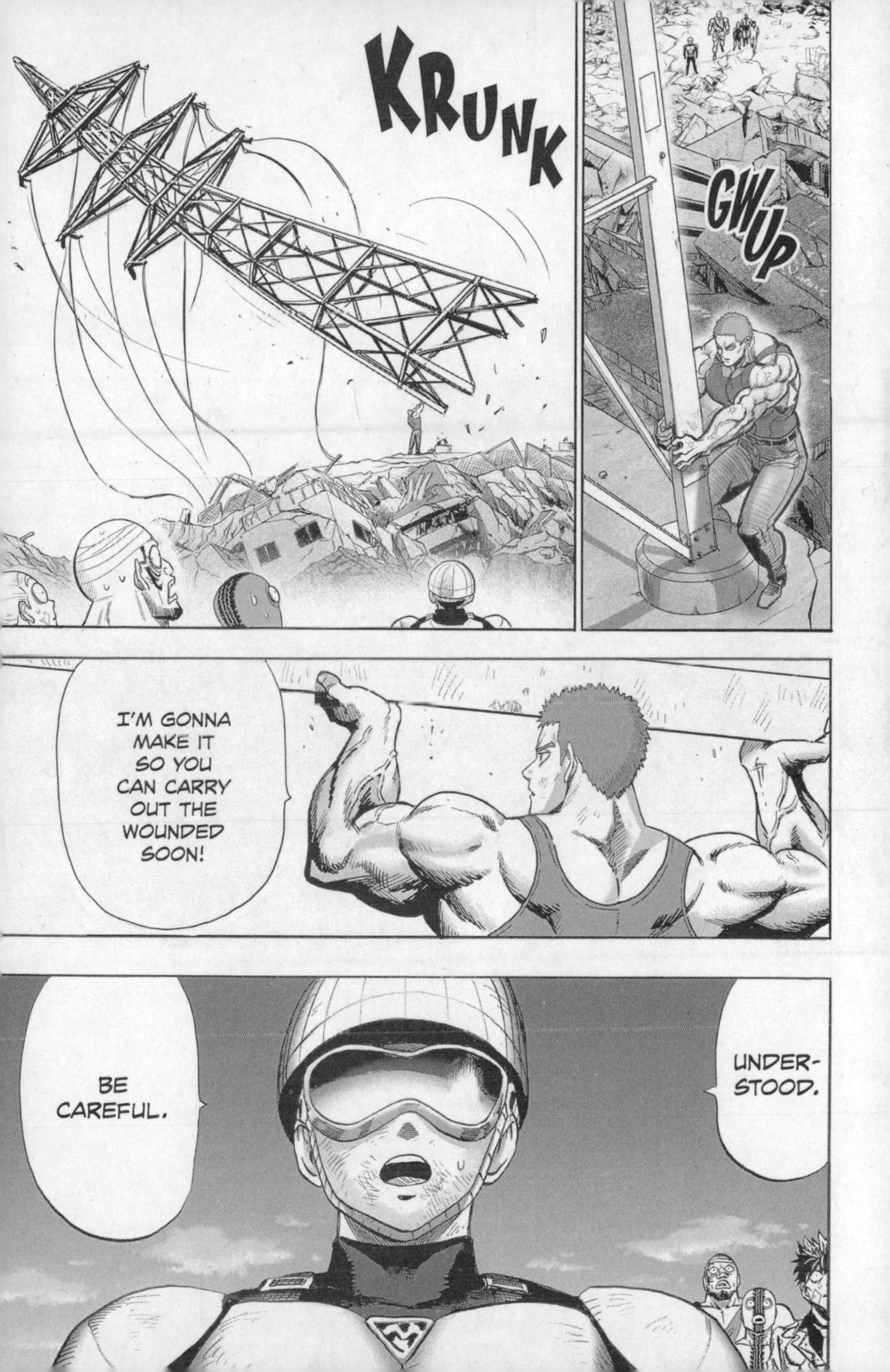
GWUP
KRUNK
I'M GONNA MAKE IT SO YOU CAN CARRY OUT THE WOUNDED SOON!
UNDER-STOOD.
BE CAREFUL.

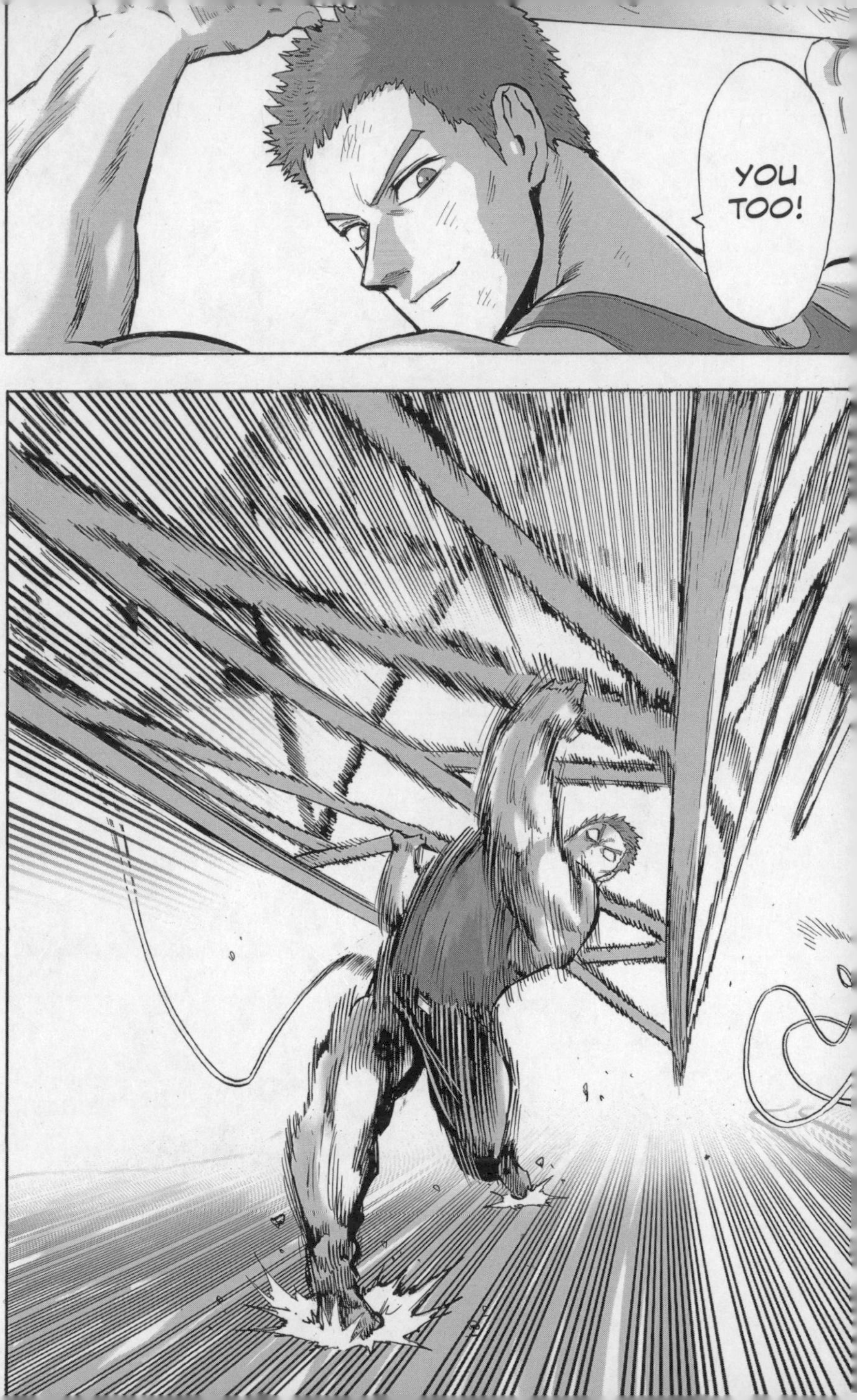
YOU TOO!

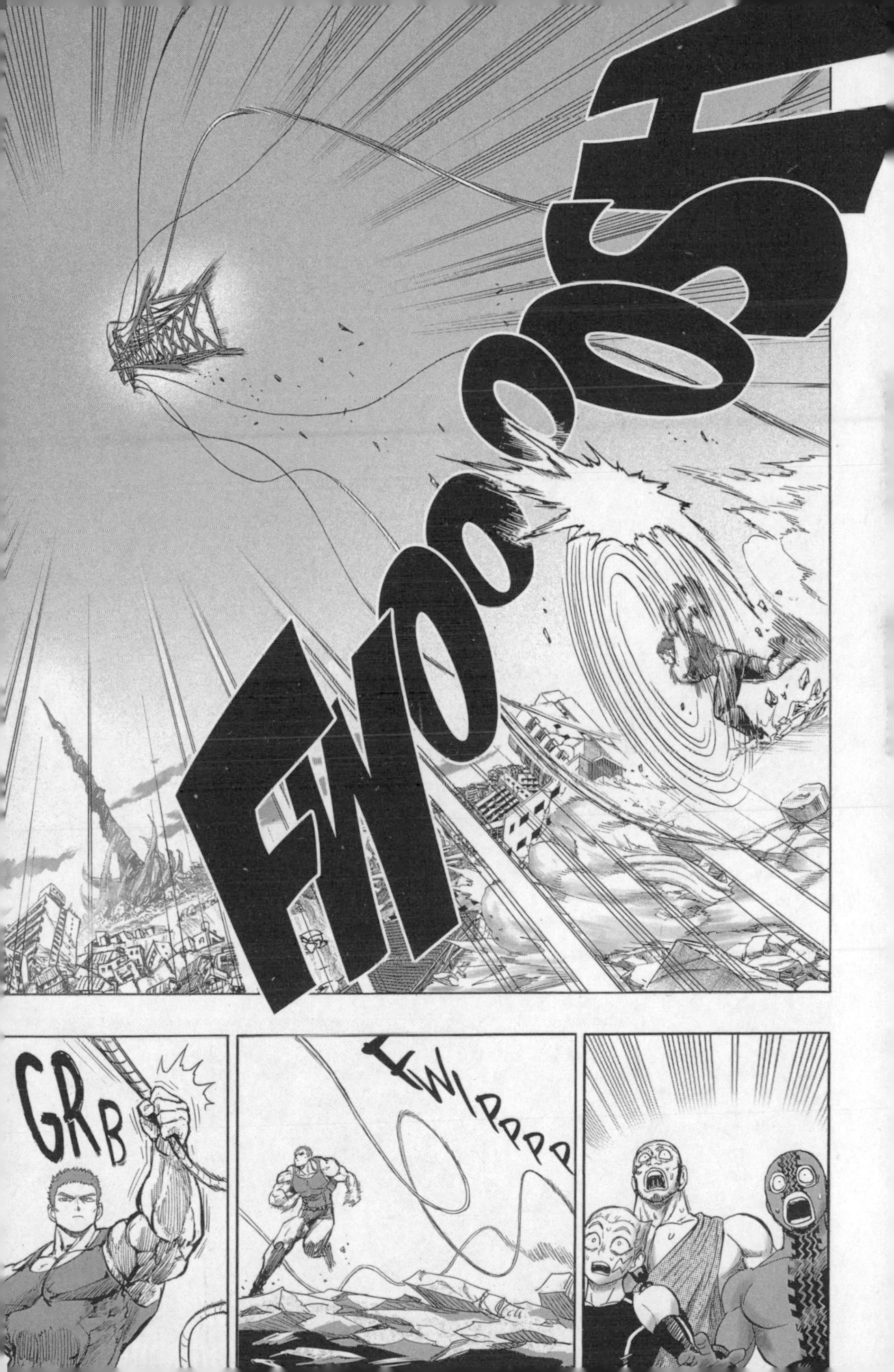
FWOOOOSH
KWIPPPPP
GRB

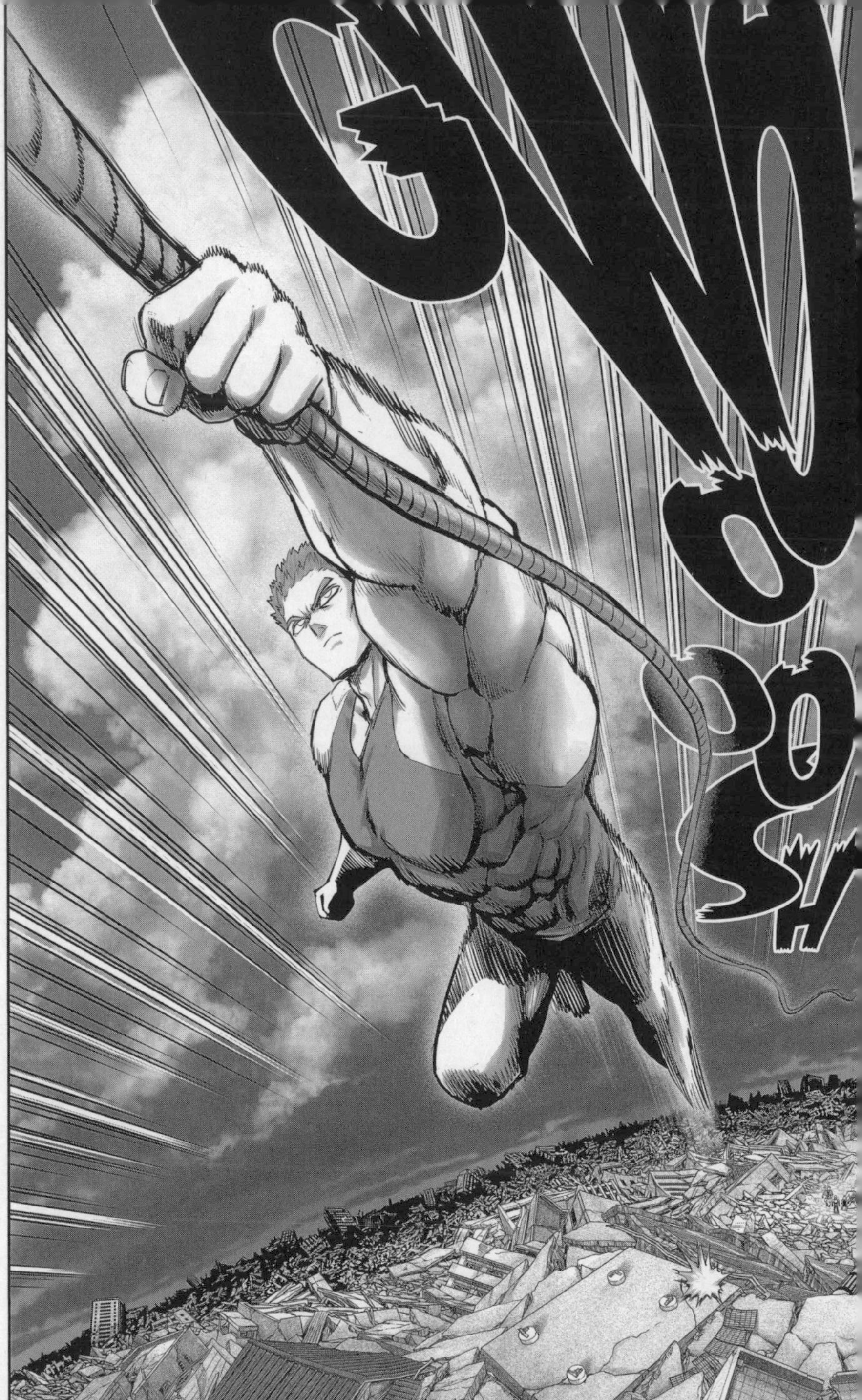
GWOOOOSH

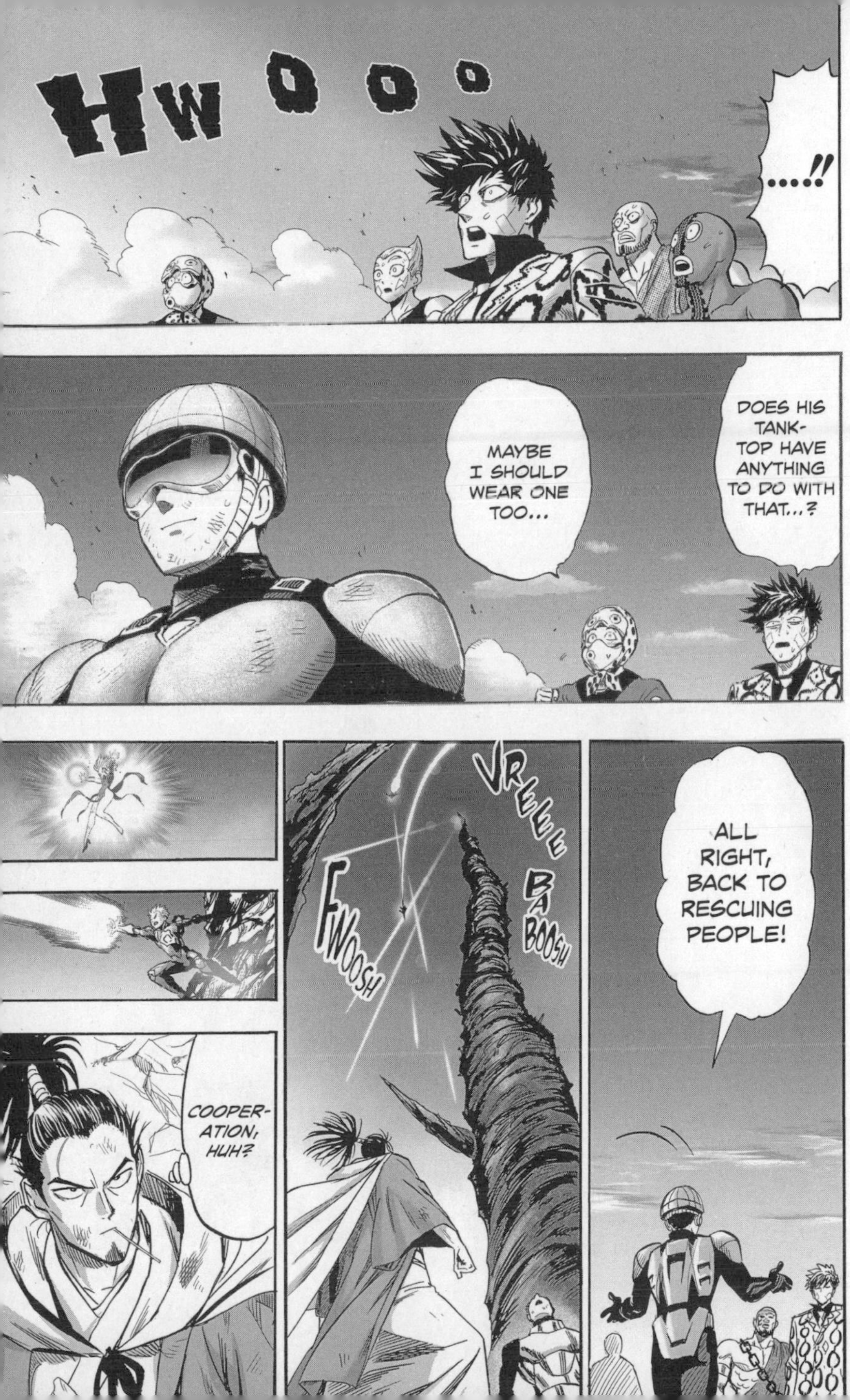
....!!
HWOOO
DOES HIS TANK-TOP HAVE ANYTHING TO DO WITH THAT...?
MAYBE I SHOULD WEAR ONE TOO...
ALL RIGHT, BACK TO RESCUING PEOPLE!
VREEE
BABOOSH
FWOOSH
COOPER-ATION, HUH?

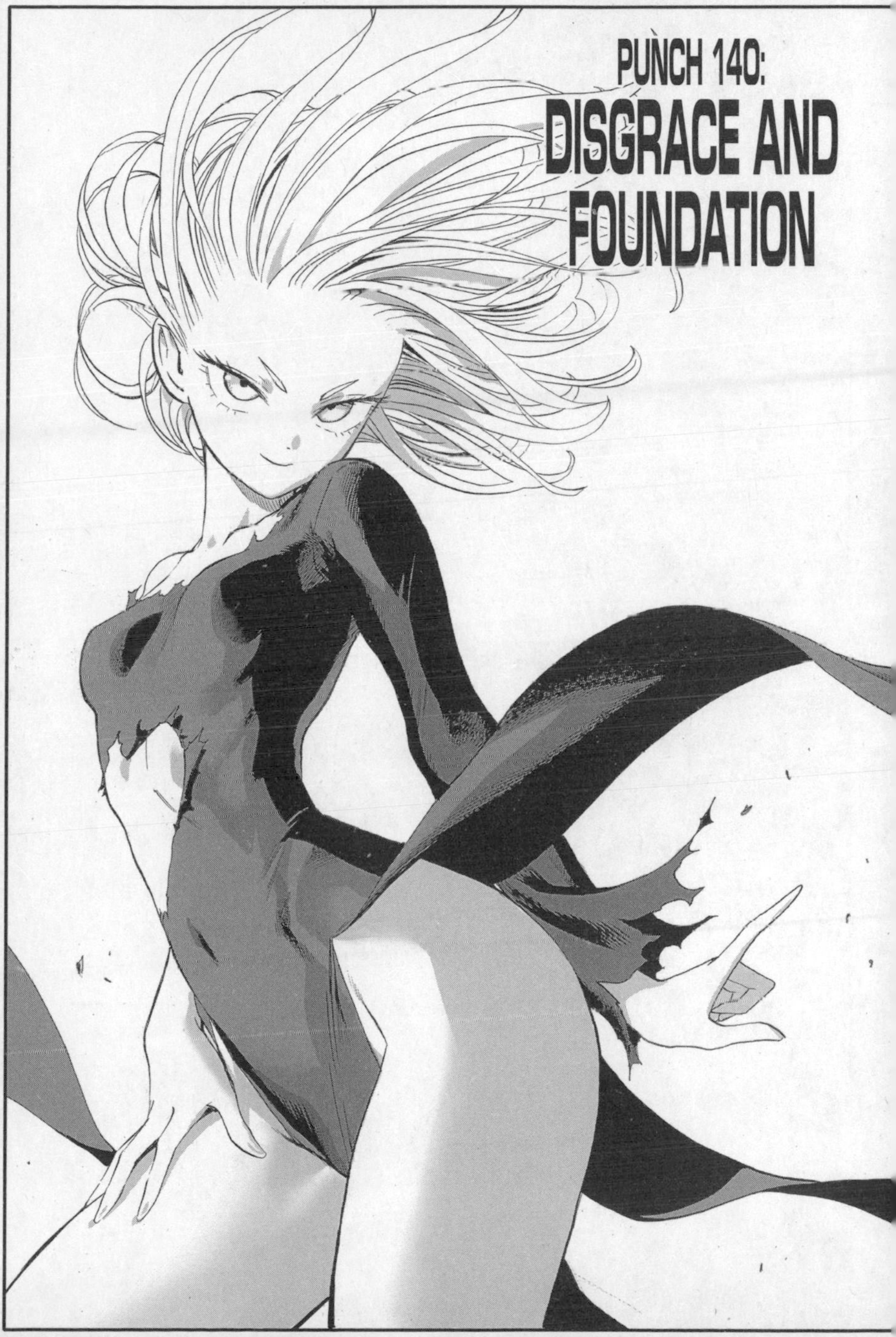
PUNCH 140:
DISGRACE AND FOUNDATION

VREEE

Five minutes ago...

...AND NOW TERRIBLE TORNADO IS BATTLING THE MONSTER ASSOCIATION'S LEADER!

RMMM RMMM

A TOWER SPLIT THE EARTH'S CRUST AND ROSE OVERHEAD...

KRAKKRAK

FWAAA

I'D LIKE TO TAKE SAMPLES OF THE FLESH LYING AROUND, BUT I'M LOW ON ENERGY.

KRAKL KRAKL

SO I'LL HELP MYSELF!

VMM

TOMP

THIS IS JUST WHAT I NEED.

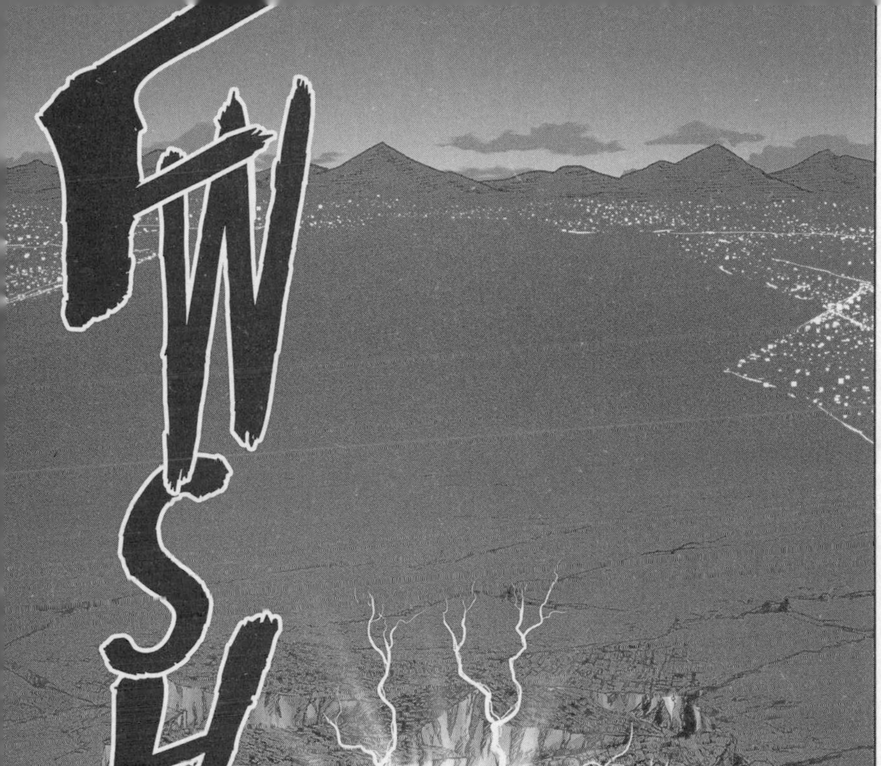
FWSH
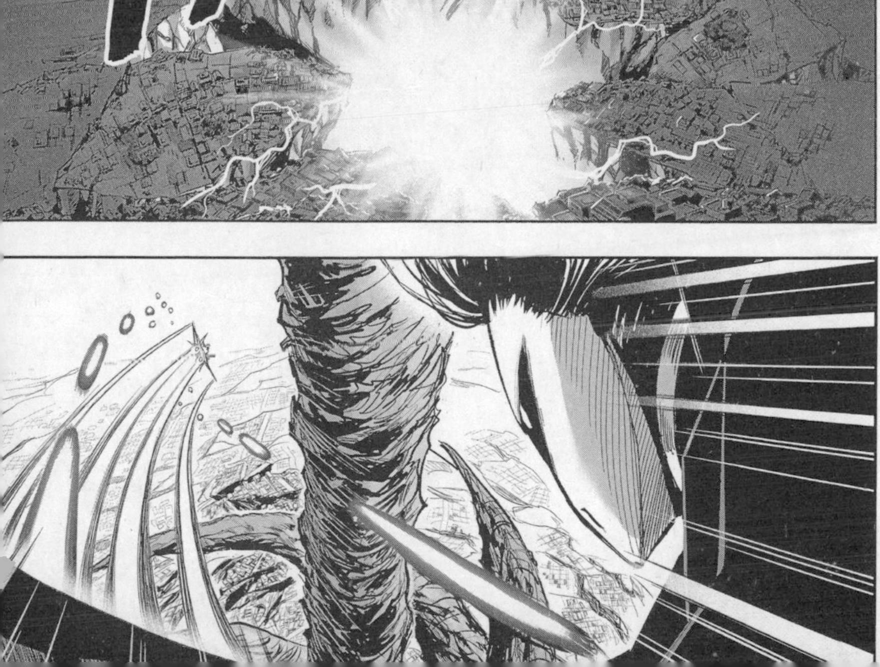

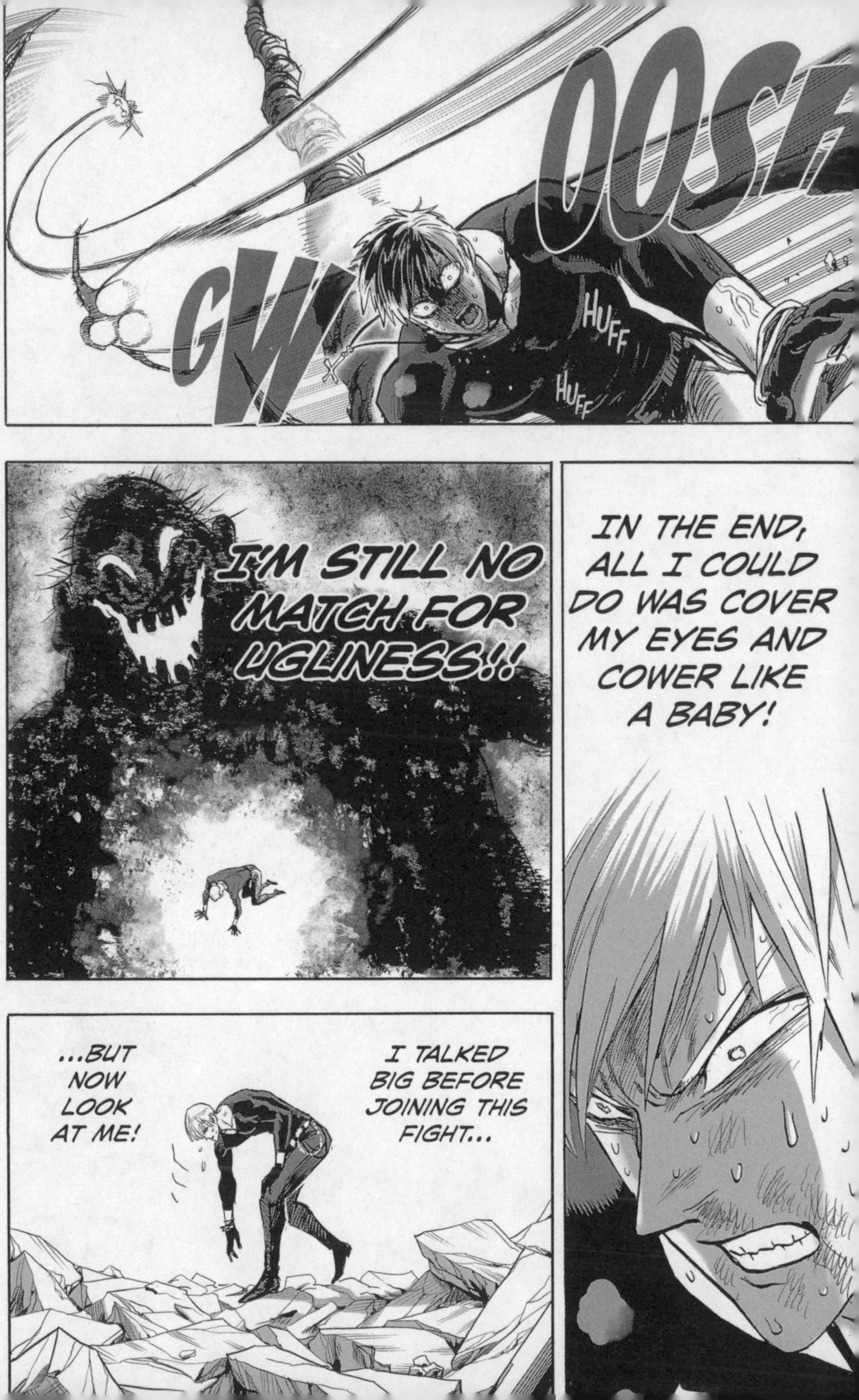
OOSH
HUFF
HUFF
GW
IN THE END, ALL I COULD DO WAS COVER MY EYES AND COWER LIKE A BABY!
I'M STILL NO MATCH FOR UGLINESS!!
I TALKED BIG BEFORE JOINING THIS FIGHT...
...BUT NOW LOOK AT ME!

HUH ?!

DID THEY OVERHEAR ME PANICKING TO TORNADO OVER MY TRANSMITTER?!

GASP

WHY ARE THEY STARING AT ME?

URGH...

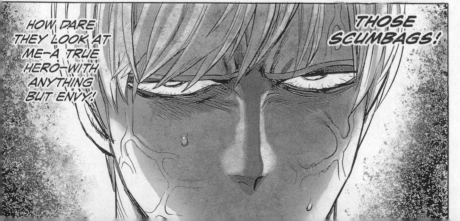

HOW DARE THEY LOOK AT ME—A TRUE HERO—WITH ANYTHING BUT ENVY!!

THOSE SCUMBAGS!

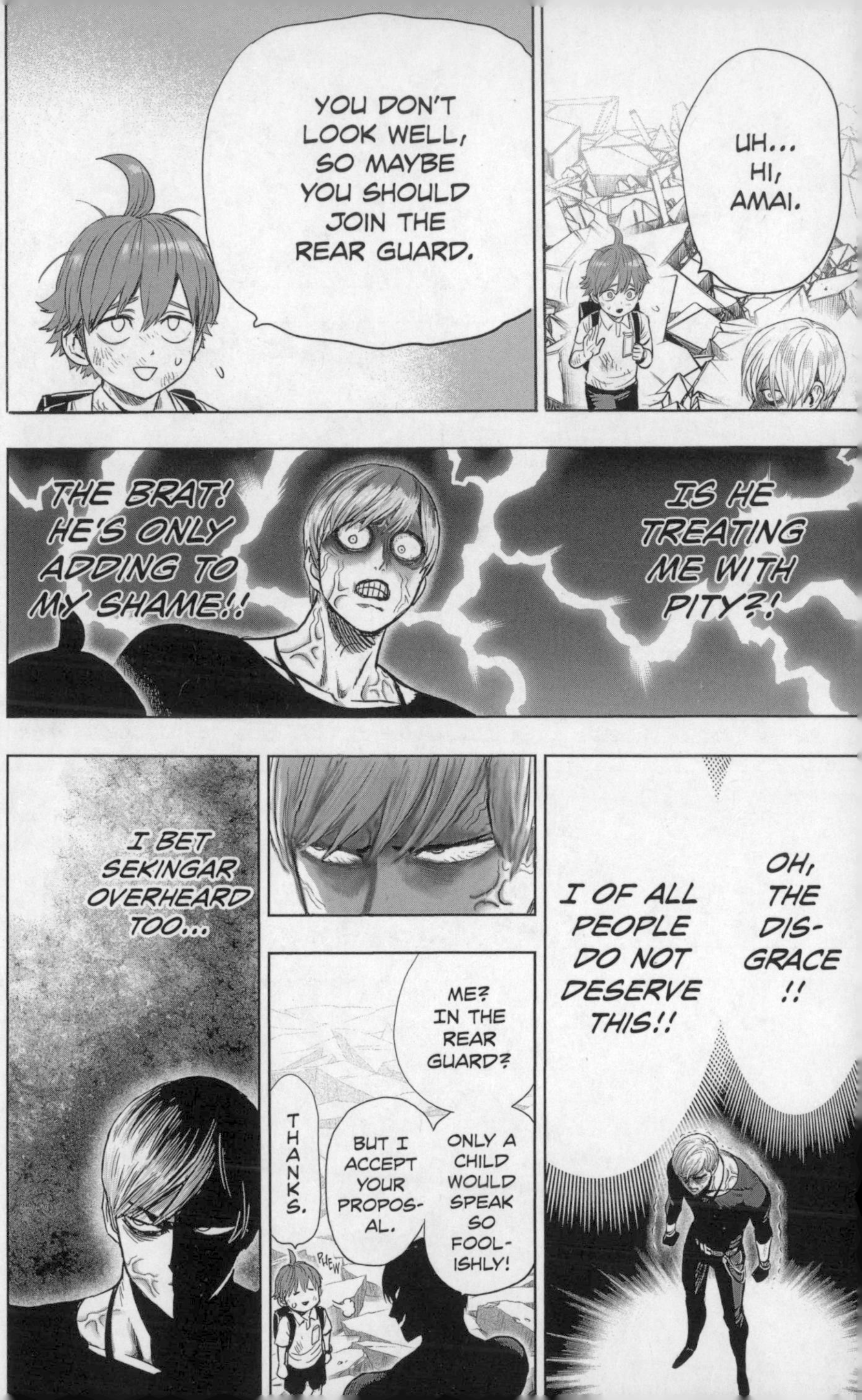
UH... HI, AMAI.
YOU DON'T LOOK WELL, SO MAYBE YOU SHOULD JOIN THE REAR GUARD.
IS HE TREATING ME WITH PITY?!
THE BRAT! HE'S ONLY ADDING TO MY SHAME!!
OH, THE DIS-GRACE !!
I OF ALL PEOPLE DO NOT DESERVE THIS!!
ME? IN THE REAR GUARD?
ONLY A CHILD WOULD SPEAK SO FOOL-ISHLY!
BUT I ACCEPT YOUR PROPOS-AL.
THANKS.
PHEW
I BET SEKINGAR OVERHEARD TOO...

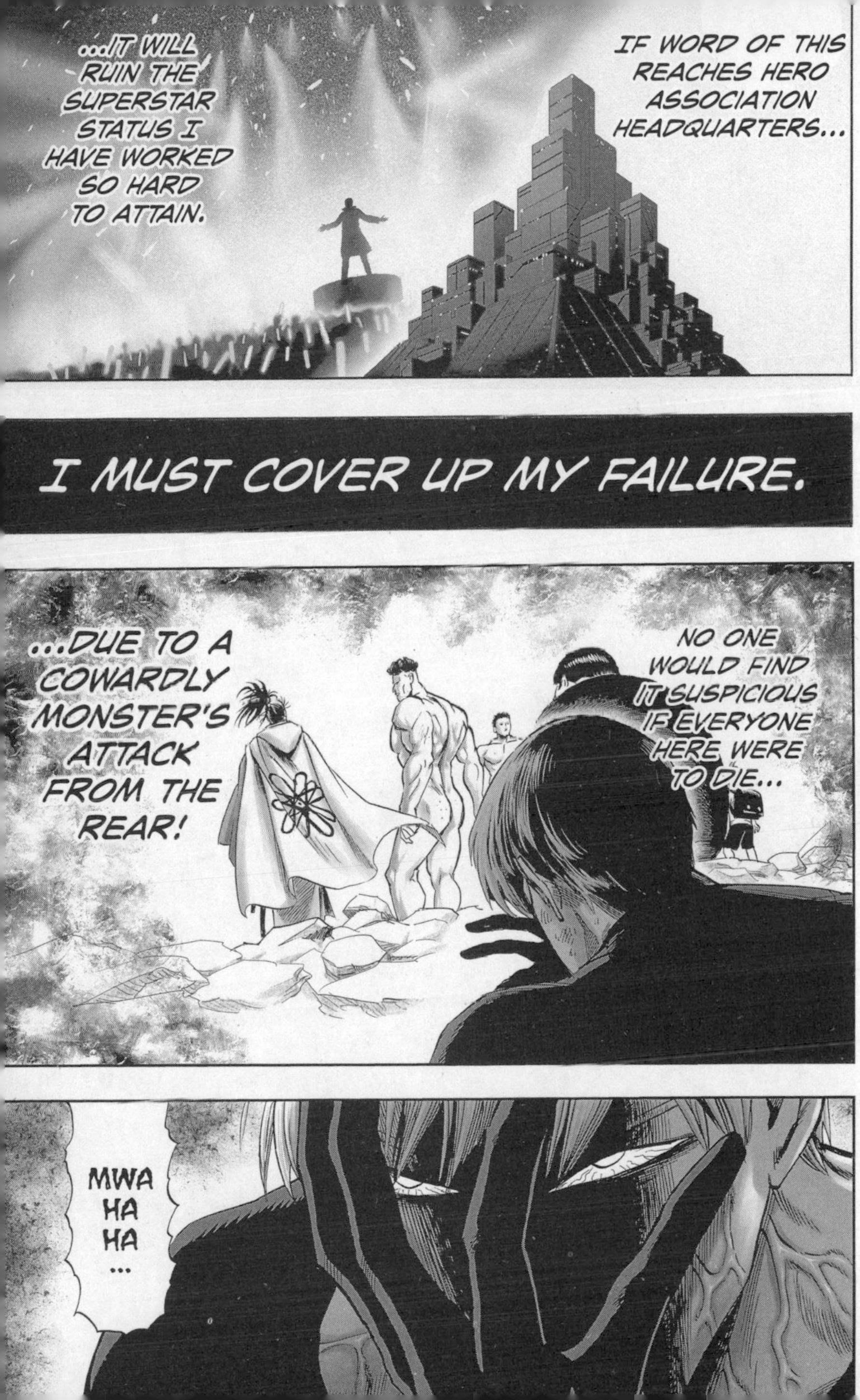
IF WORD OF THIS REACHES HERO ASSOCIATION HEADQUARTERS...
...IT WILL RUIN THE SUPERSTAR STATUS I HAVE WORKED SO HARD TO ATTAIN.
I MUST COVER UP MY FAILURE.
NO ONE WOULD FIND IT SUSPICIOUS IF EVERYONE HERE WERE TO DIE...
...DUE TO A COWARDLY MONSTER'S ATTACK FROM THE REAR!
MWA HA HA ...

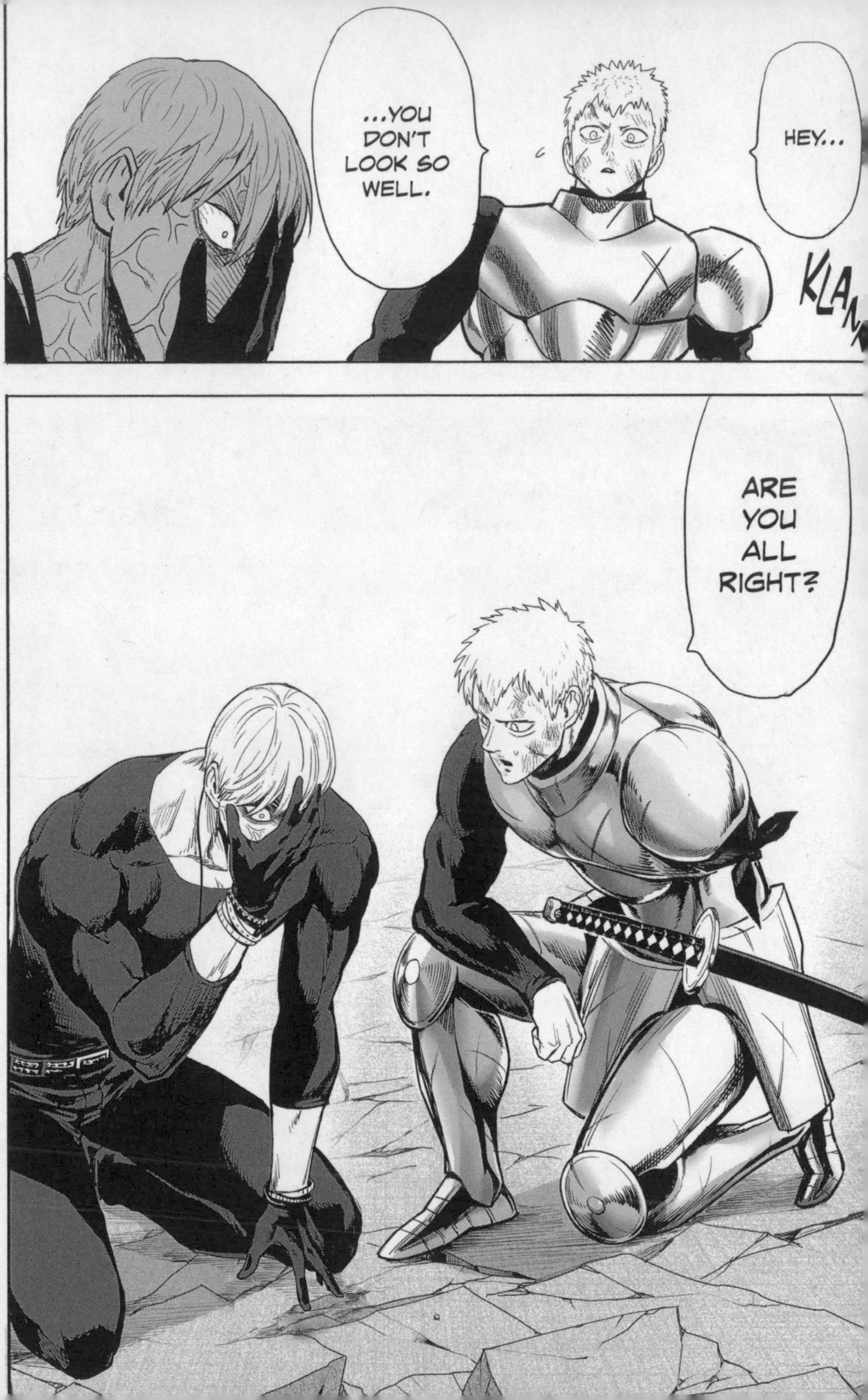
HEY...
KLAN
...YOU DON'T LOOK SO WELL.
ARE YOU ALL RIGHT?

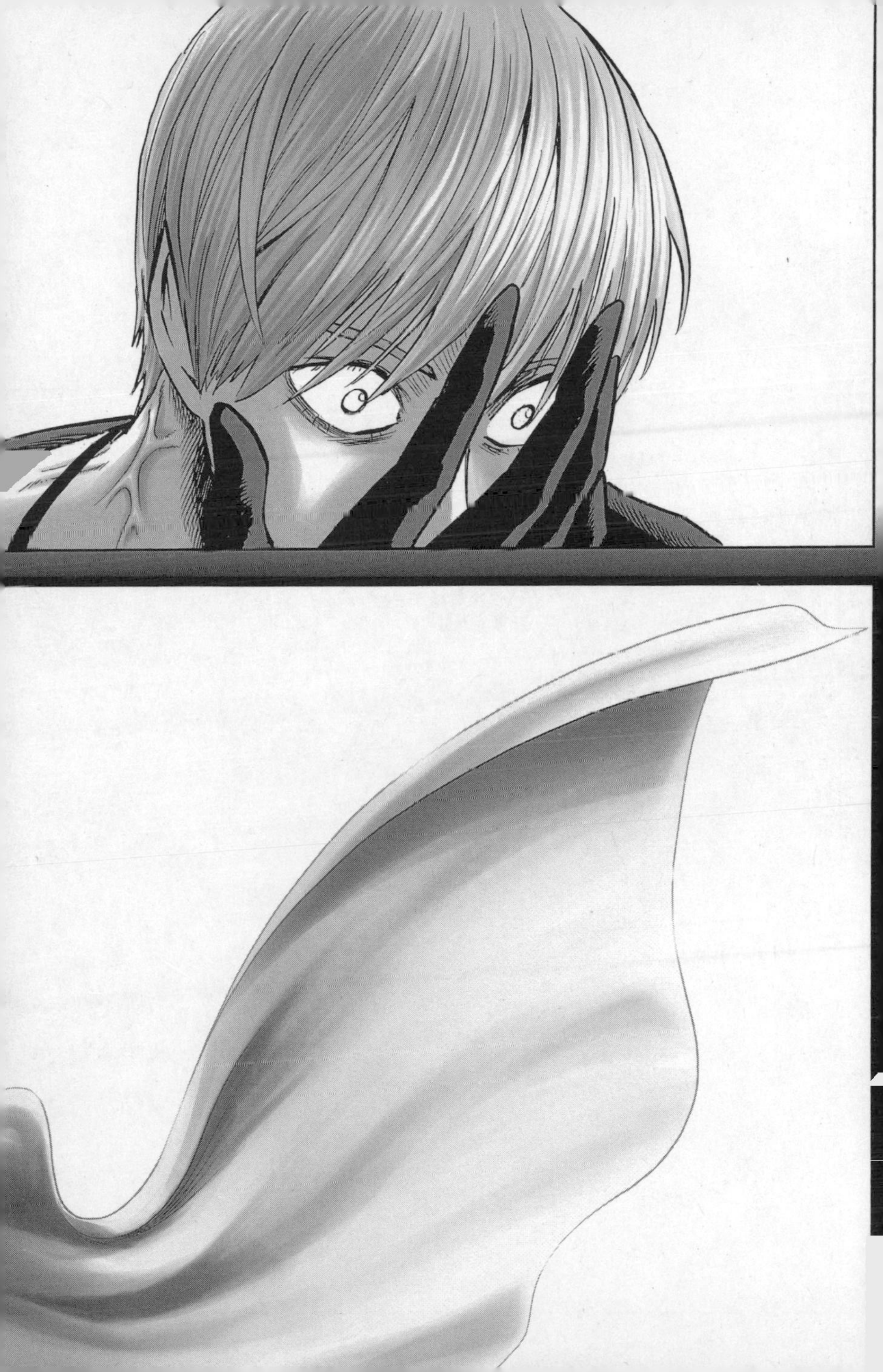

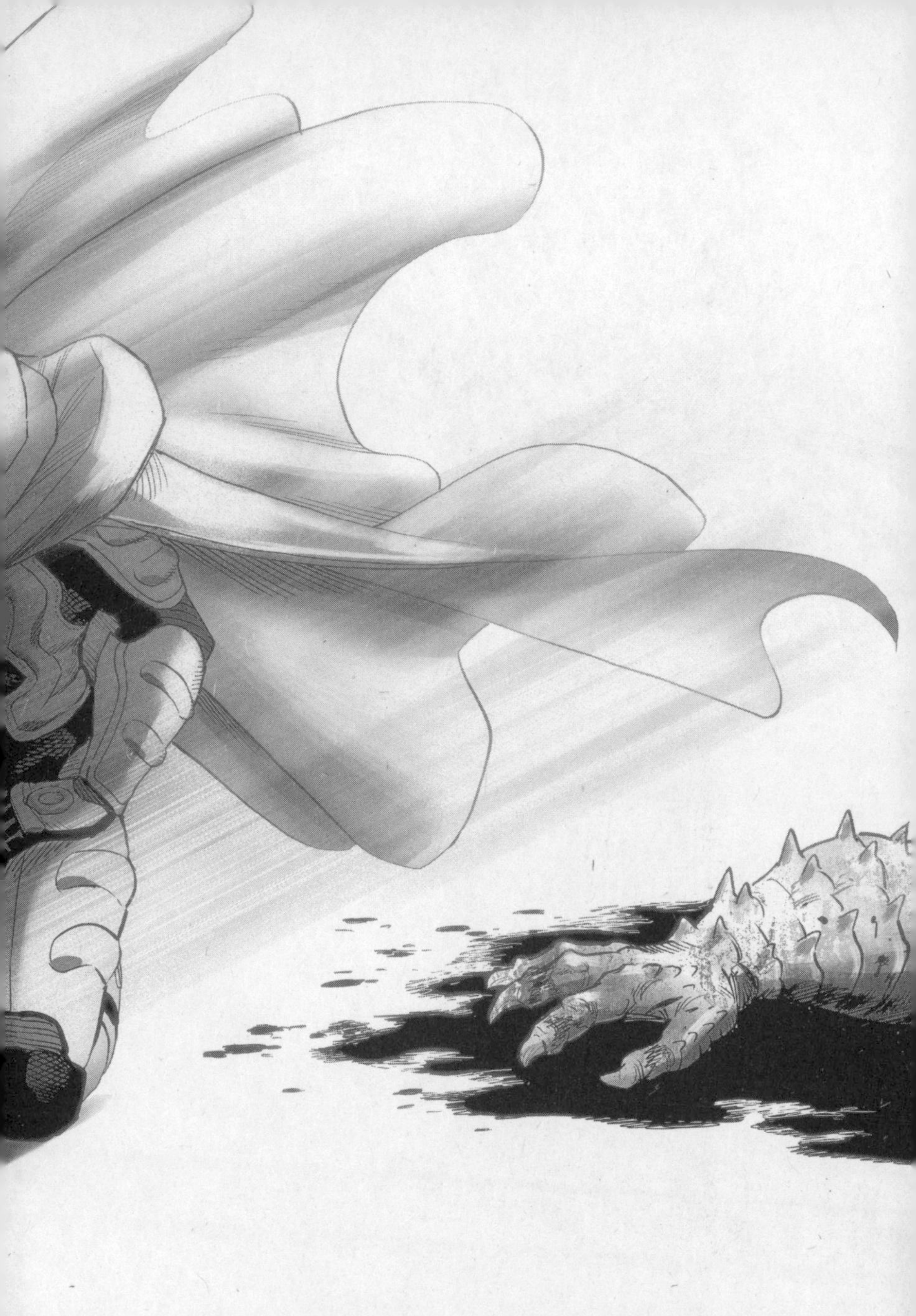

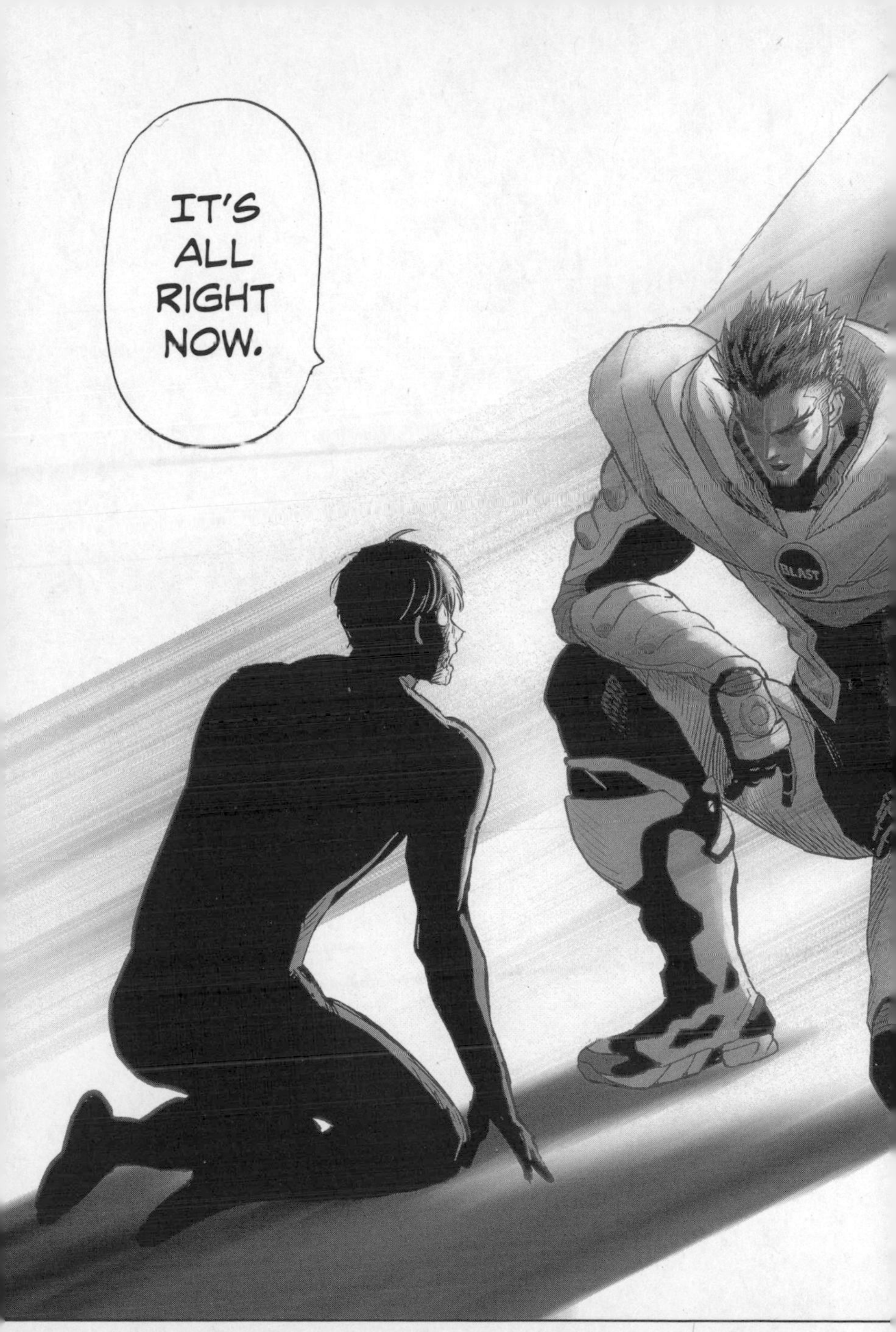
IT'S ALL RIGHT NOW.
BLAST

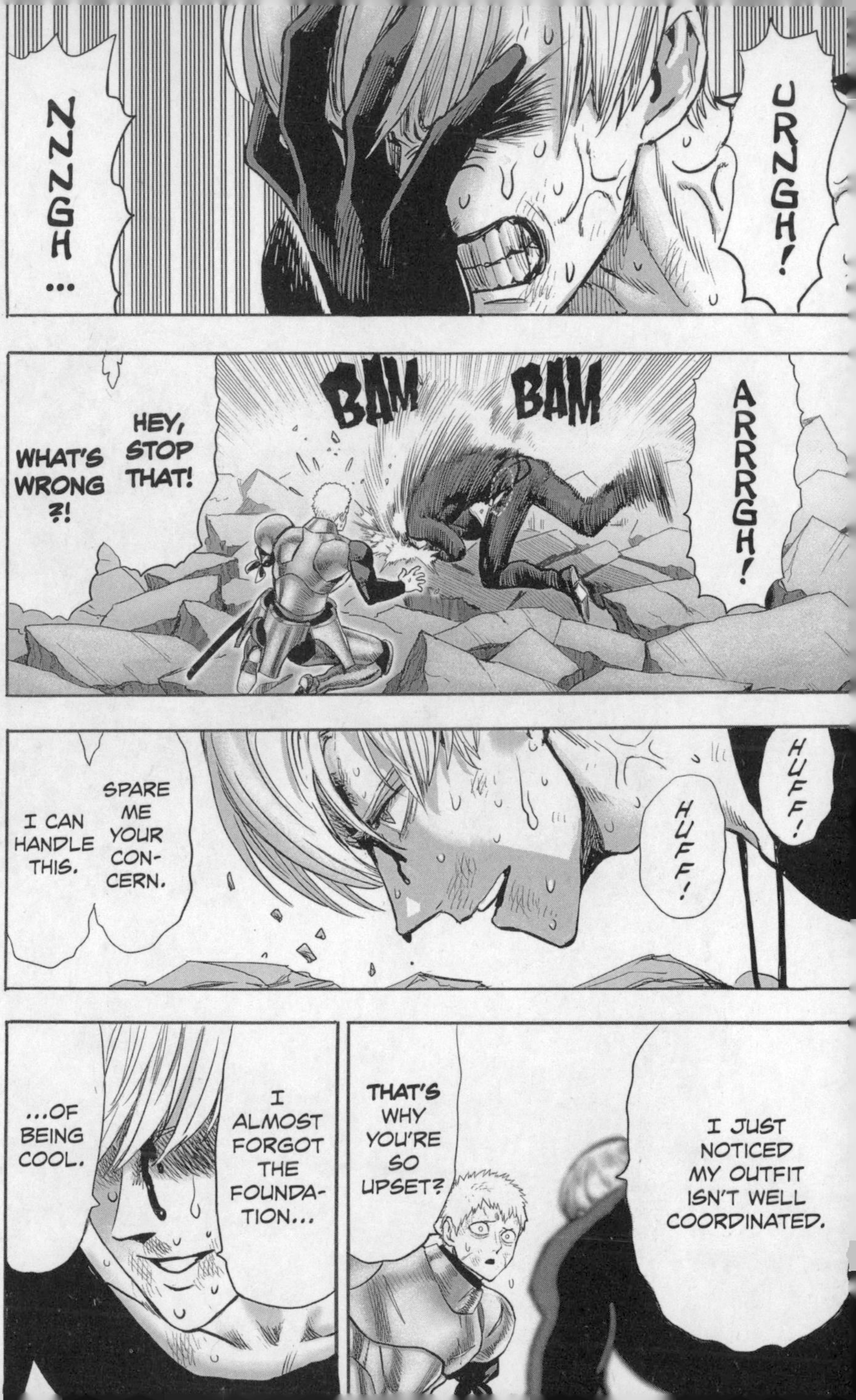
URNGH!
NNNGH...
ARRRGH!
BAM BAM
HEY, STOP THAT!
WHAT'S WRONG?!
HUFF! HUFF!
SPARE ME YOUR CONCERN.
I CAN HANDLE THIS.
I JUST NOTICED MY OUTFIT ISN'T WELL COORDINATED.
THAT'S WHY YOU'RE SO UPSET?
I ALMOST FORGOT THE FOUNDATION...
...OF BEING COOL.

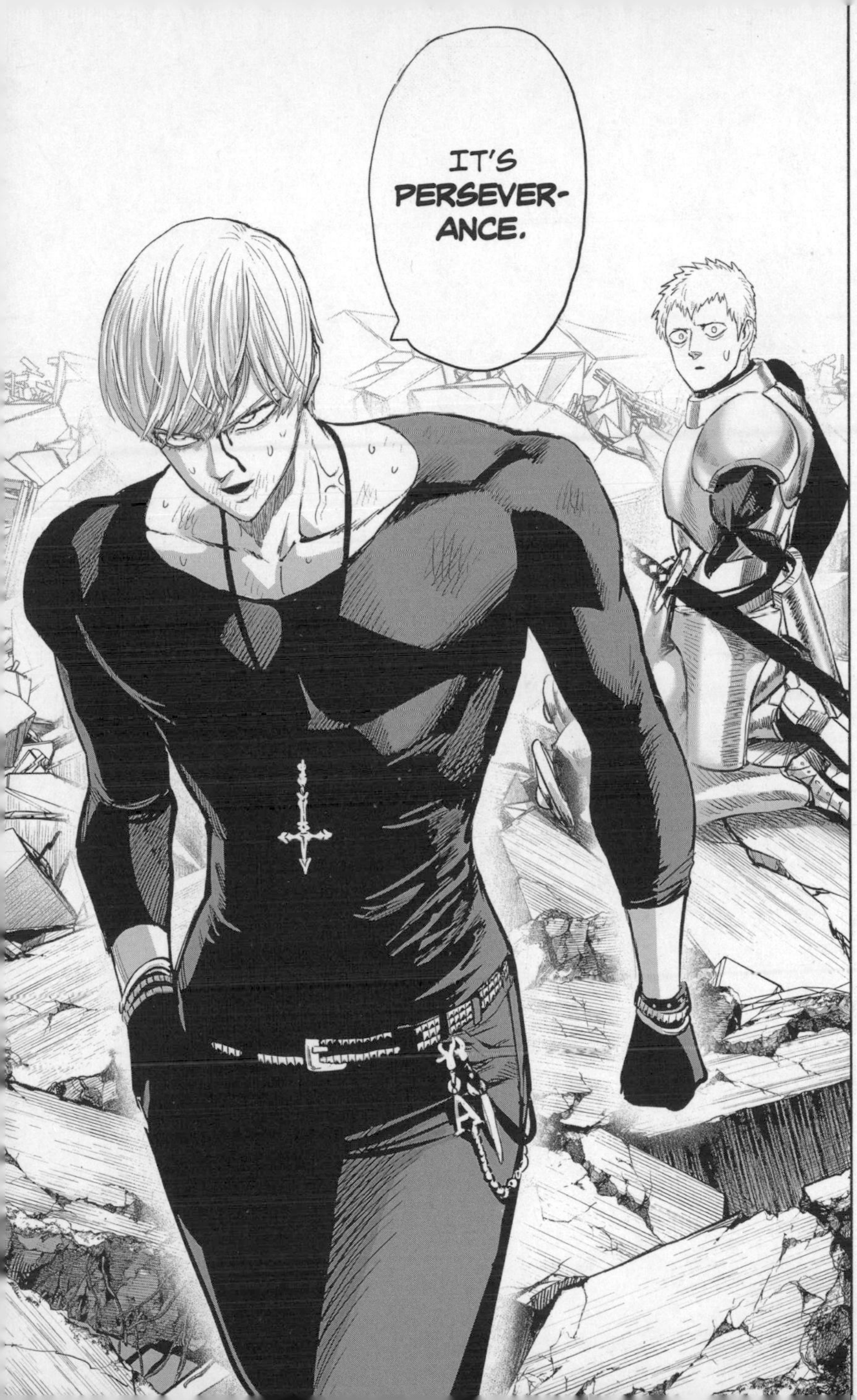
IT'S PERSEVER-ANCE.

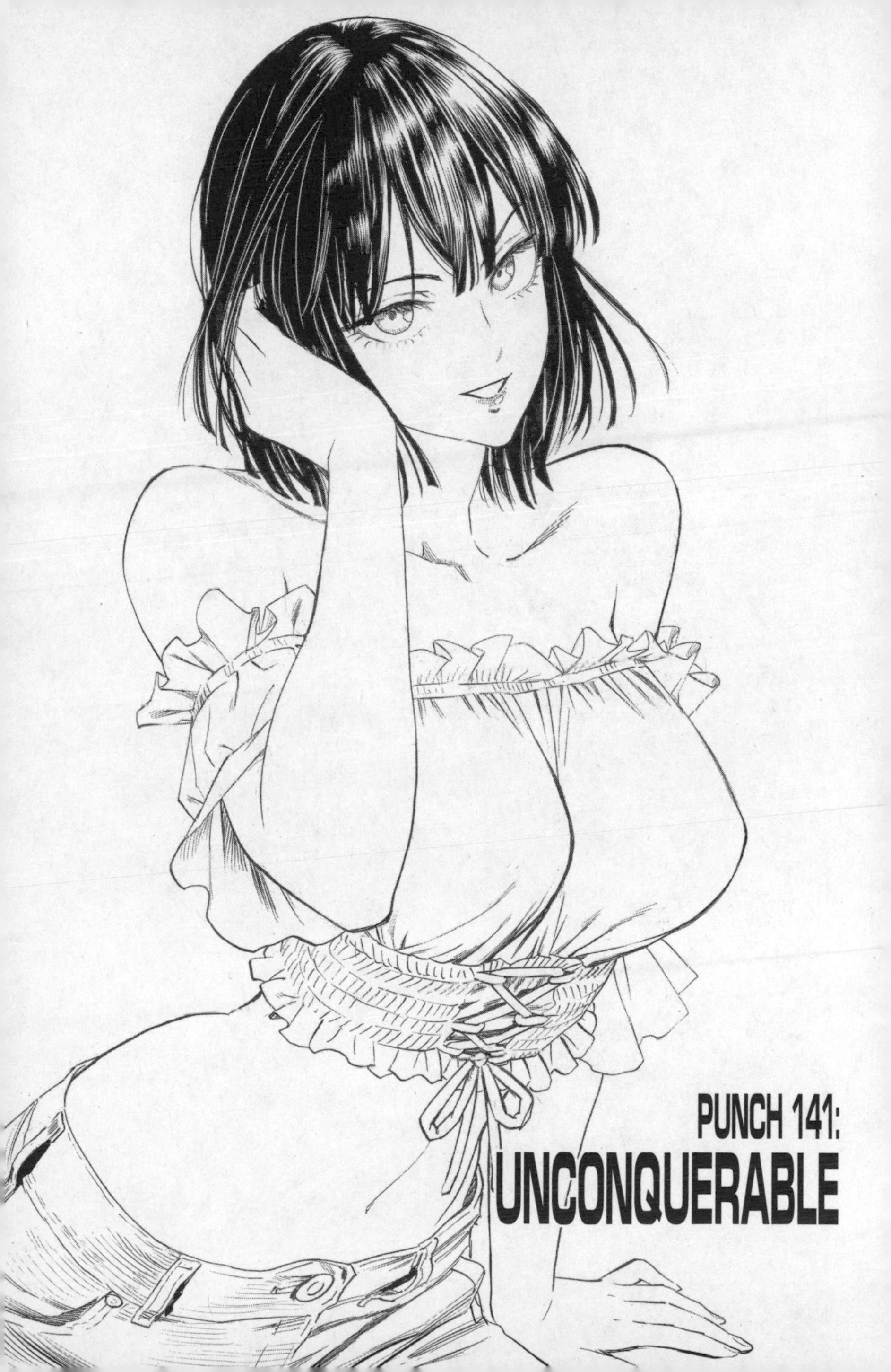

PUNCH 141: UNCONQUERABLE

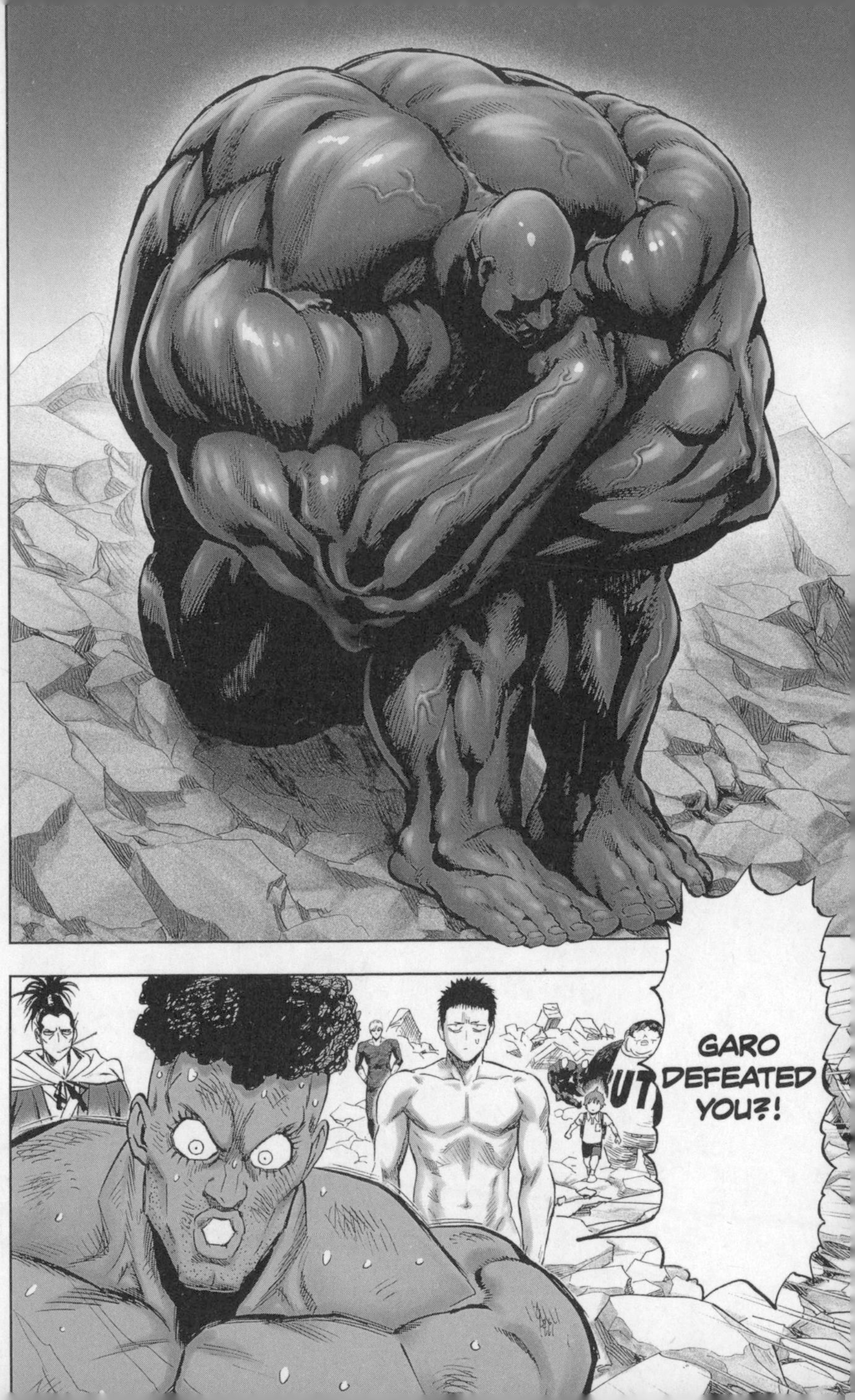
GARO DEFEATED YOU?!

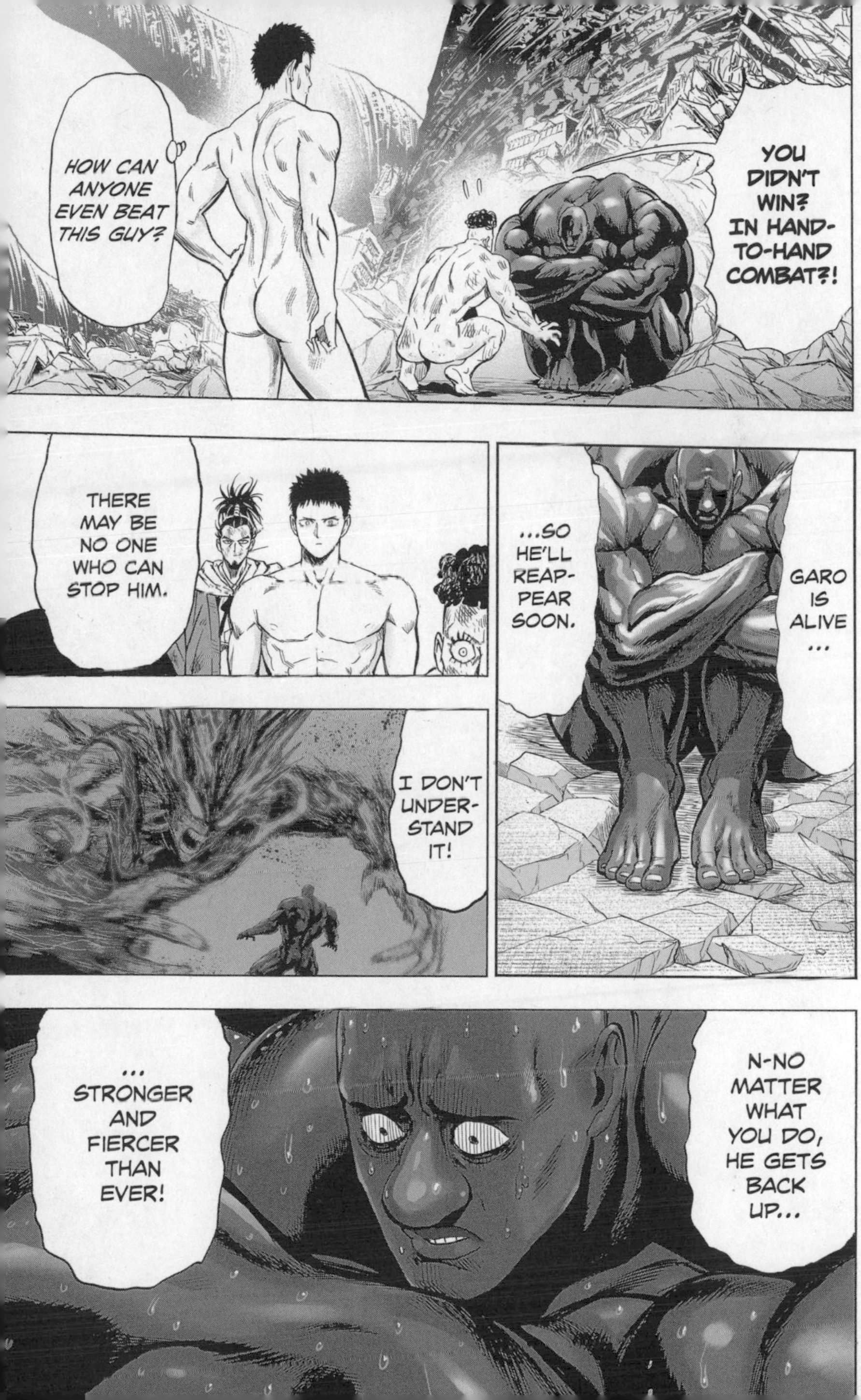
YOU DIDN'T WIN? IN HAND-TO-HAND COMBAT?!
HOW CAN ANYONE EVEN BEAT THIS GUY?
GARO IS ALIVE...
...SO HE'LL REAP-PEAR SOON.
THERE MAY BE NO ONE WHO CAN STOP HIM.
I DON'T UNDER-STAND IT!
N-NO MATTER WHAT YOU DO, HE GETS BACK UP...
... STRONGER AND FIERCER THAN EVER!

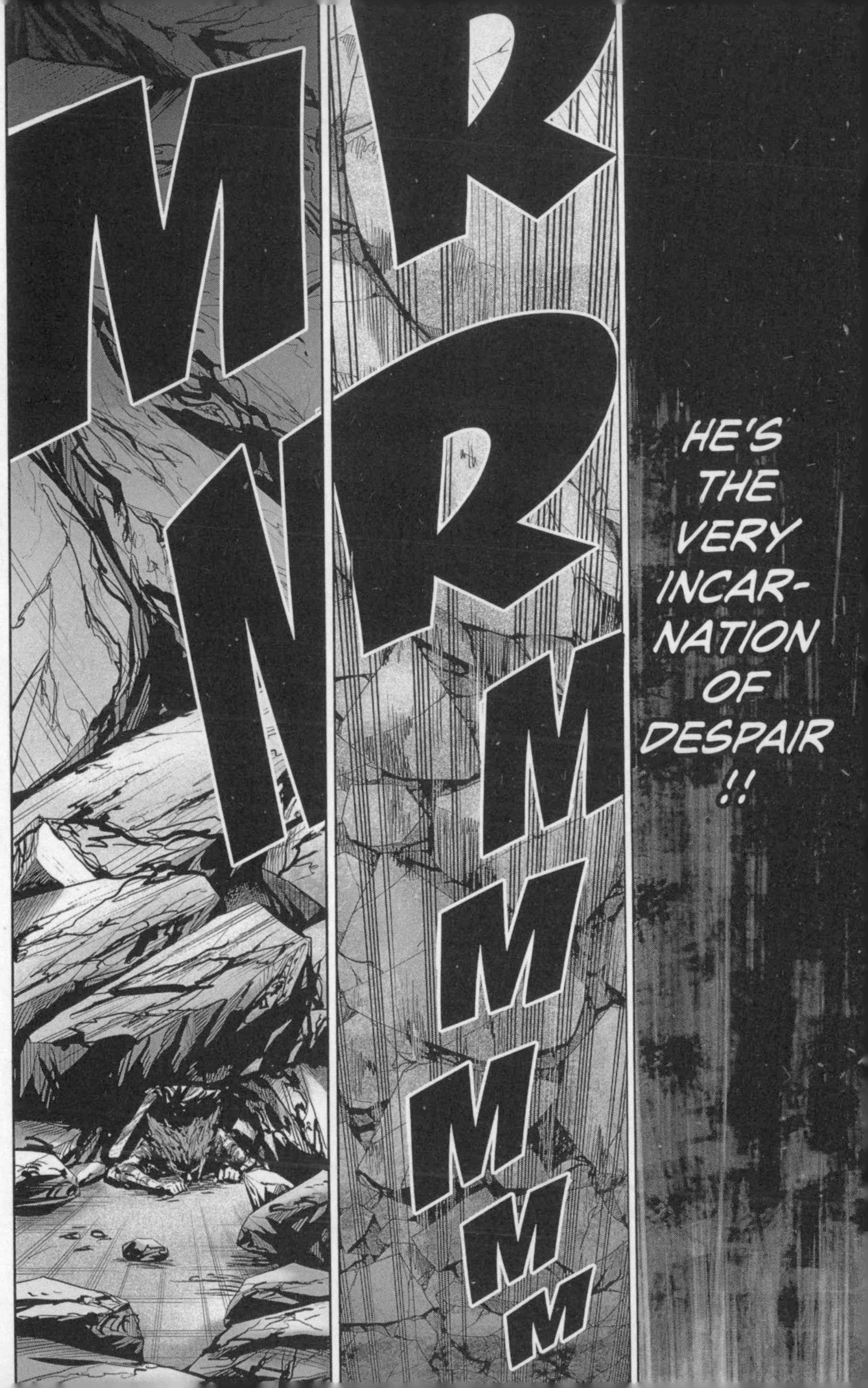
HE'S THE VERY INCAR-NATION OF DESPAIR !!

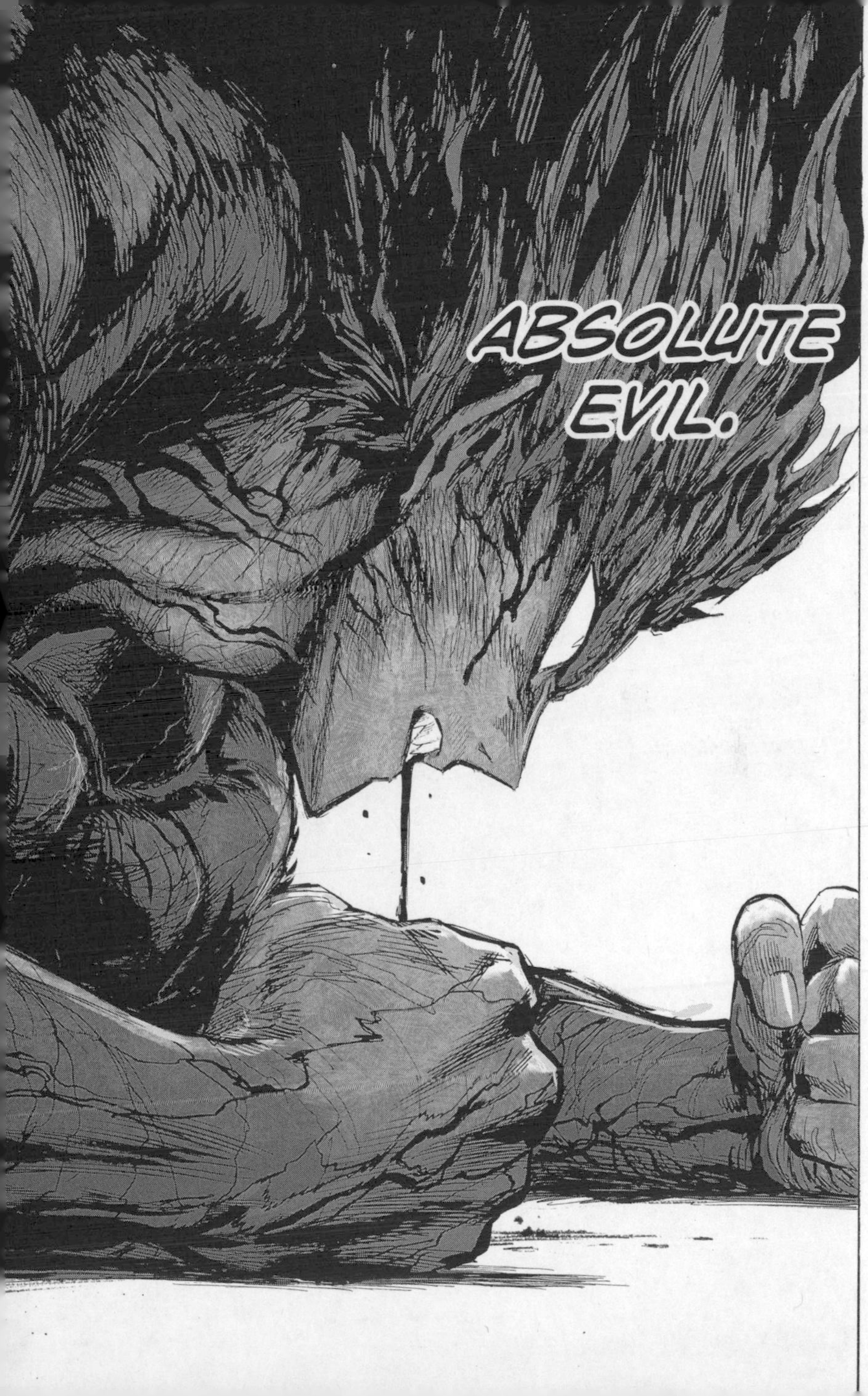
ABSOLUTE EVIL.

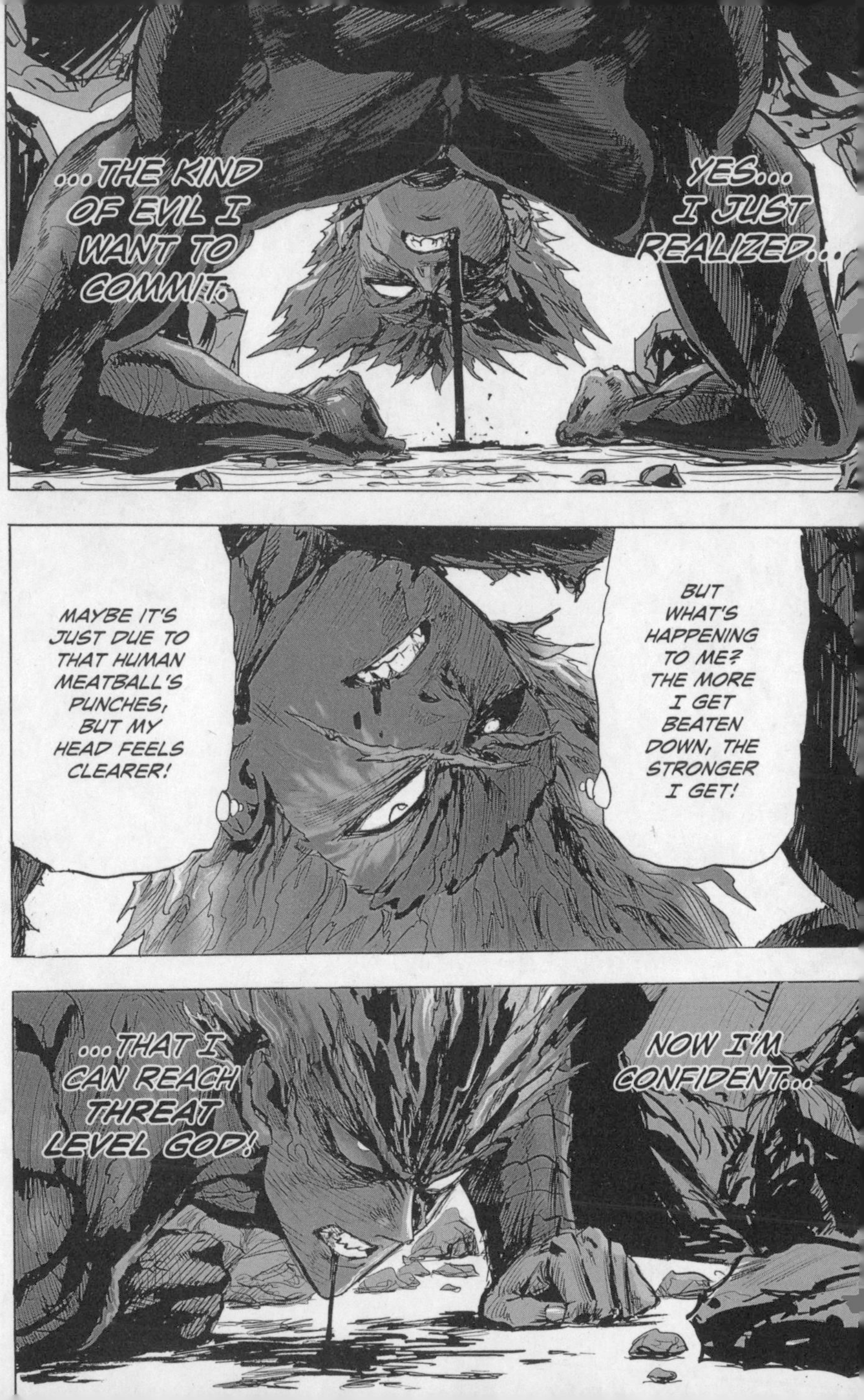
YES... I JUST REALIZED...
...THE KIND OF EVIL I WANT TO COMMIT.
BUT WHAT'S HAPPENING TO ME? THE MORE I GET BEATEN DOWN, THE STRONGER I GET!
MAYBE IT'S JUST DUE TO THAT HUMAN MEATBALL'S PUNCHES, BUT MY HEAD FEELS CLEARER!
NOW I'M CONFIDENT...
...THAT I CAN REACH THREAT LEVEL GOD!

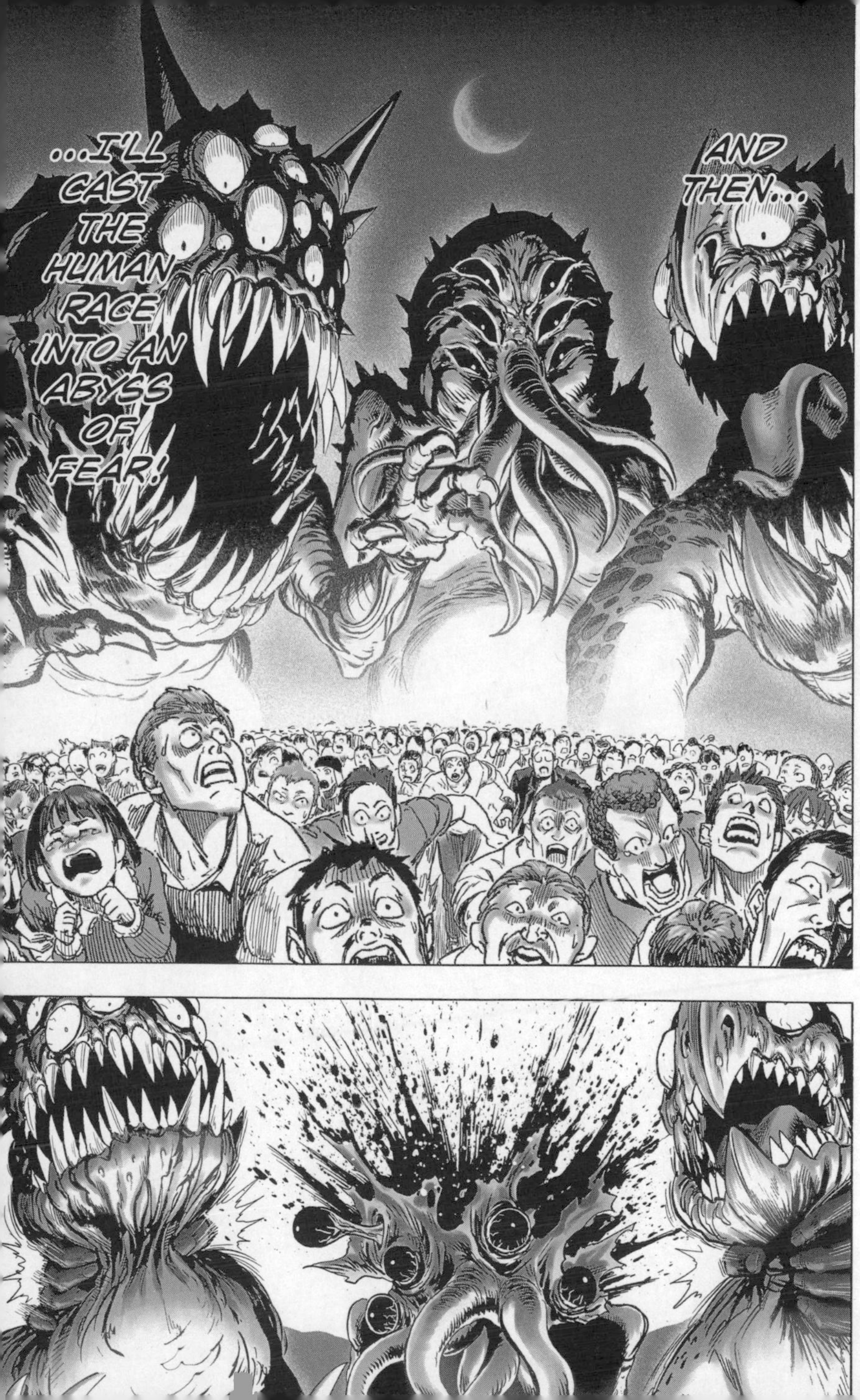
AND THEN...
...I'LL CAST THE HUMAN RACE INTO AN ABYSS OF FEAR!

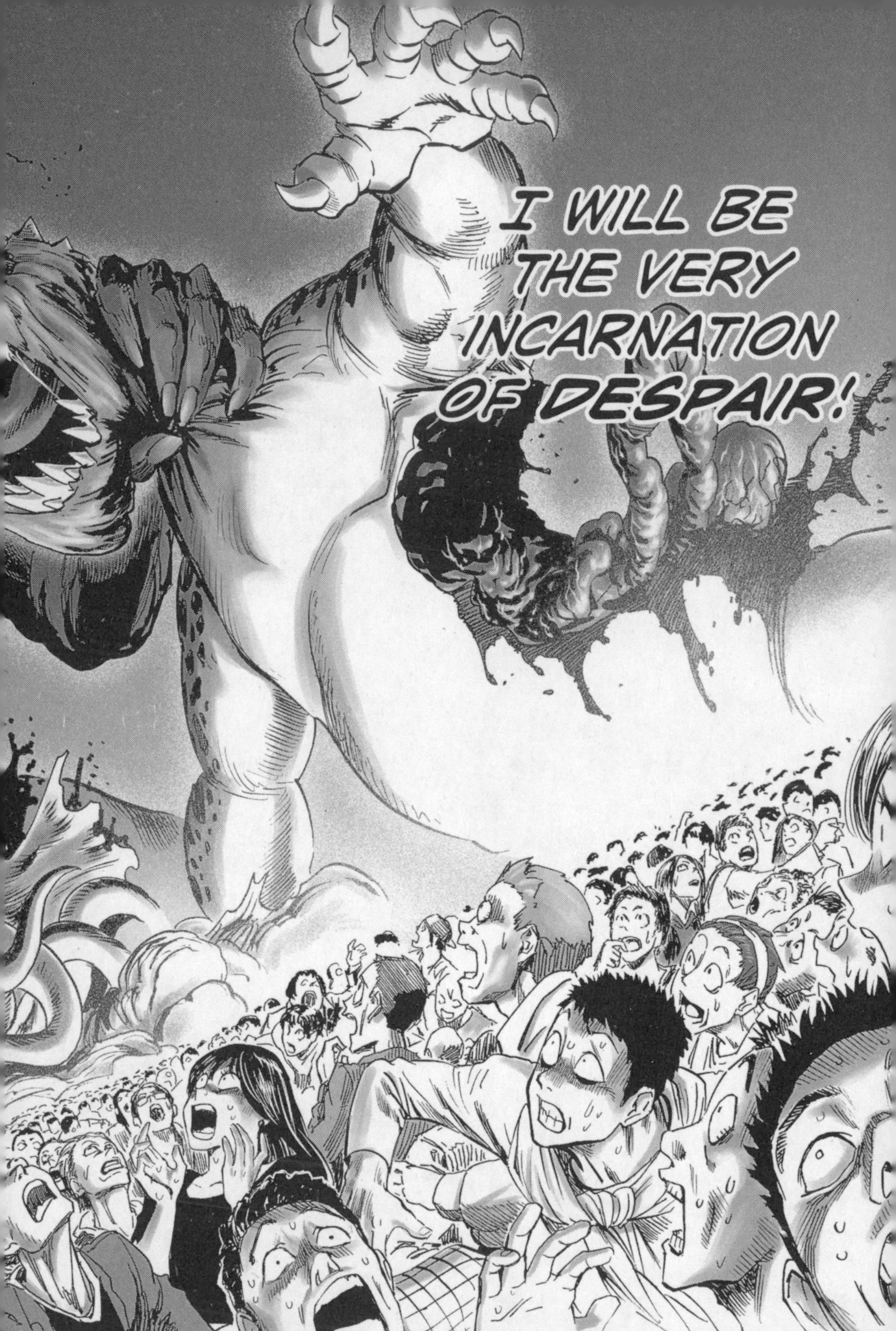
I WILL BE THE VERY INCARNATION OF DESPAIR!

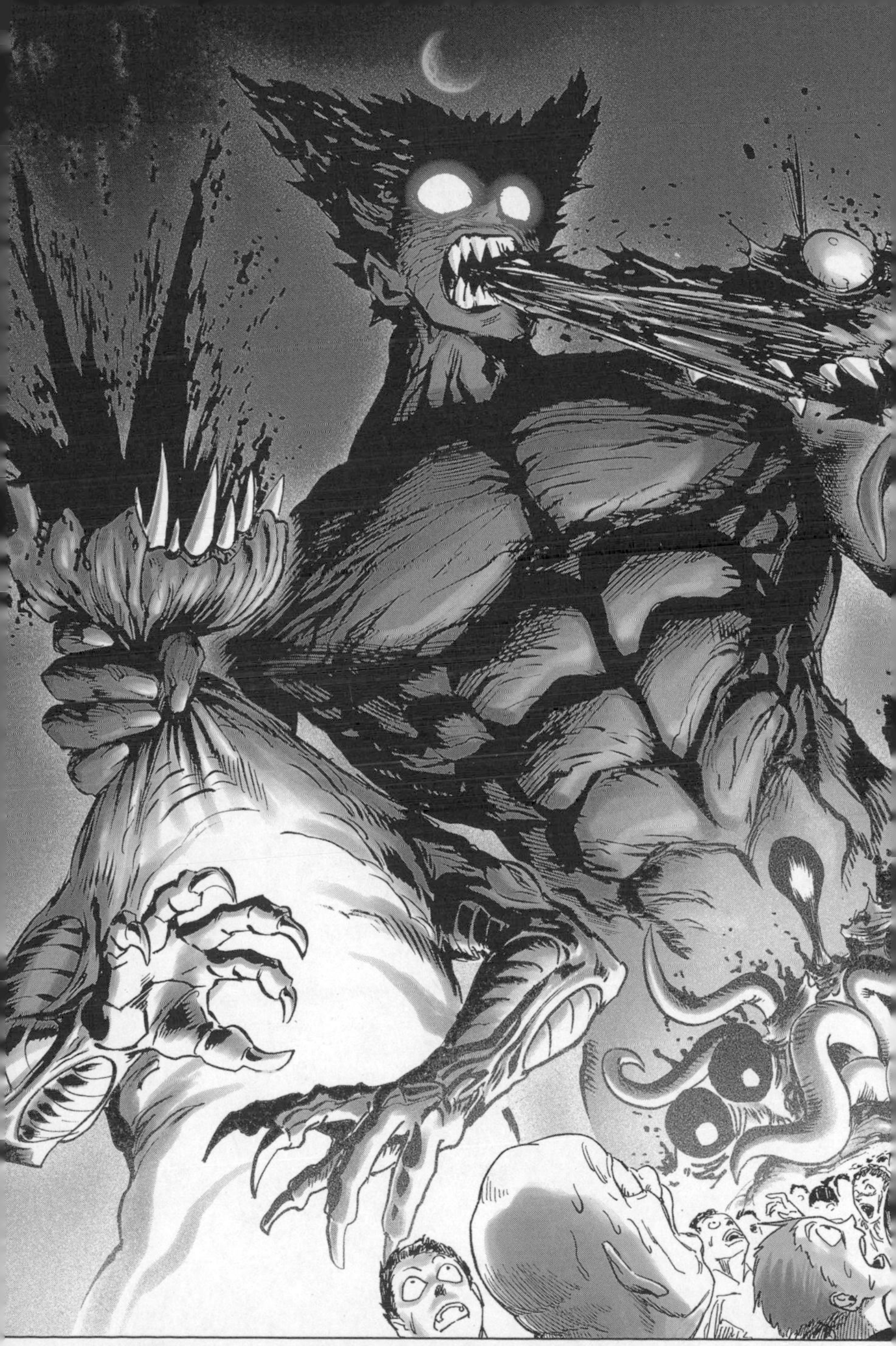

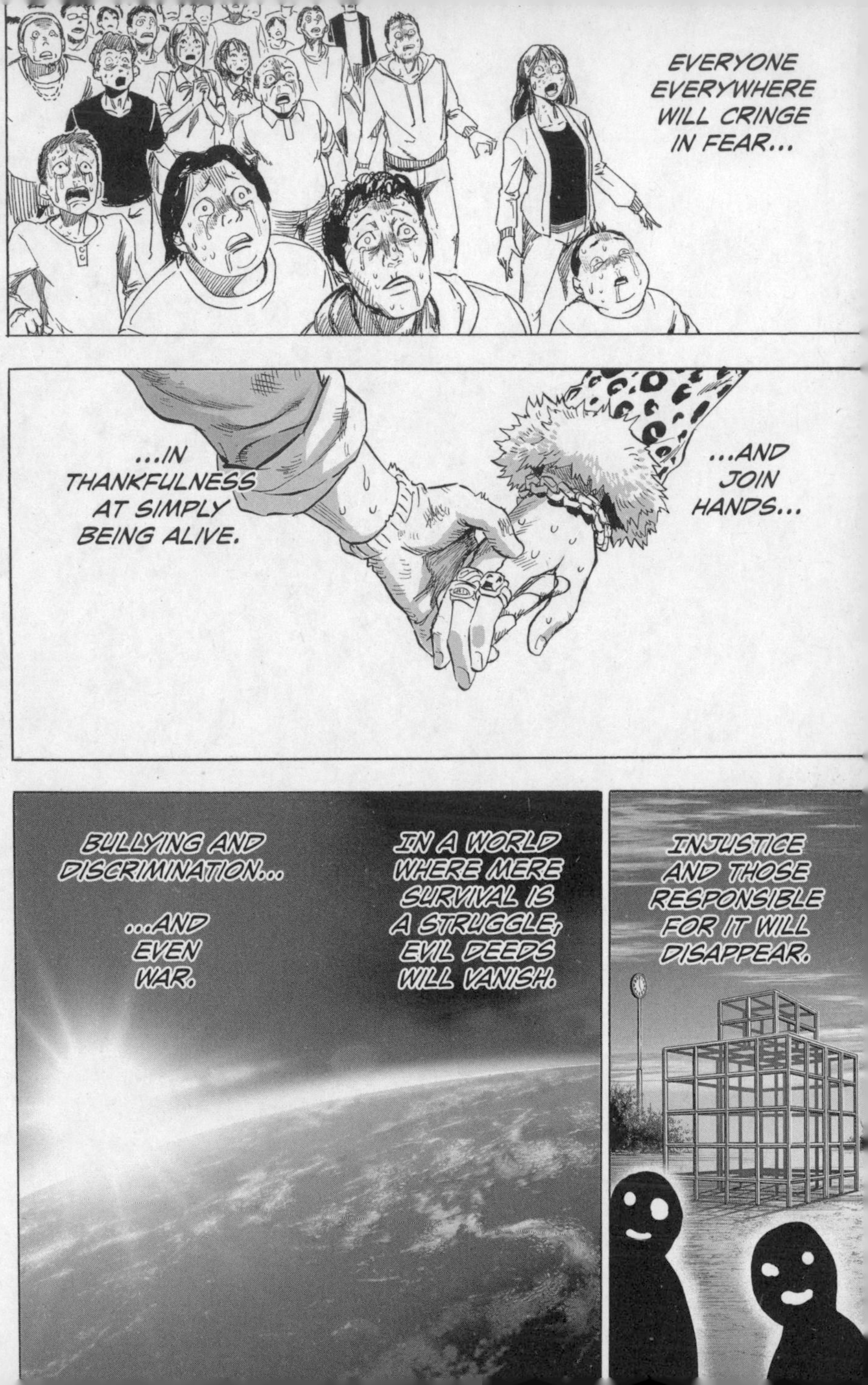
EVERYONE EVERYWHERE WILL CRINGE IN FEAR...
...AND JOIN HANDS...
...IN THANKFULNESS AT SIMPLY BEING ALIVE.
INJUSTICE AND THOSE RESPONSIBLE FOR IT WILL DISAPPEAR.
IN A WORLD WHERE MERE SURVIVAL IS A STRUGGLE, EVIL DEEDS WILL VANISH.
BULLYING AND DISCRIMINATION...
...AND EVEN WAR.

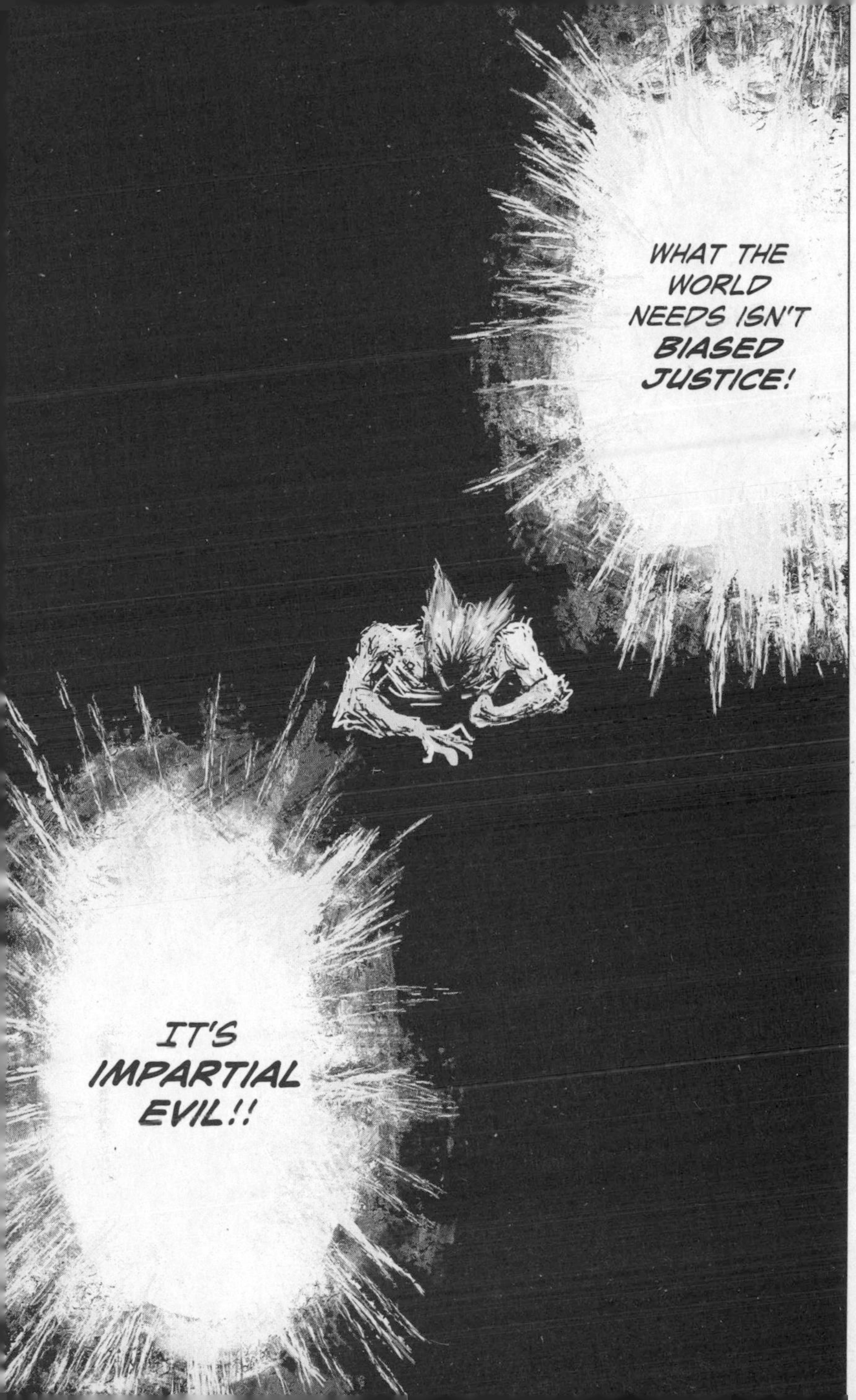
WHAT THE WORLD NEEDS ISN'T BIASED JUSTICE!
IT'S IMPARTIAL EVIL!!

THE SNOTTY BRAT?!

H-HOW WERE YOU ABLE TO FIND ME?

OLD DUDE!

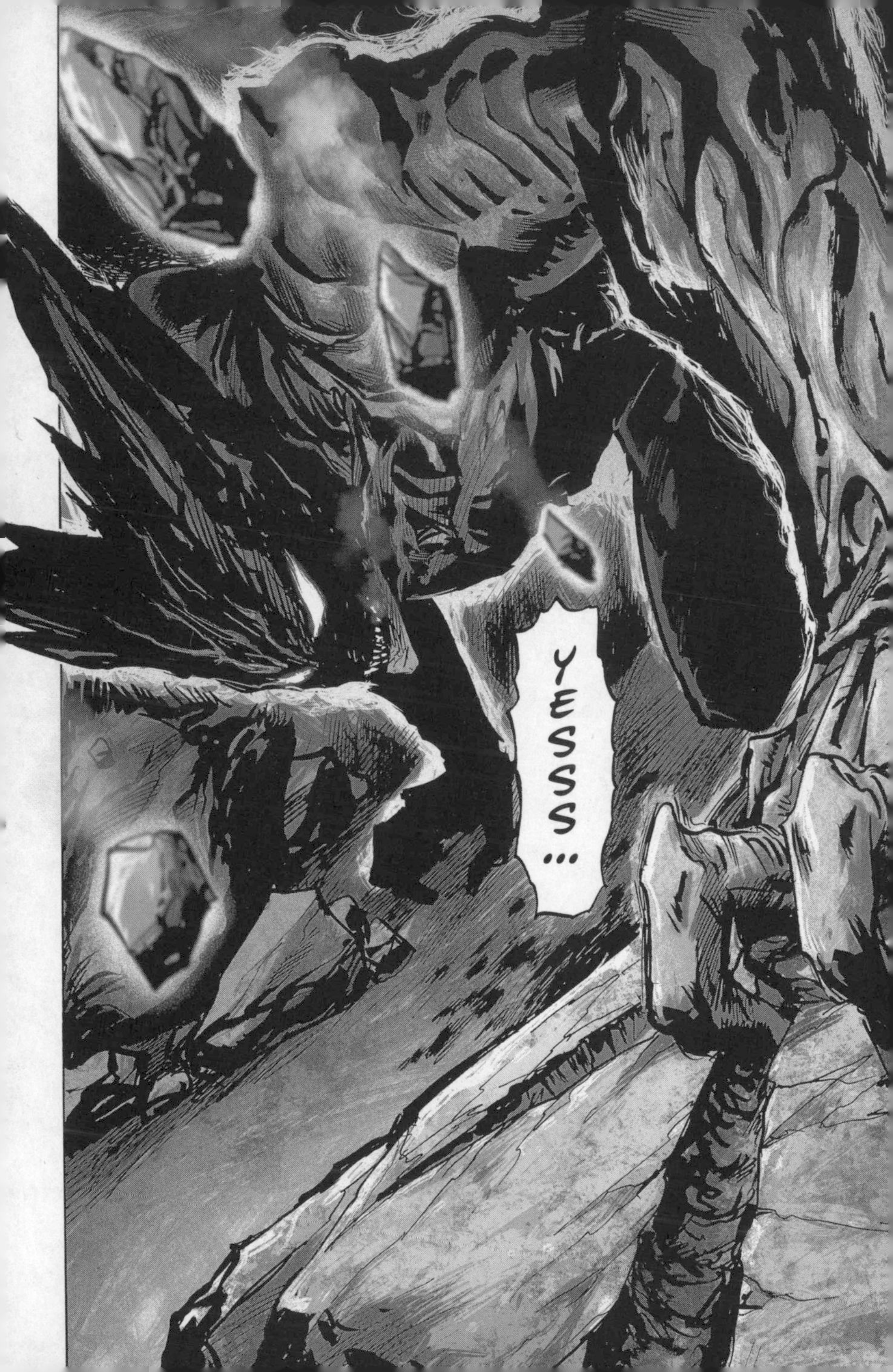
YESSS...

I DON'T ACTUALLY CARE ABOUT JUSTICE OR—

I UNDERSTAND YOUR ANGER.

AMAI MASK...

KA
WHOK
WHOK
WHOK
WHOK

HEY!

WE DON'T NEED COWARDS HERE, SO GET LOST!

ARE YOU A HERO OR NOT?!

SELF-PITY! WHINING! AND EXCUSES!

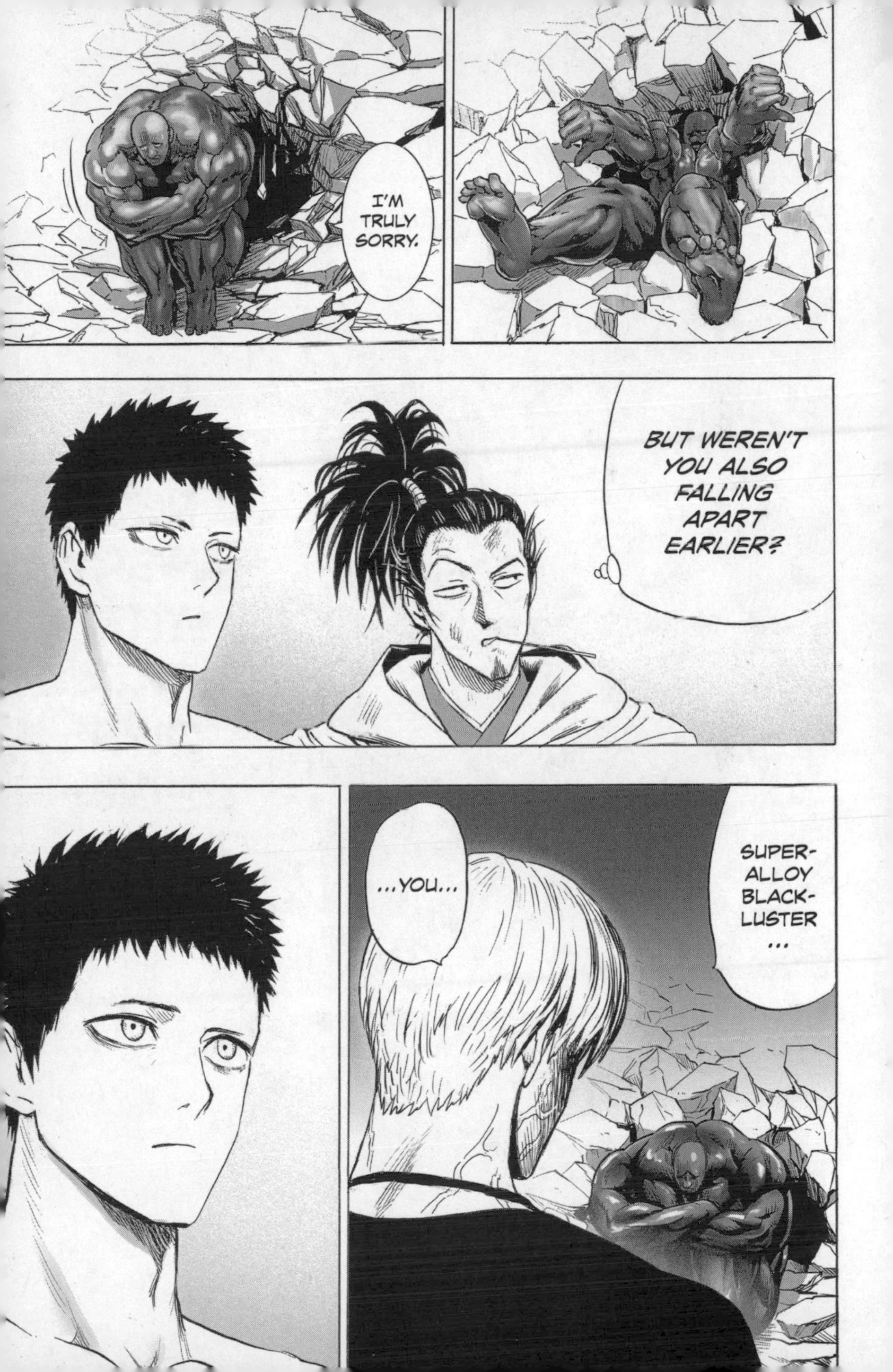
I'M TRULY SORRY.
BUT WEREN'T YOU ALSO FALLING APART EARLIER?
SUPER-ALLOY BLACK-LUSTER ...
...YOU...

HEY, YOU HAVE NO RIGHT TO—

YOU'RE STILL A HUNK OF MUSCLE! AND SUPER-STRONG!

B-BUT EVEN THOSE KICKS FROM AMAI DIDN'T HURT YOU!

WE WILL DEFINITELY NEED YOUR STRENGTH...

GARO AND THE LEADERS OF THE MONSTER ASSOCIATION ARE STILL ALIVE.

...TO BEAT THEM!

BUT NOW YOU'RE JUST GONNA COWER?

DO THAT AND YOU'LL LOSE WHO'S MOST IMPORTANT! YOUR-SELF!

...AND SEE HOW IT TREM-BLES.

LOOK AT YOUR BODY...

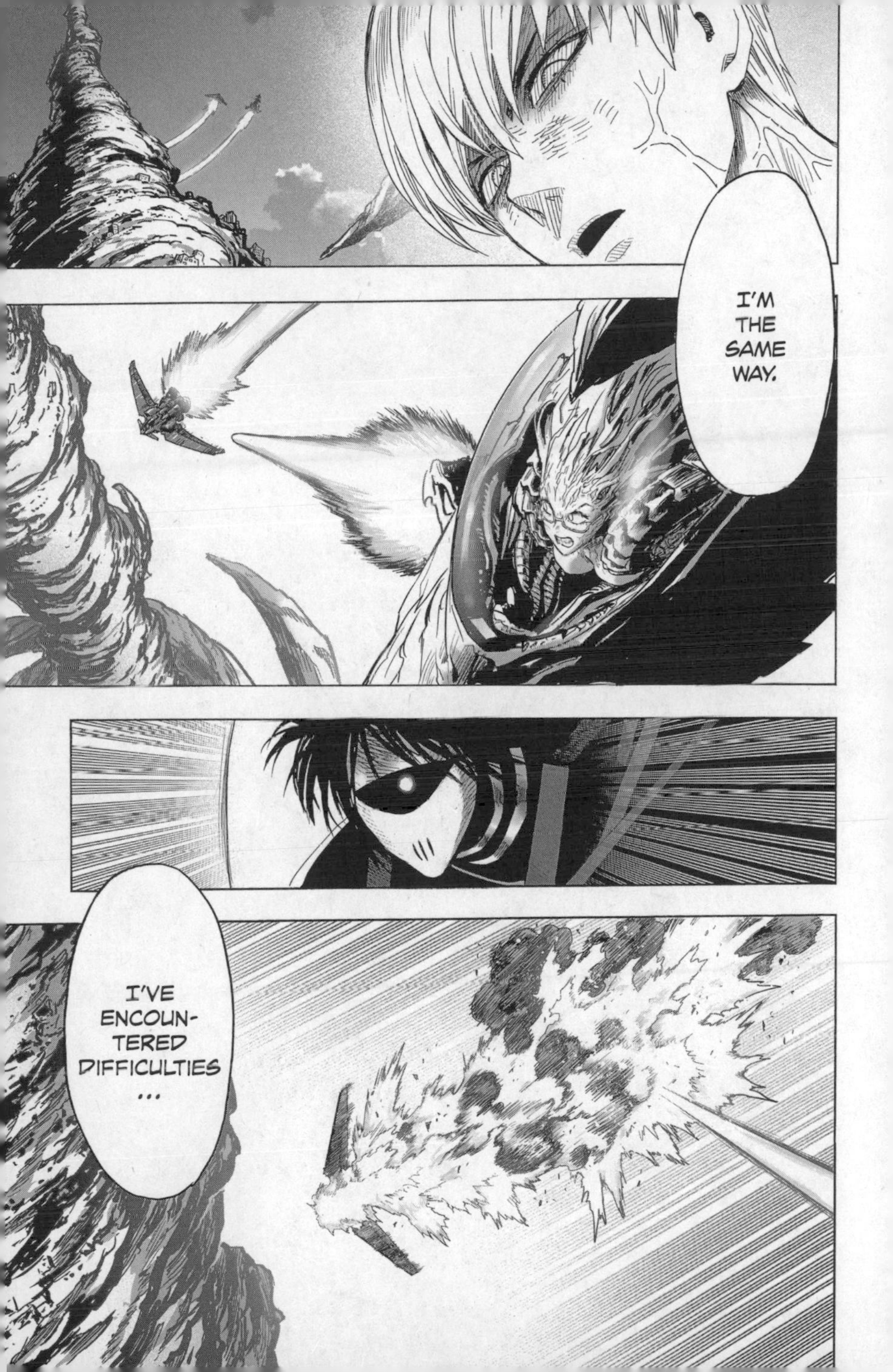
I'M THE SAME WAY.
I'VE ENCOUNTERED DIFFICULTIES ...

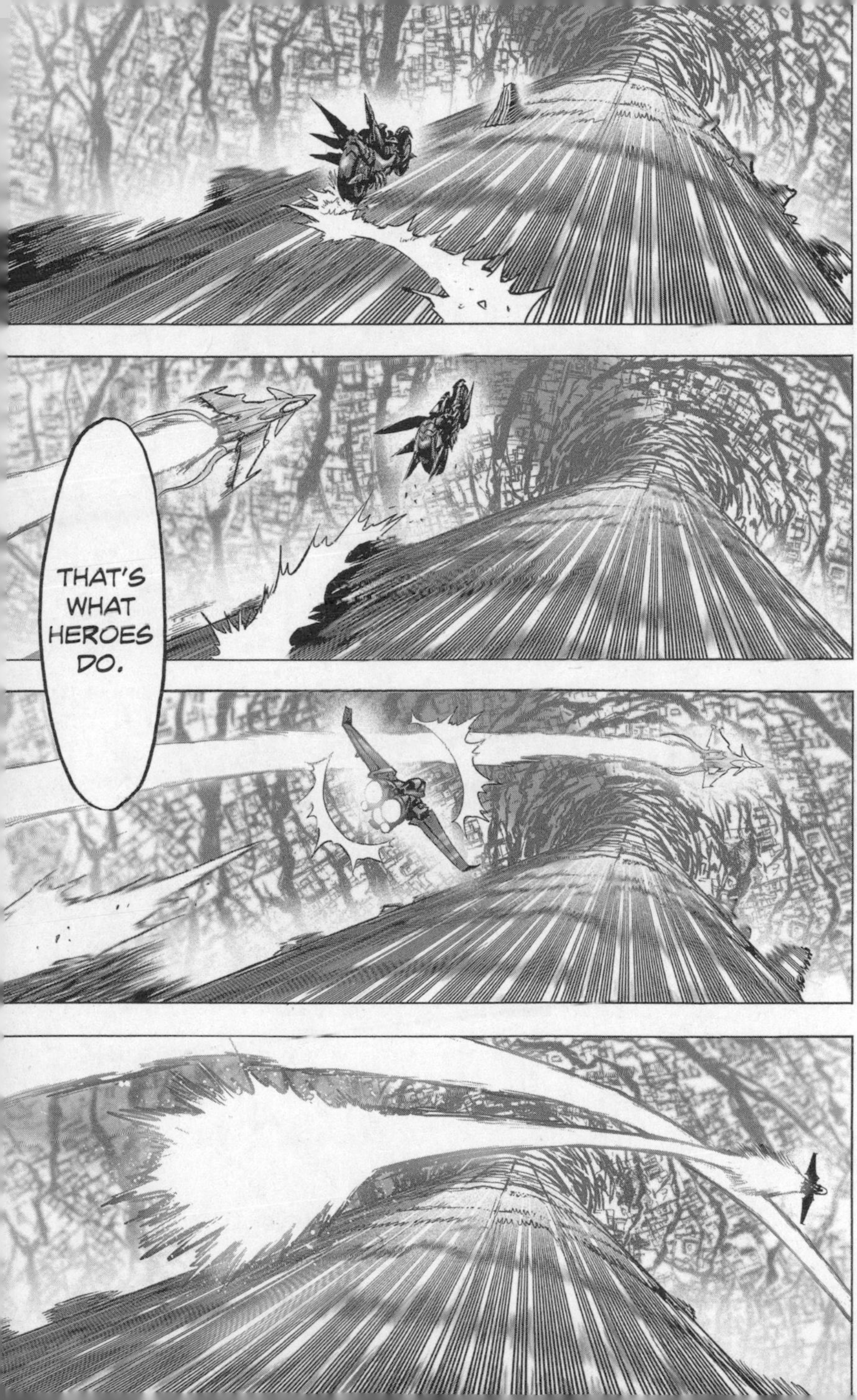
THAT'S WHAT HEROES DO.

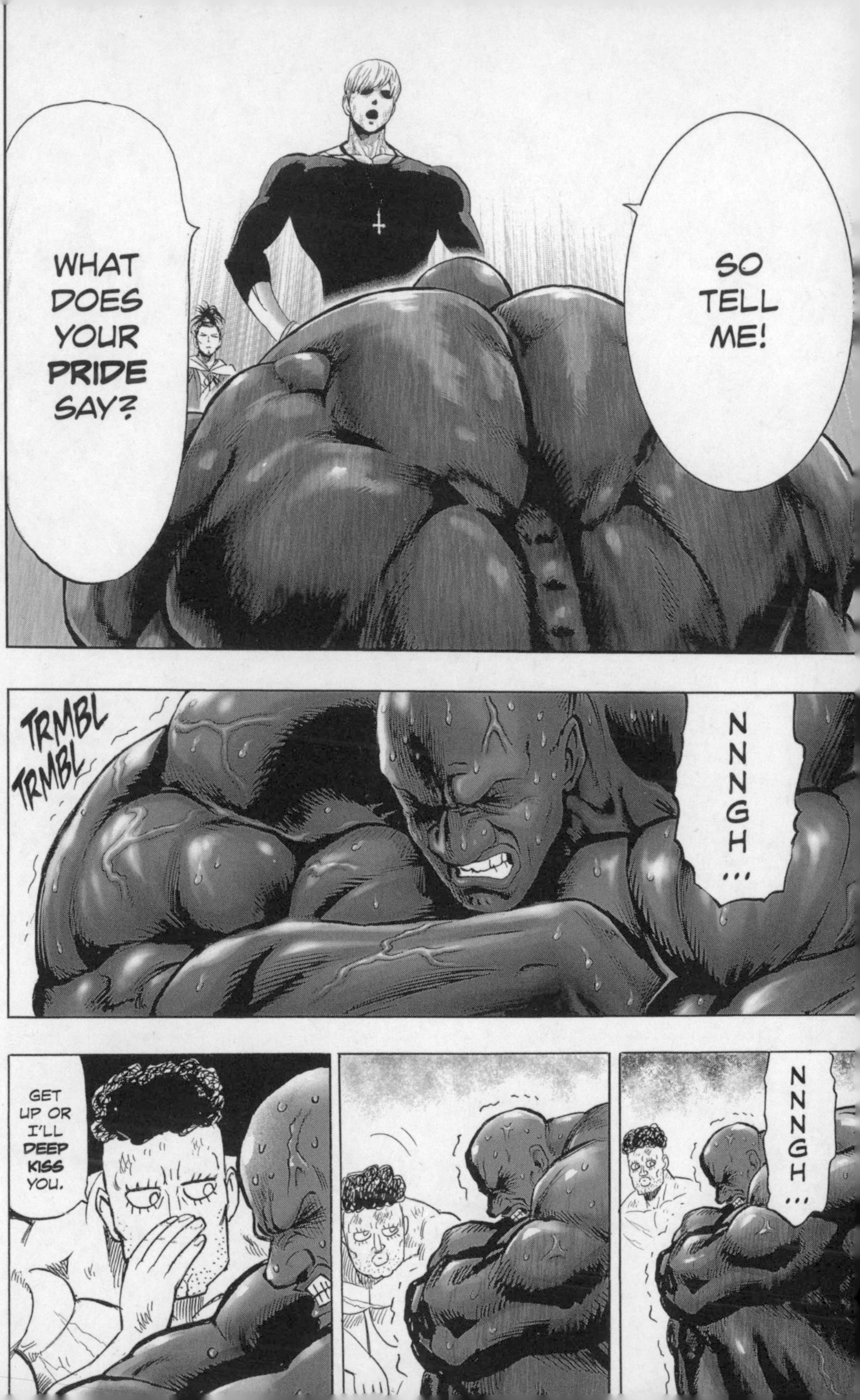
SO TELL ME!
WHAT DOES YOUR PRIDE SAY?
NNNGH...
TRMBL TRMBL
NNNGH...
GET UP OR I'LL DEEP KISS YOU.

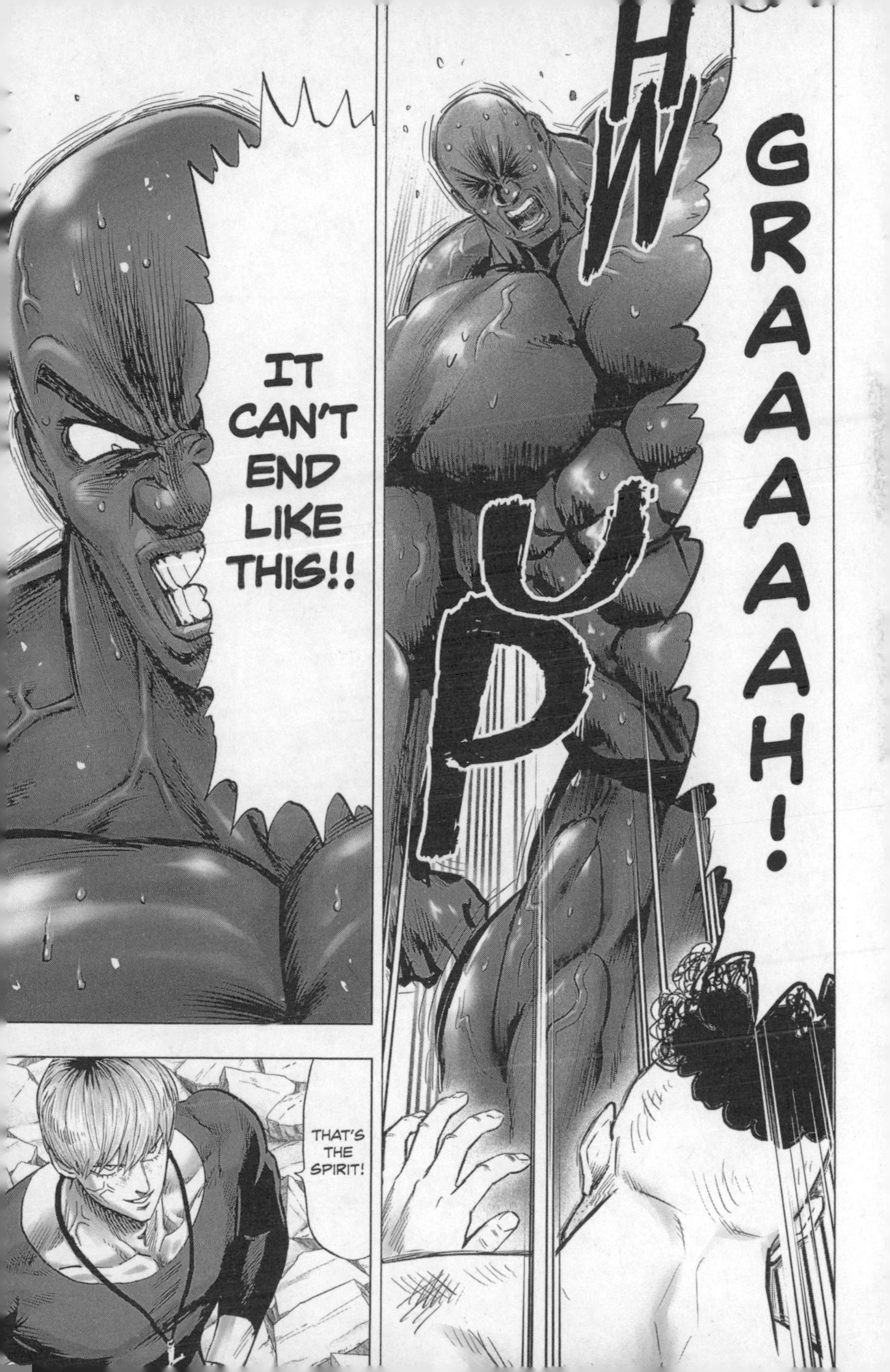

HWUP
GRAAAAH!
IT CAN'T END LIKE THIS!!
THAT'S THE SPIRIT!

IN THAT CASE...

...WE SHOULD COOPERATE IN TAKING THAT THING DOWN!!

...

YOU WANT TO COOPERATE?!

HUH?!

SHALL I STRIKE YOU ALL DOWN?

CAREFUL WHAT YOU EAT.

HAVE YOU EATEN SOMETHING WEIRD?

YOU'D PUT YOUR BUTT IN OUR HANDS?!

YOU? THE HIGH-AND-MIGHTY WARRIOR?

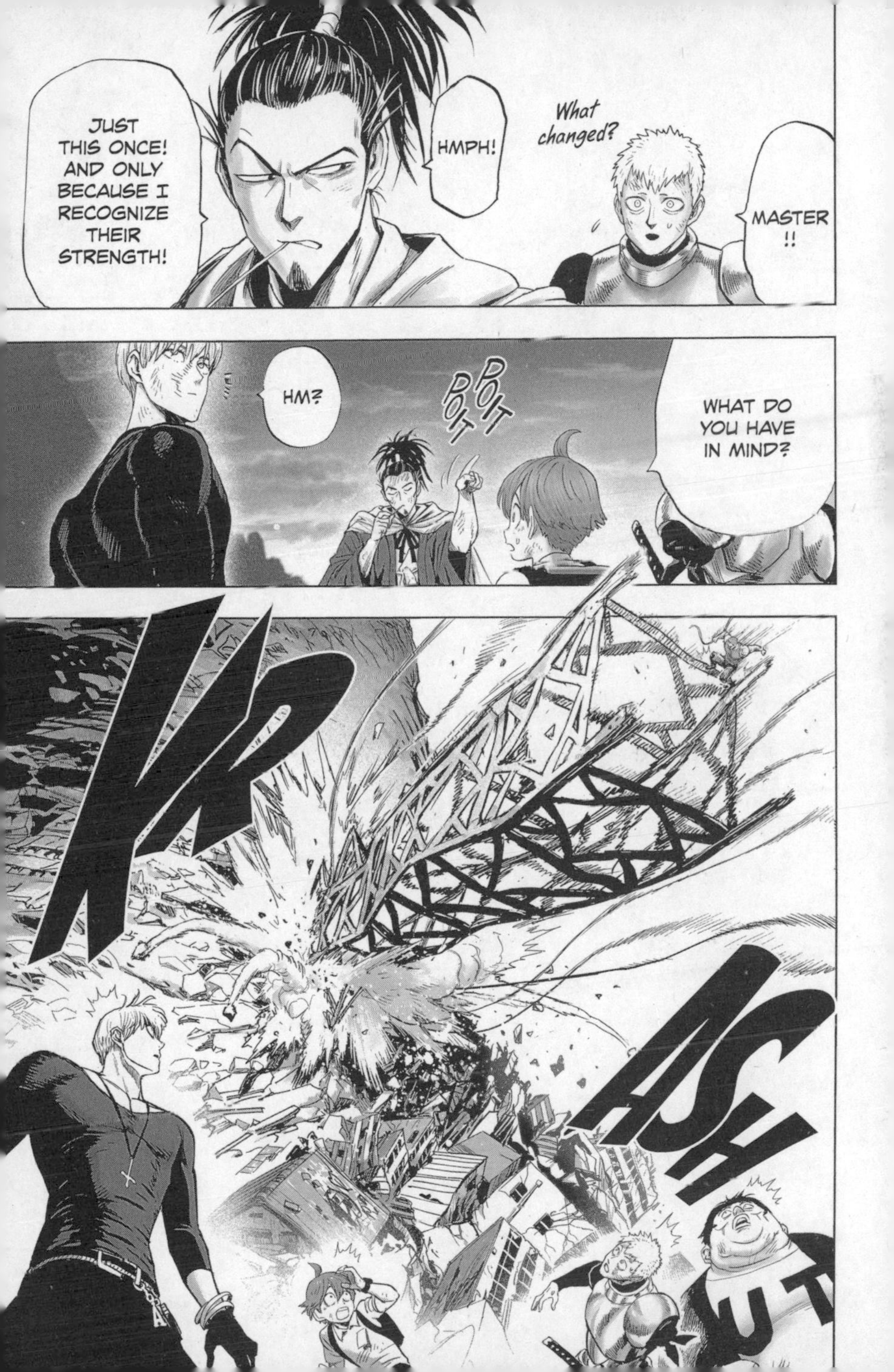
MASTER !!
What changed?
HMPH!
JUST THIS ONCE! AND ONLY BECAUSE I RECOGNIZE THEIR STRENGTH!
WHAT DO YOU HAVE IN MIND?
POIT POIT
HM?
KRASH!

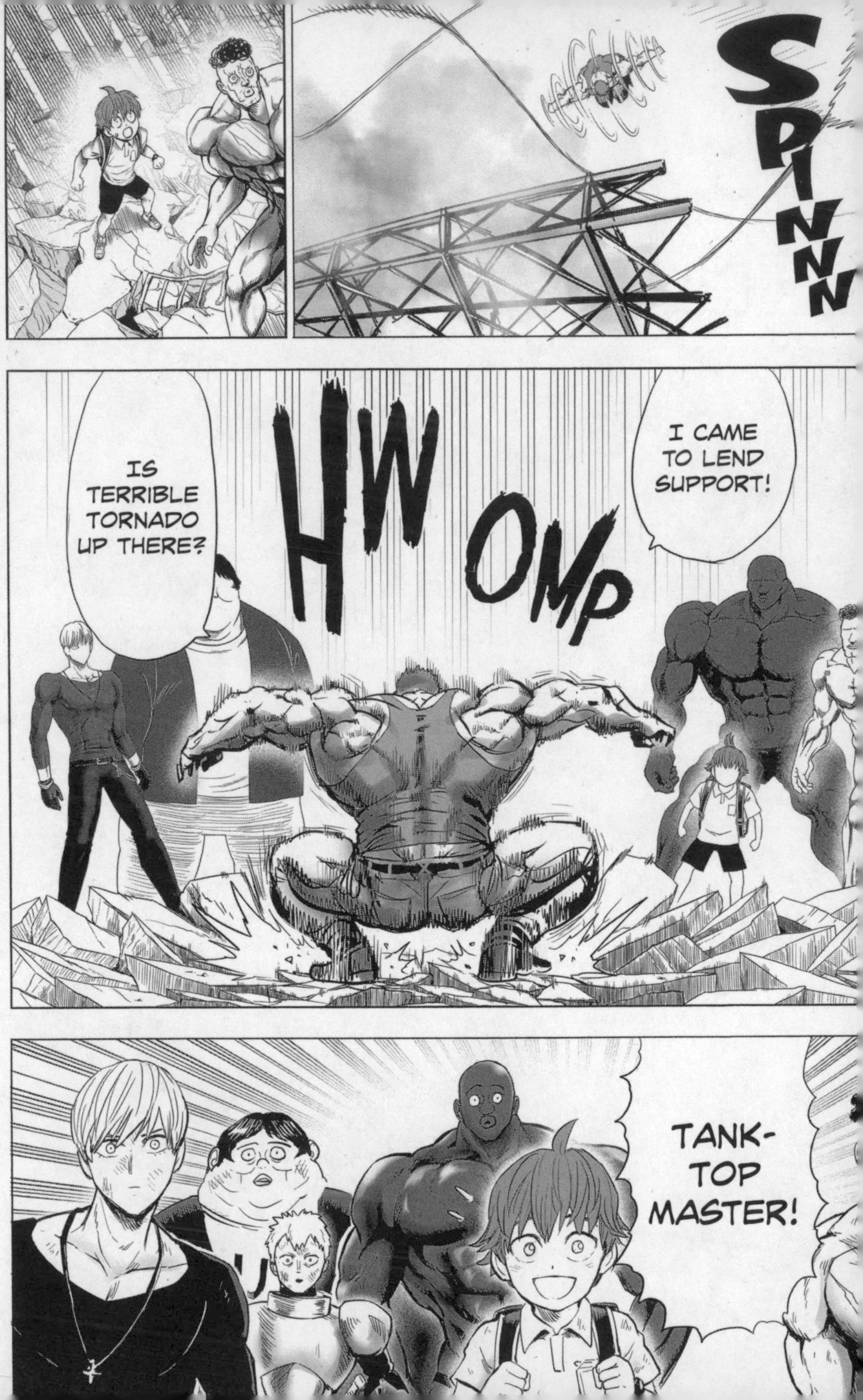
SPINNN
I CAME TO LEND SUPPORT!
HWOMP
IS TERRIBLE TORNADO UP THERE?
TANK-TOP MASTER!

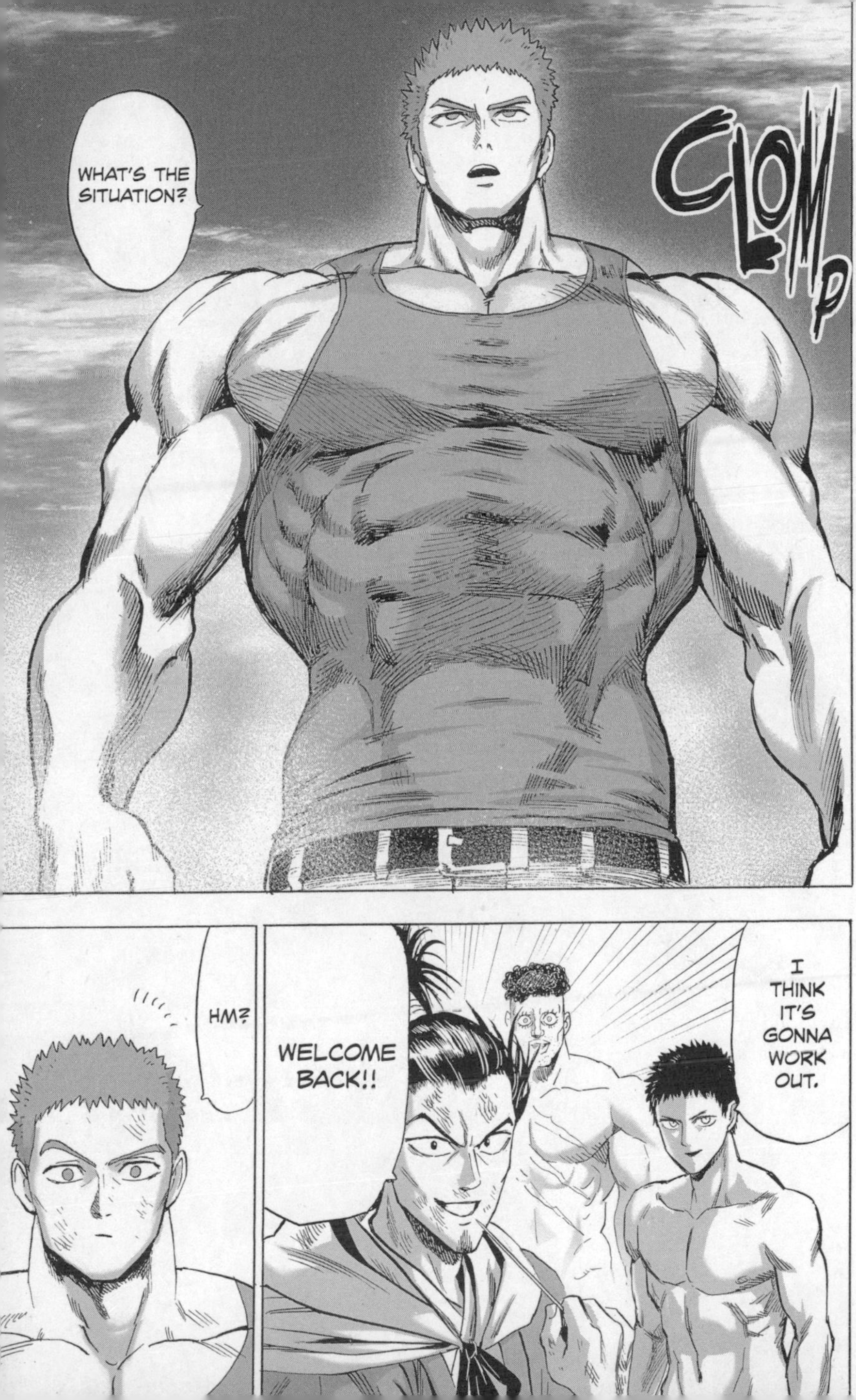
WHAT'S THE SITUATION?
CLOMP
I THINK IT'S GONNA WORK OUT.
WELCOME BACK!!
HM?

AMAI
MASK
...

...BUT
I'VE
CHANGED
MY MIND.

I
THOUGHT
YOU
WERE
ALL
TALK...

HA
HA
HA!

YOU
REALLY
ARE
CREEPY...

WHY
NOW?

...

I NEVER THOUGHT THEY WOULD COOPERATE.

THEY REALLY **ARE** CLASS-S HEROES!

THEY RAN INTO A WALL, BUT GREW AND FOUND A NEW WAY FORWARD!

NO, DON'T FIGHT!

DON'T WORRY, **AWRY MASK**.

...BUT DON'T HOLD ME BACK.

I DON'T EXPECT MUCH FROM A GUY THE ENEMY **DENUDED** ...

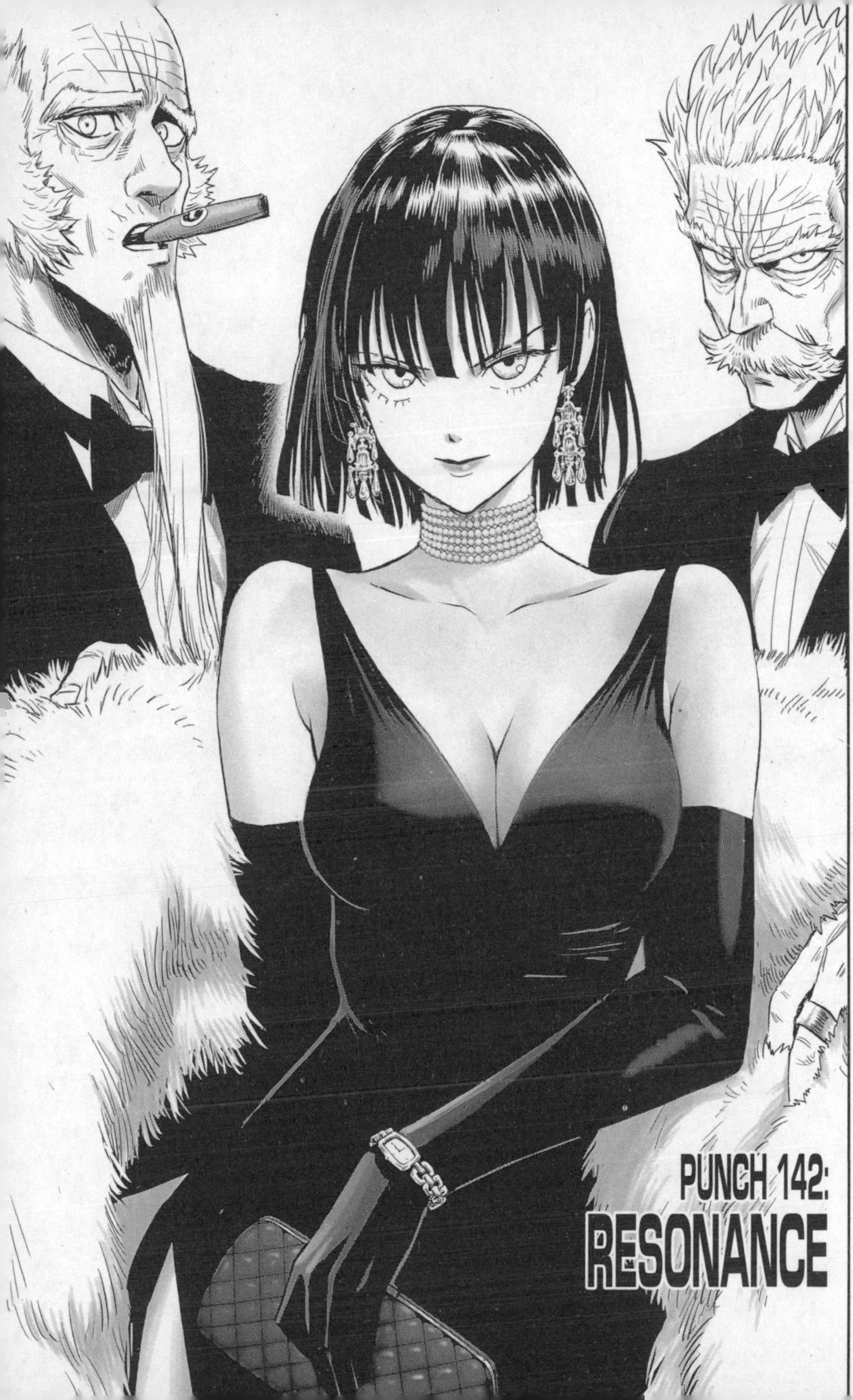
PUNCH 142:
RESONANCE

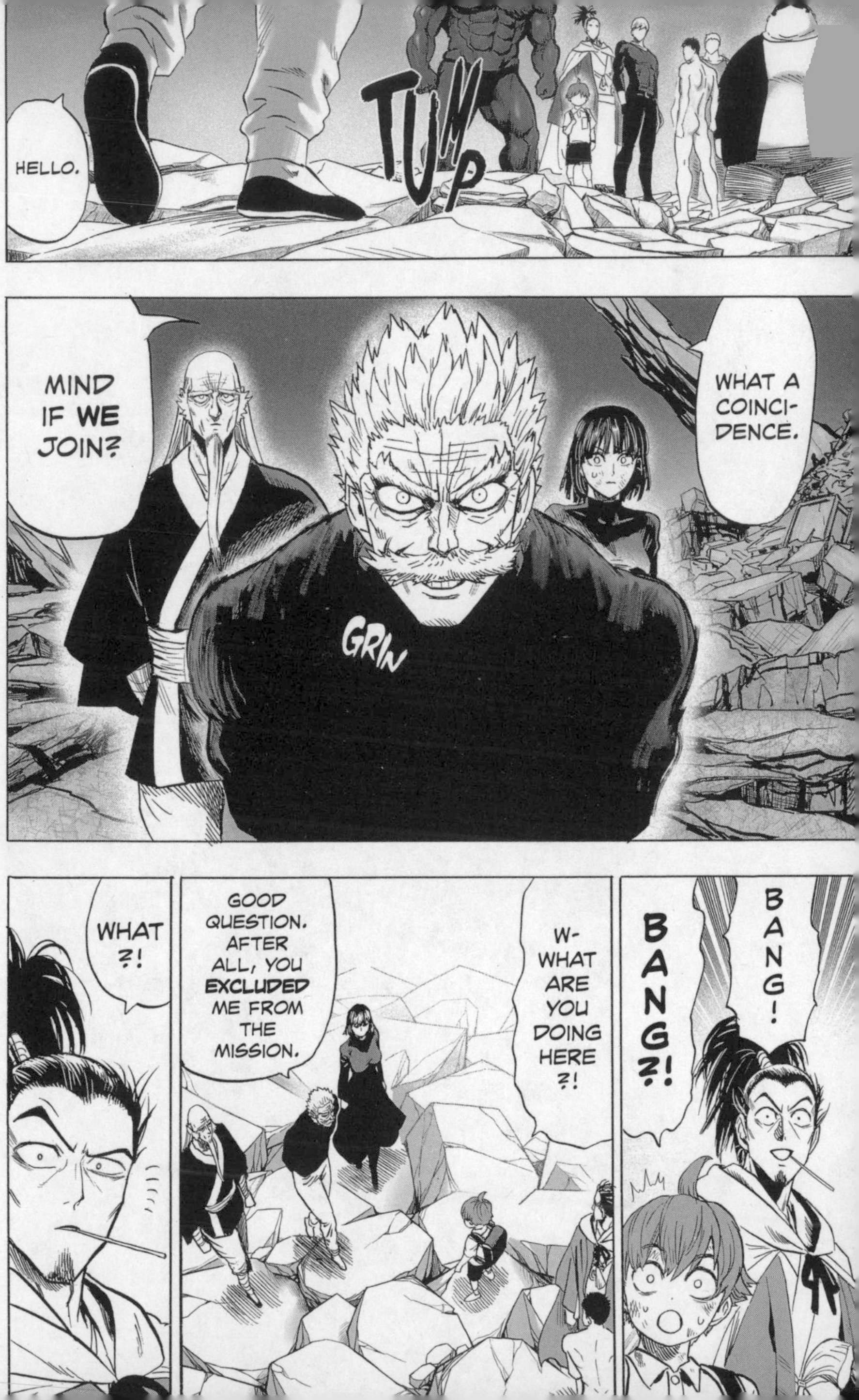

TUMP
HELLO.
WHAT A COINCIDENCE.
GRIN
MIND IF WE JOIN?
BANG!
BANG?!
W-WHAT ARE YOU DOING HERE?!
GOOD QUESTION. AFTER ALL, YOU EXCLUDED ME FROM THE MISSION.
WHAT?!

YEAH, W-WELL...

...I HAD A REASON FOR THAT.

YOU SAID HE WASN'T PARTICIPATING BECAUSE YOU COULDN'T REACH HIM.

WHAT DOES HE MEAN, CHILD EMPEROR?

HEH... GIVEN MY RECORD, PERHAPS THAT'S UNDERSTANDABLE.

YOU WERE WORRIED THAT I'D GO SOFT ON GARO BECAUSE HE'S A FORMER PUPIL.

I WILL TAKE RESPONSIBILITY BY DEFEATING HIM WITH MY OWN FISTS.

BUT DO NOT WORRY.

SO REMOVING ME FROM THE MISSION WAS FOR THE BEST. I OWE YOU ONE, BOY.

ACTUALLY, I **PREFER** SETTLING THIS AS HIS FORMER MASTER TO DOING SO AS A HERO.

I'LL HELP IN ANY WAY I CAN!

PLEASE! WE MUST HURRY IF WE'RE TO HELP MY SISTER!!

HELLISH BLIZZARD ...

...

I SUSPECT MY SISTER IS ALREADY UNCON-SCIOUS!!

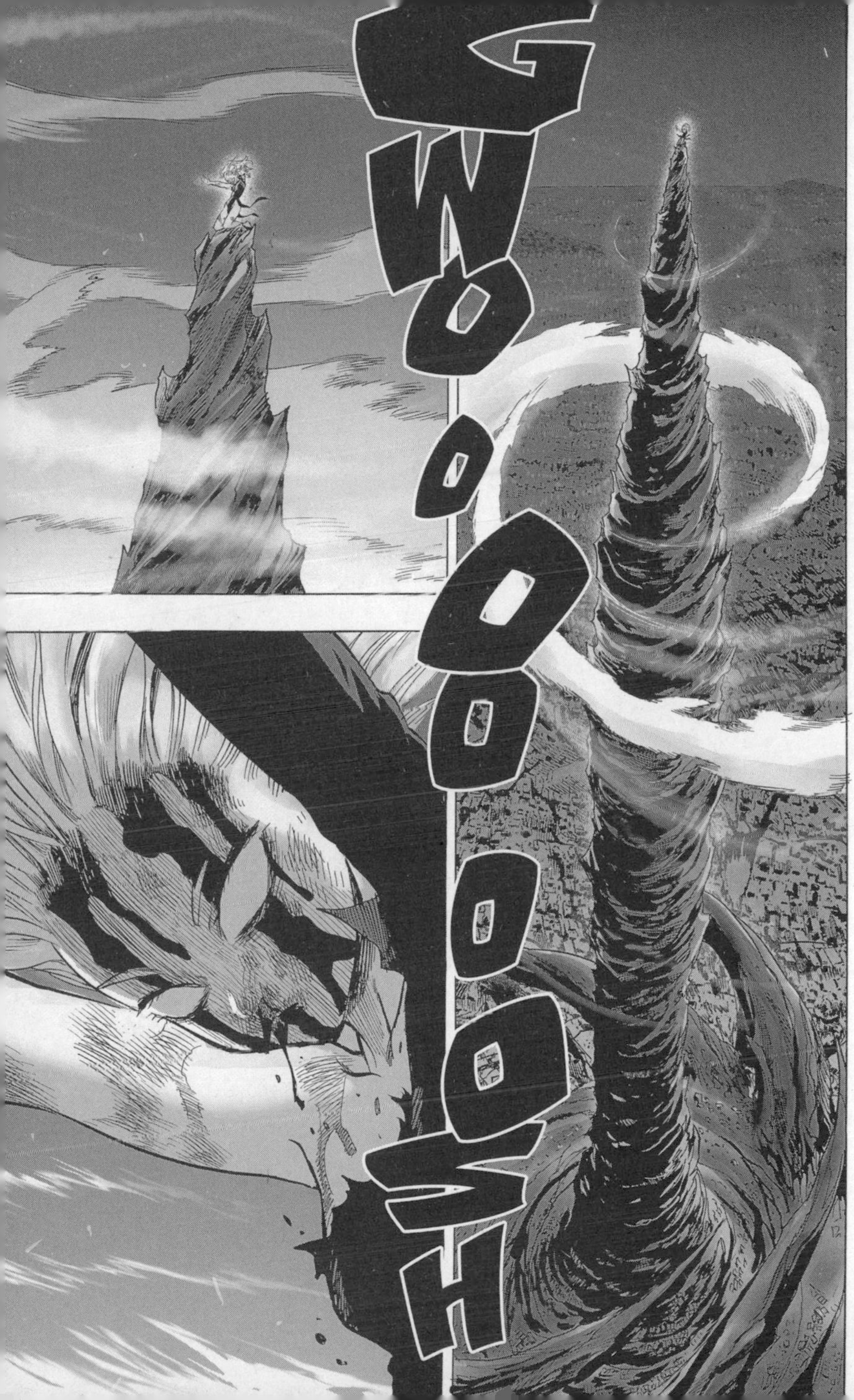
GWOOOOOOSH

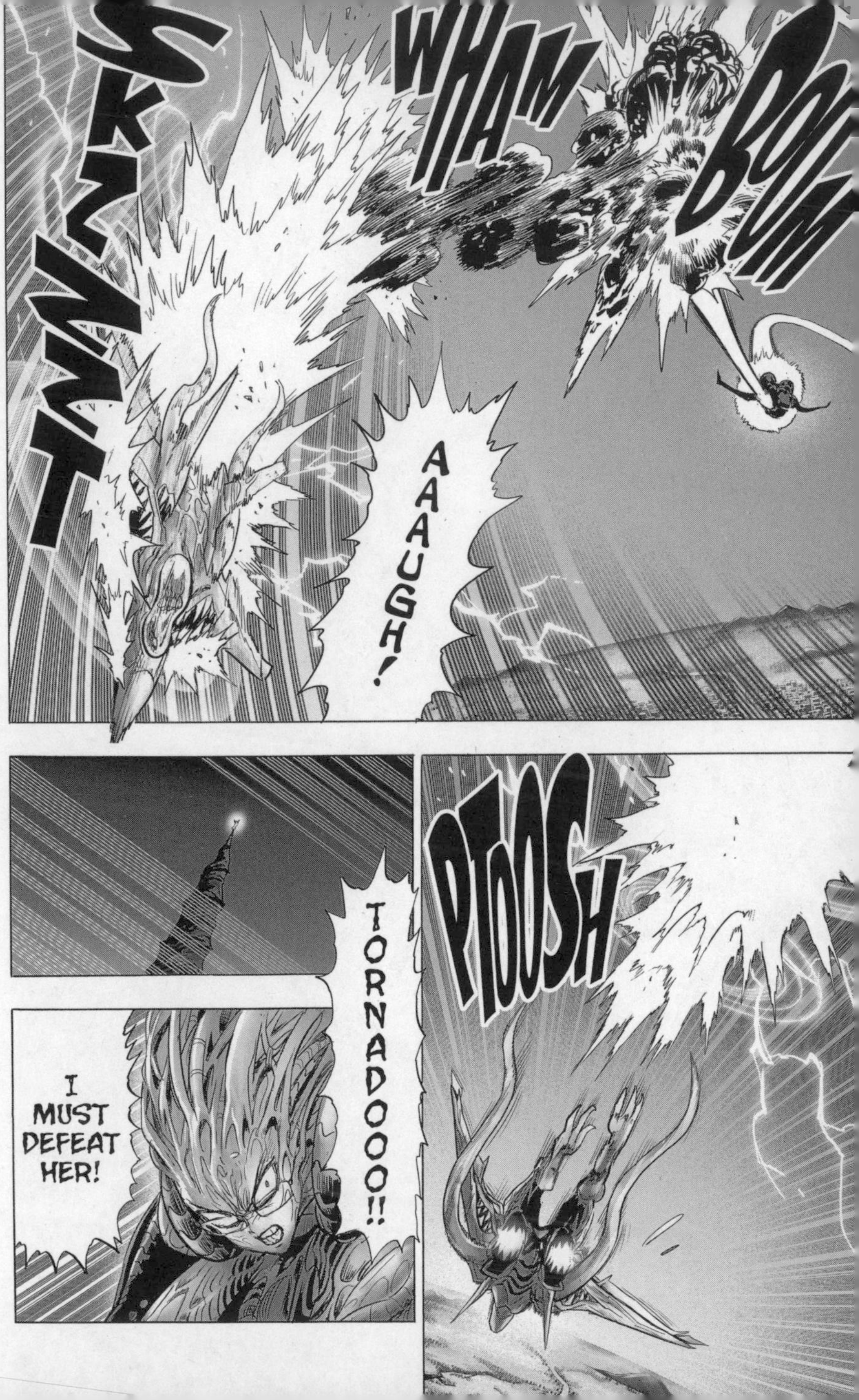
BOOM
WHAM
AAAUGH!
PTOOSH
TORNADOOOO!!
I MUST DEFEAT HER!

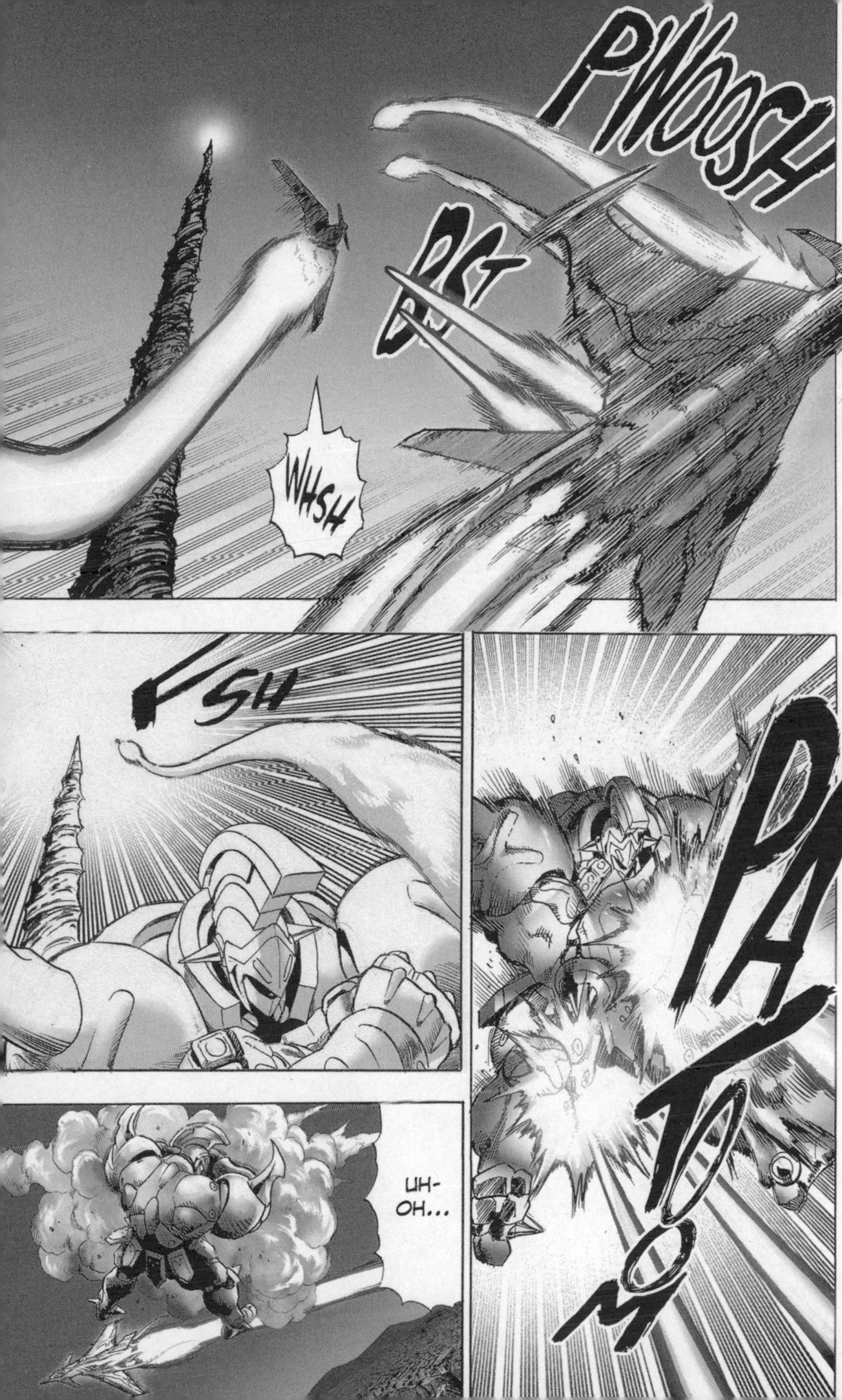
PWOOSH
DGT
WHSH
PATOOM
FSH
UH-OH...

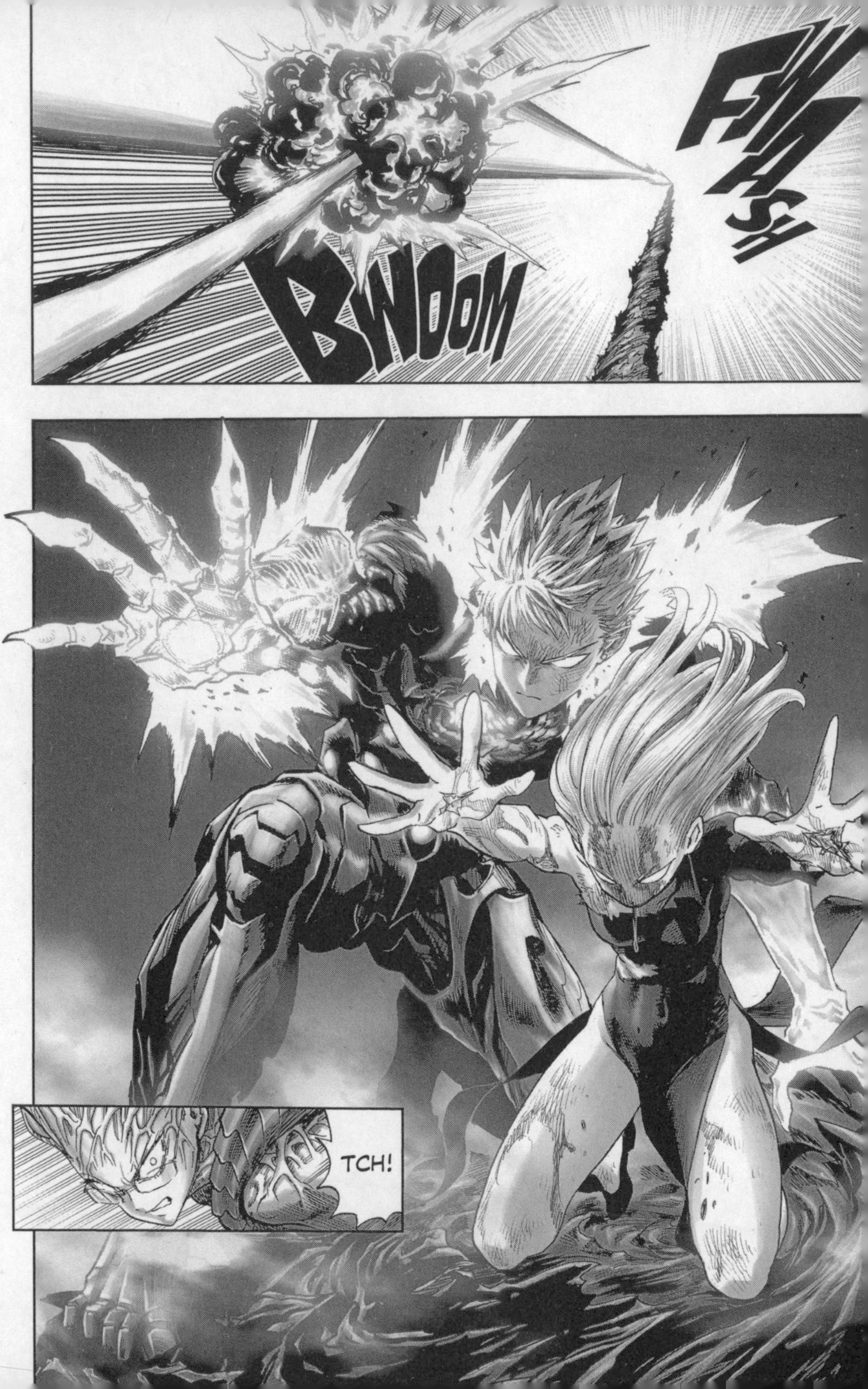
FWASH
BWOOM
TCH!

SHE'S UNCON-SCIOUS.

TORNA-DO...

WHO...?

...THAT SOMEONE WILL COME HELP.

YOU SHOULDN'T INTERFERE.

DON'T GIVE ME HOPE...

...at a certain research facility.

Eighteen years ago...

GRARRRRRR

GYAAAH! A SYNTHETIC BEAST BROKE FREE!!

RUUUN!

VREEE VREEE

LET ME OUT OF HERE!

DON'T LEAVE ME!

WAIT!

101

ALL PERSONNEL, EVACUATE!

TROMP TROMP TROMP

PRIORITIZE SAVING SUBJECTS WITH GREATER PROMISE!

NO! HER NUMBERS HAVE LEVELED OFF!

YES, SIR!

DIRECTOR! THAT GIRL!

FWOO

KLOMP

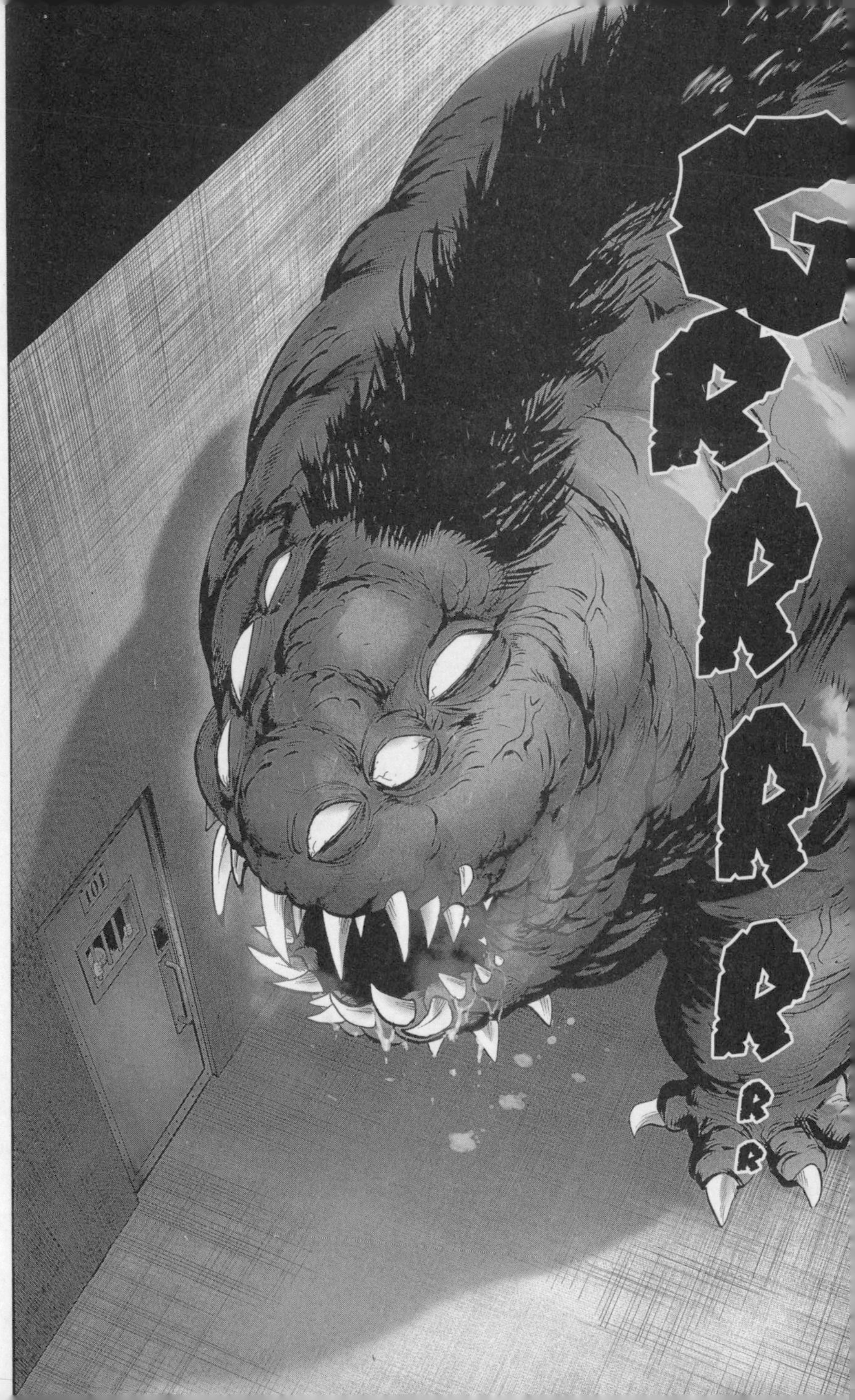

101
GRRRRRR

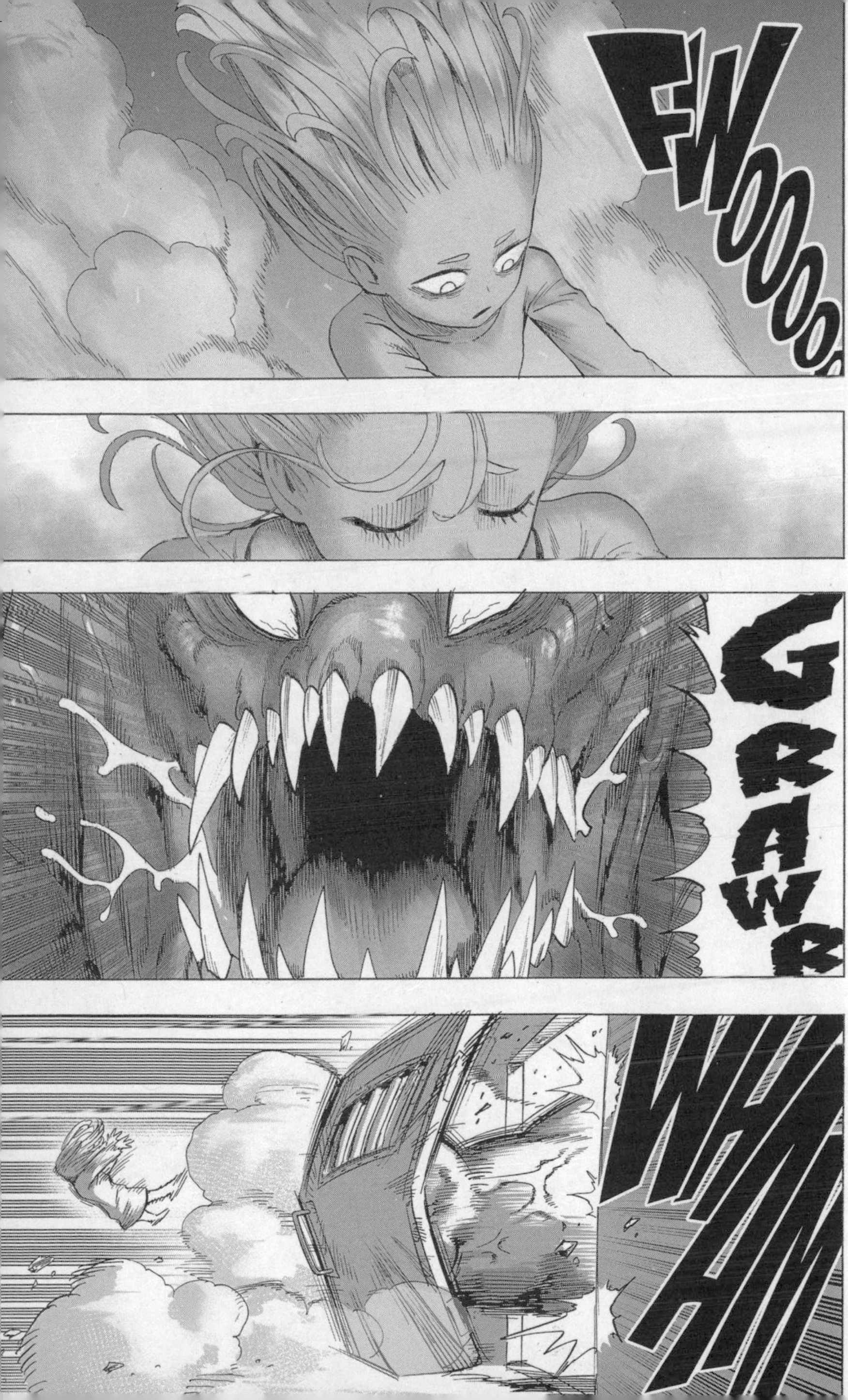
FWOOOO
GRAWR

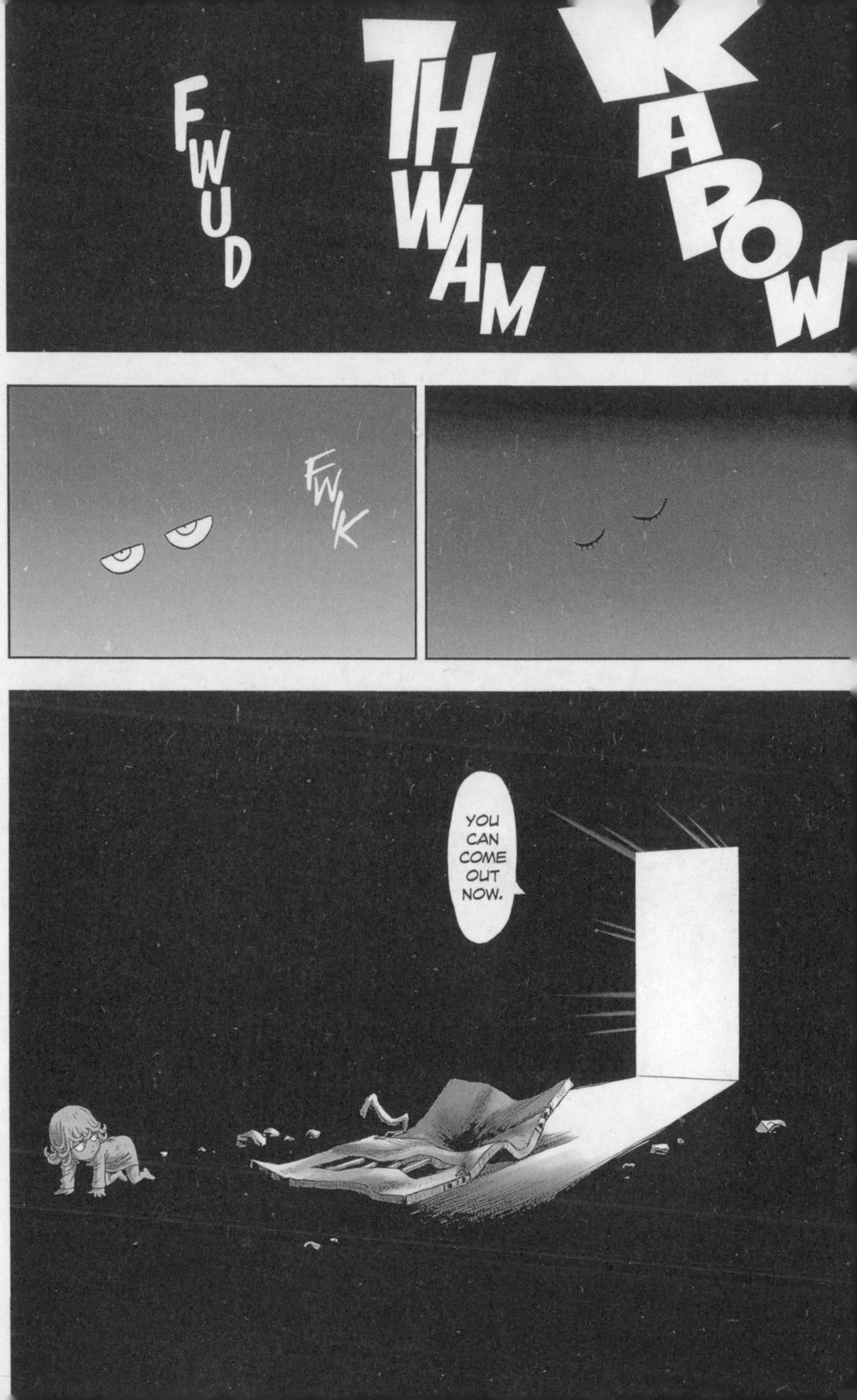
KAPOW
THWAM
FWUD
FWIK
YOU CAN COME OUT NOW.

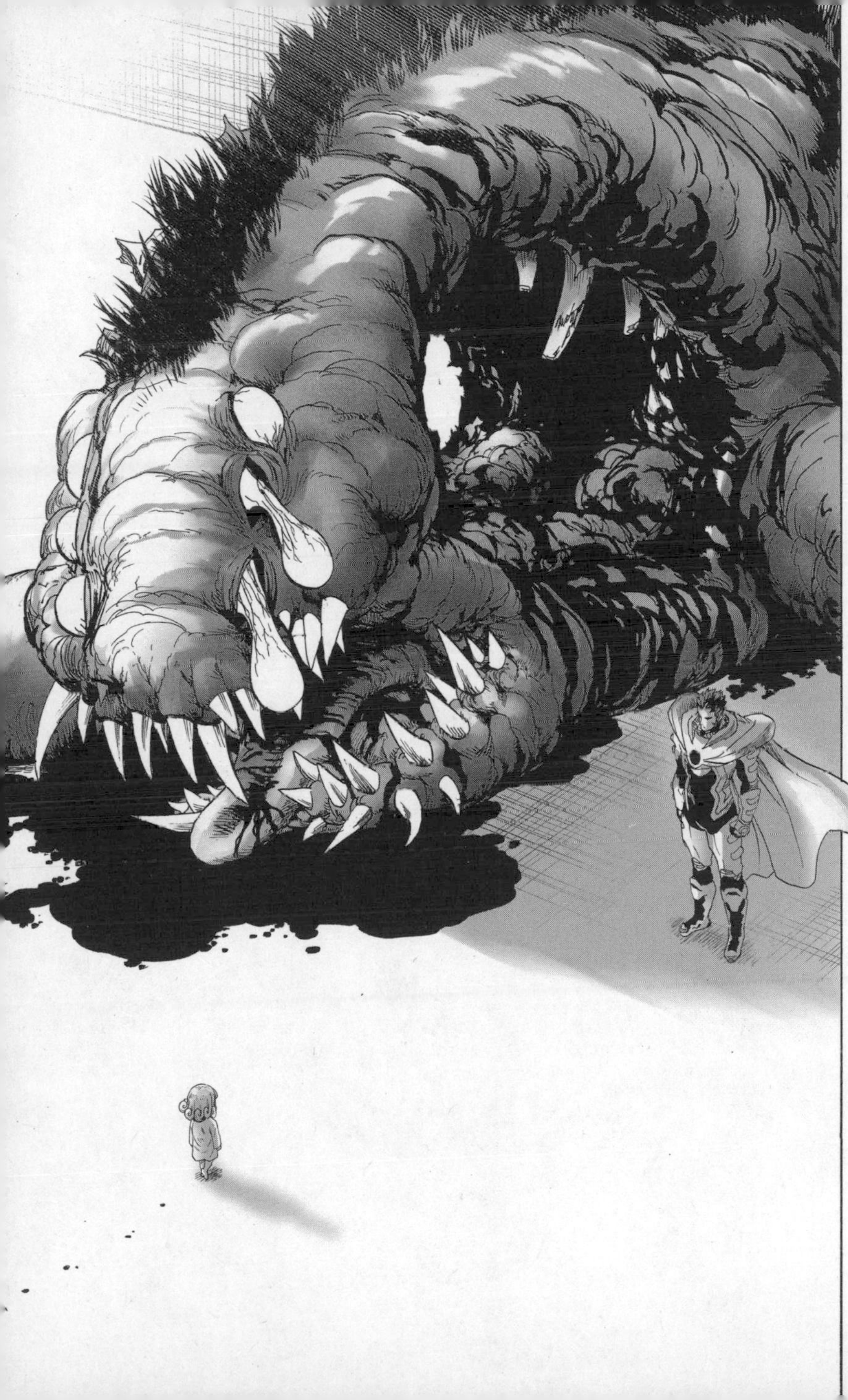

...SO THIS IS JUST FOR FUN.

I USUALLY WORK AT A JOB JUST LIKE ANYONE ELSE, THOUGH...

WHY DIDN'T YOU USE YOUR **POWER?**

HERO ?

NO, YOU'RE **LYING.**

...I CAN'T USE IT ANY-MORE.

UM...

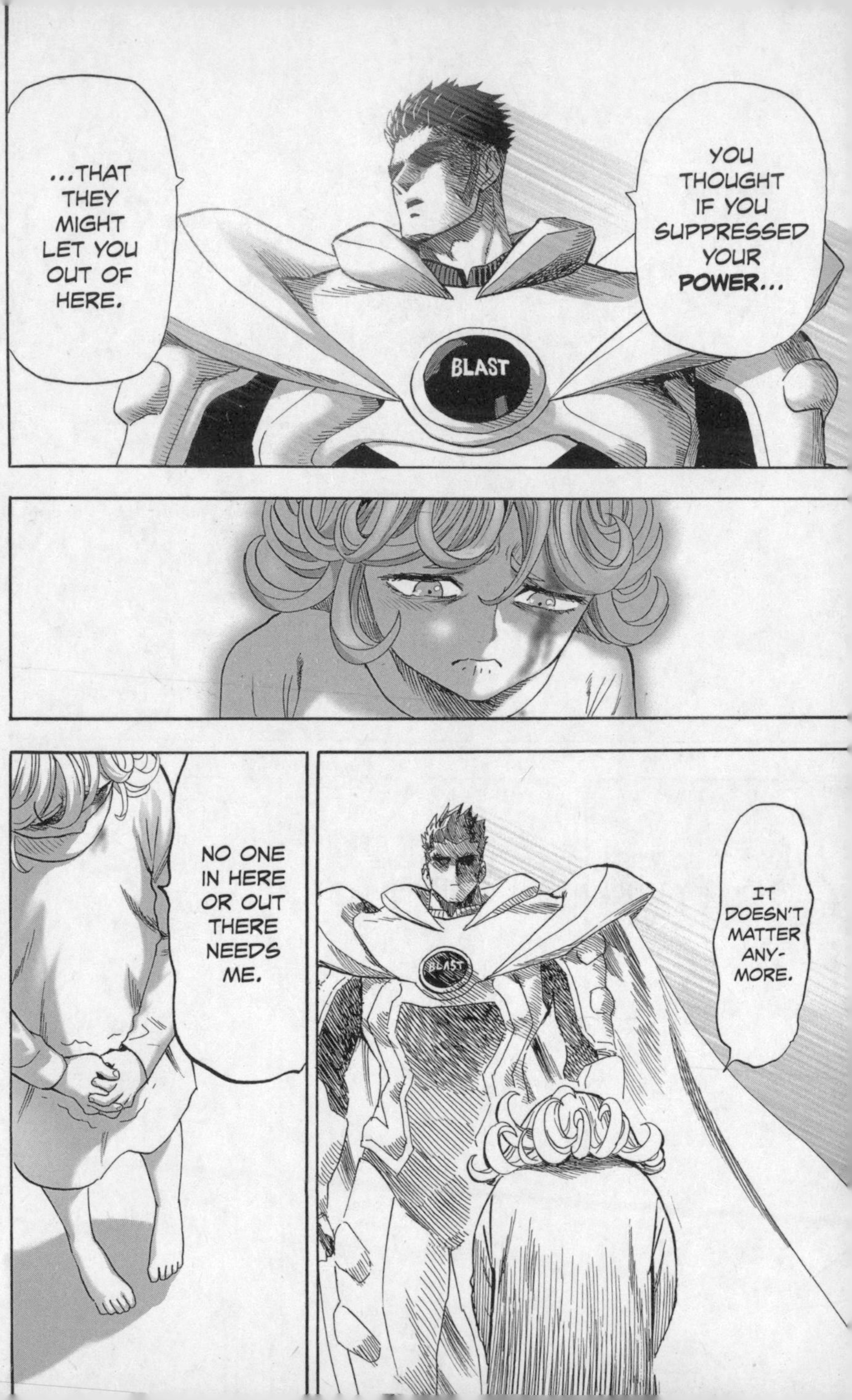
YOU THOUGHT IF YOU SUPPRESSED YOUR **POWER...**
BLAST
...THAT THEY MIGHT LET YOU OUT OF HERE.
IT DOESN'T MATTER ANY-MORE.
BLAST
NO ONE IN HERE OR OUT THERE NEEDS ME.

MAMA AND PAPA **SOLD** ME!

YOUR DEAR LITTLE SISTER.

NO, SOMEONE **DOES** NEED YOU.

PAT

YOU MUST PROTECT YOUR FAMILY.

THOSE WHO POSSESS GREAT POWER...

OKAY? LET ME GIVE YOU SOME ADVICE.

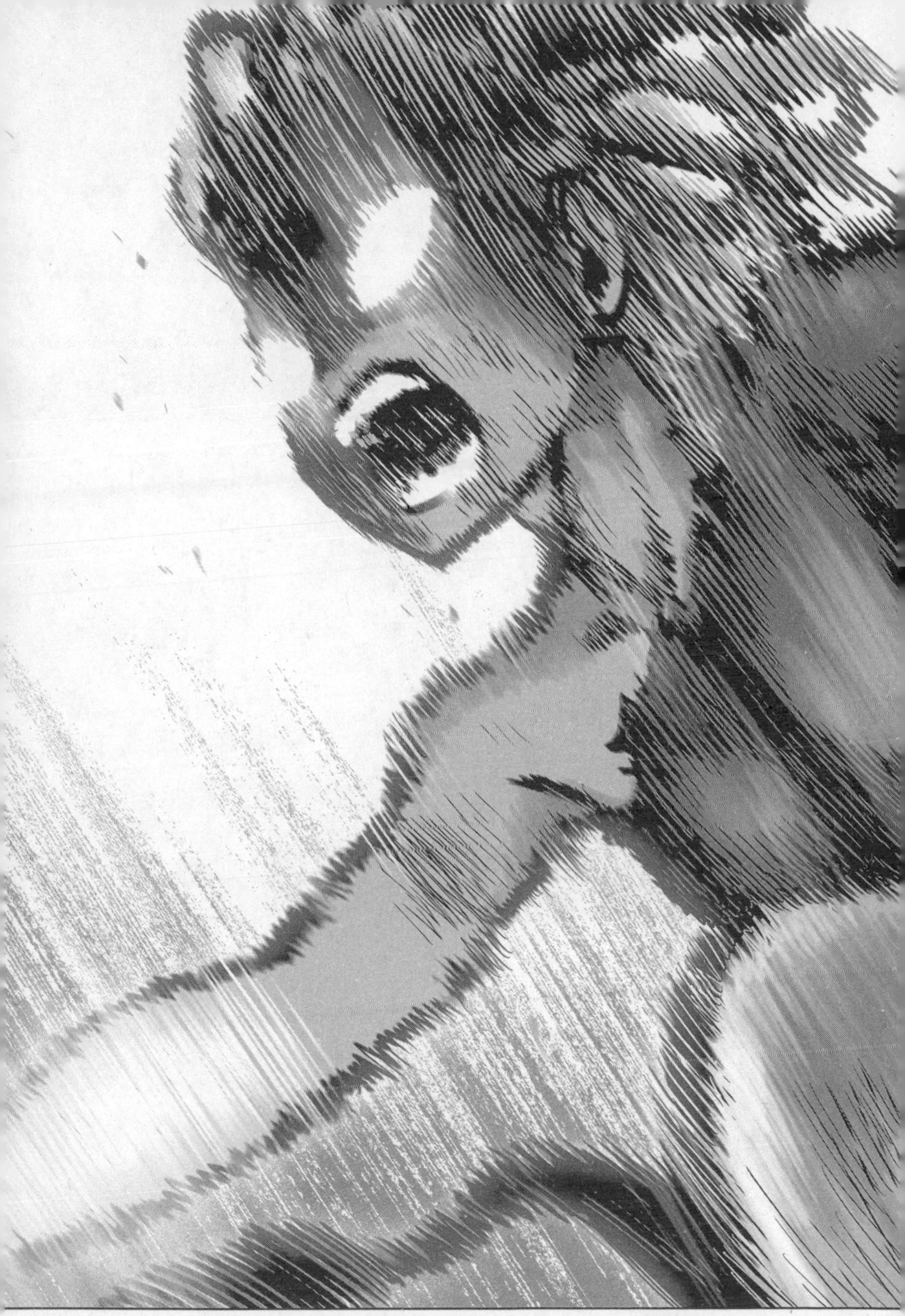

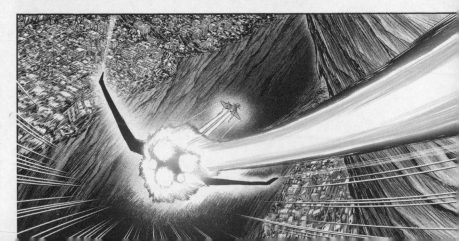

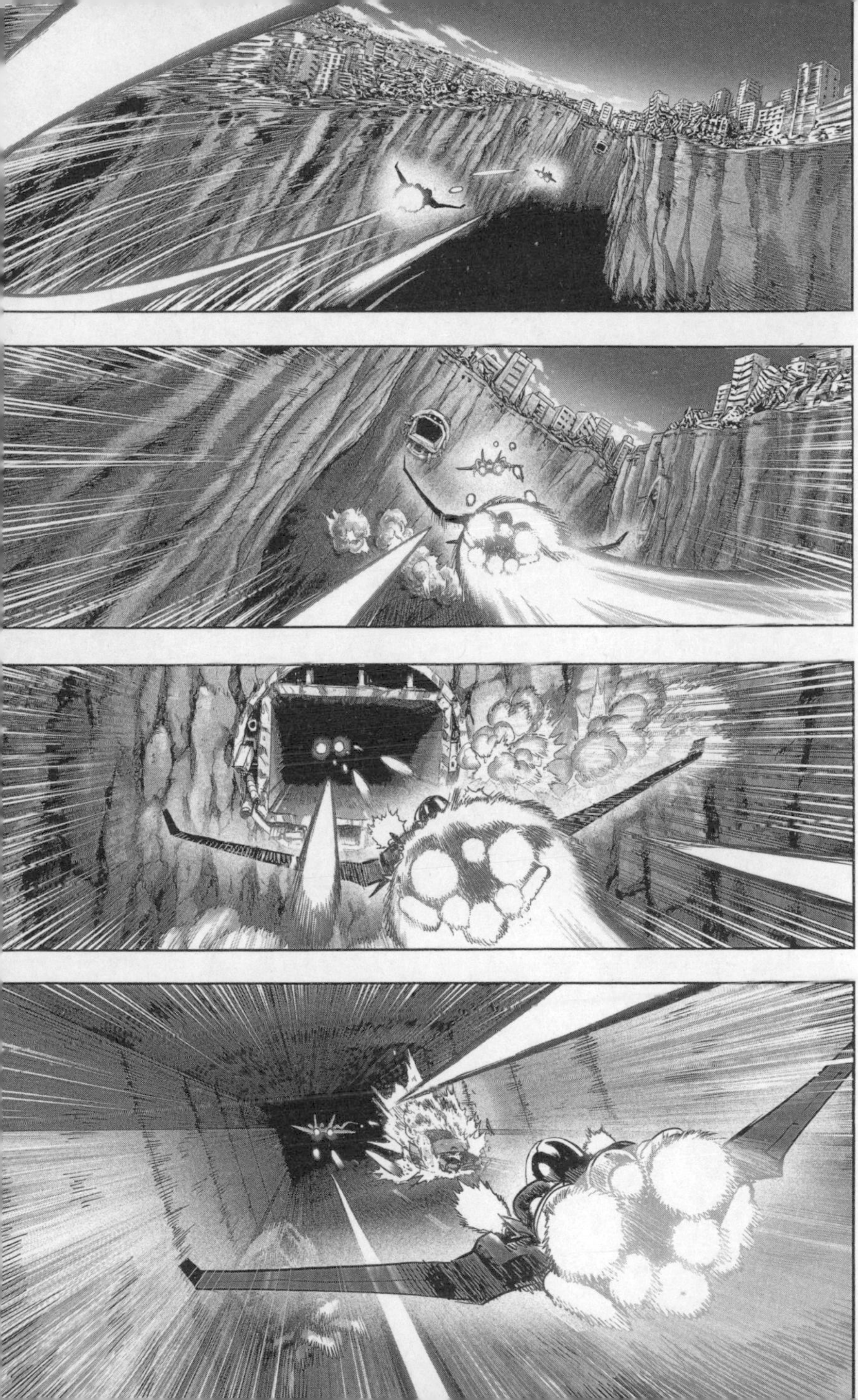

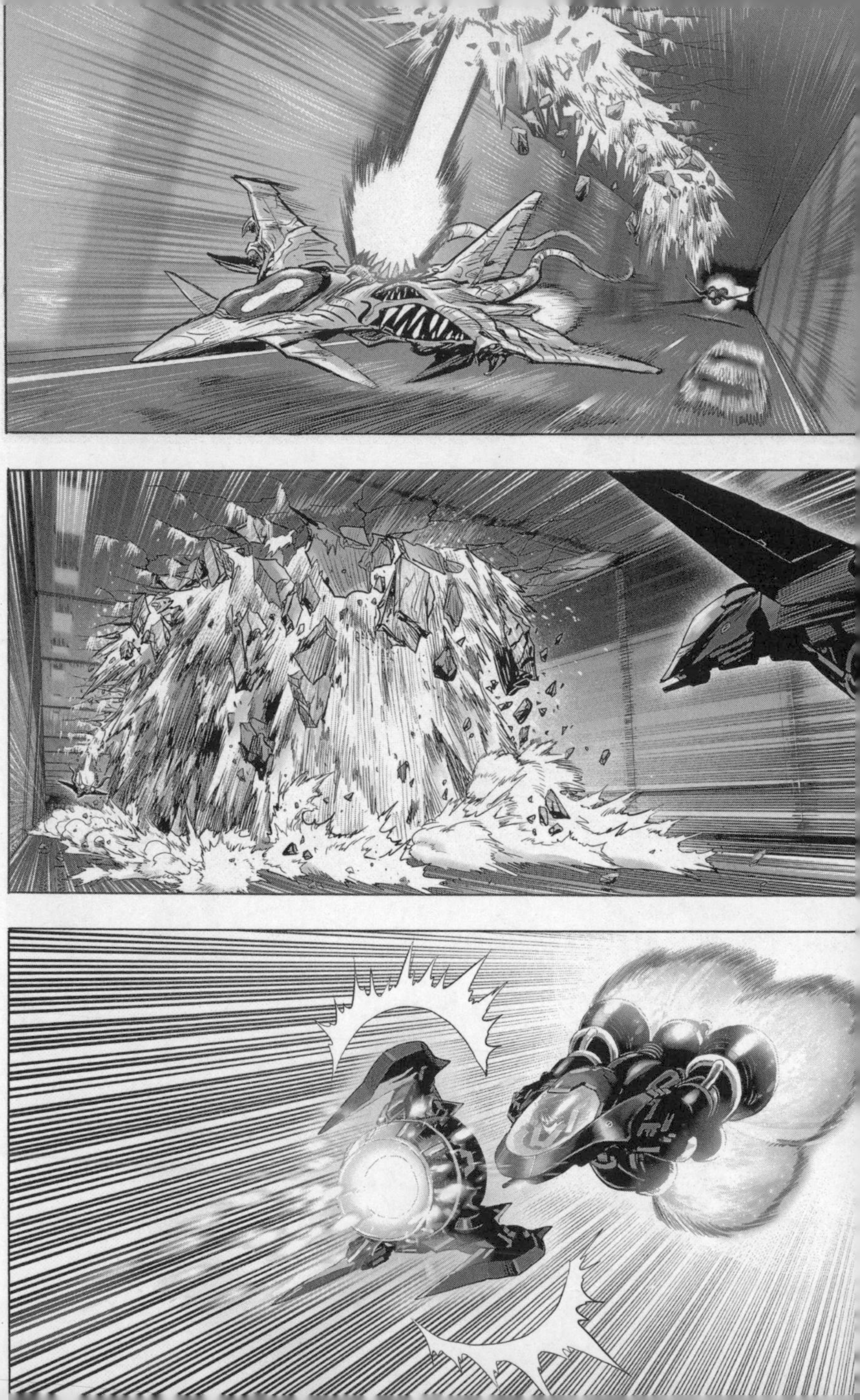

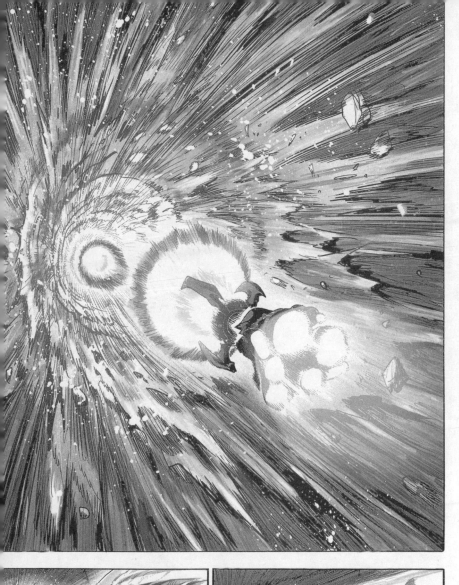

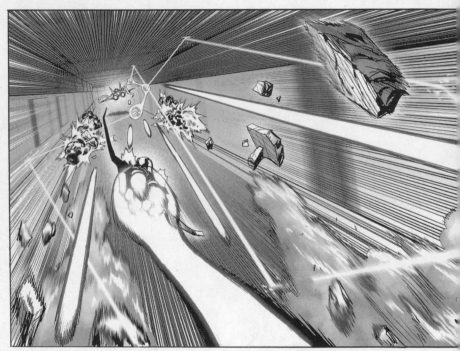

IT WOULD'VE BEEN EASIER FOR ME TO GET A SAMPLE IF SHE HAD BEEN OFF THE MARK A BIT.

TORNADO IS SUCH A BEAST!

BUT IT'S ALL DAMAGED ON A CELLULAR LEVEL!

IT DUG INTO THE EARTH LIKE ROOTS, HUH?

ARE THESE...

...THE REMAINS OF THE MONSTER KING?

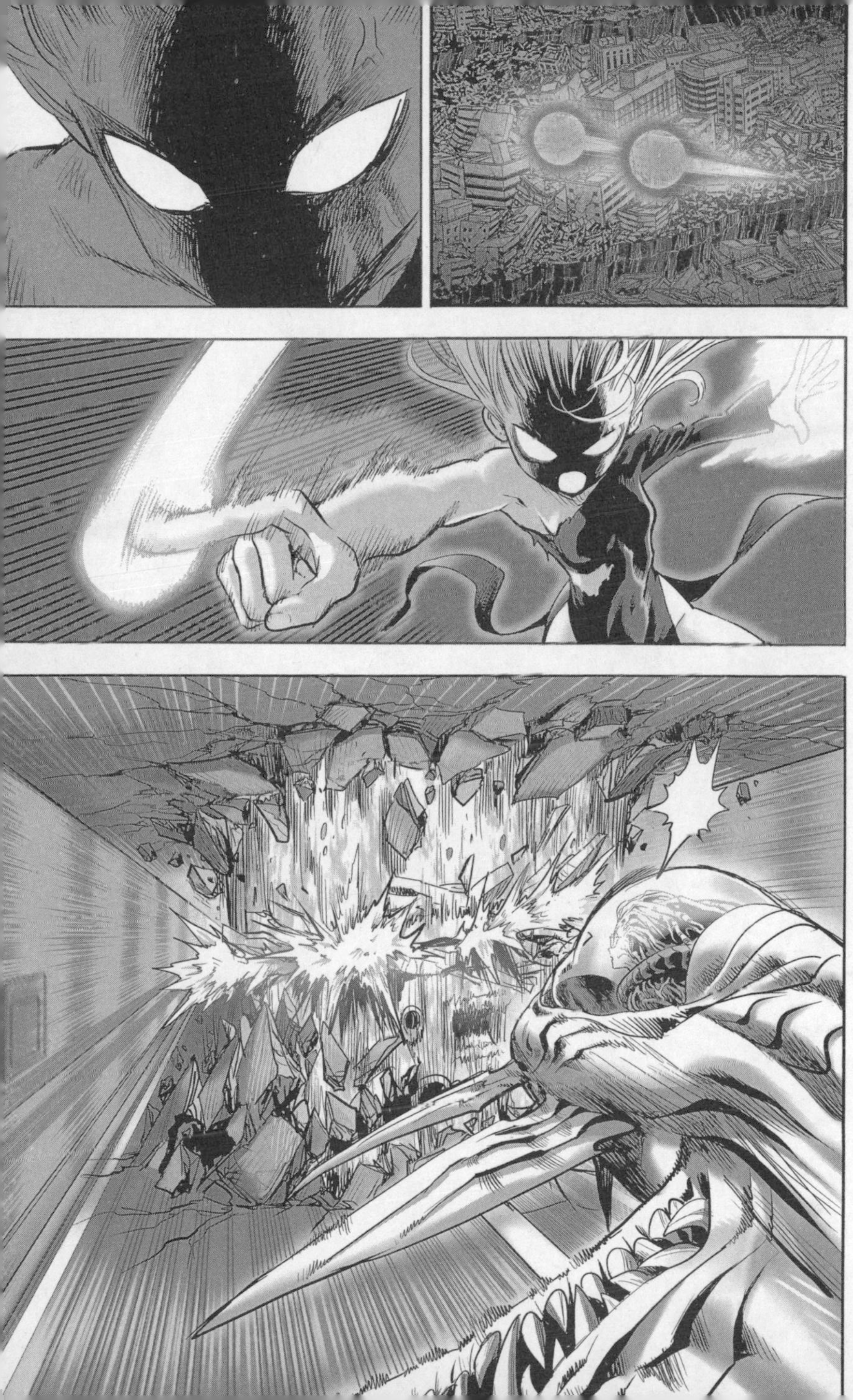

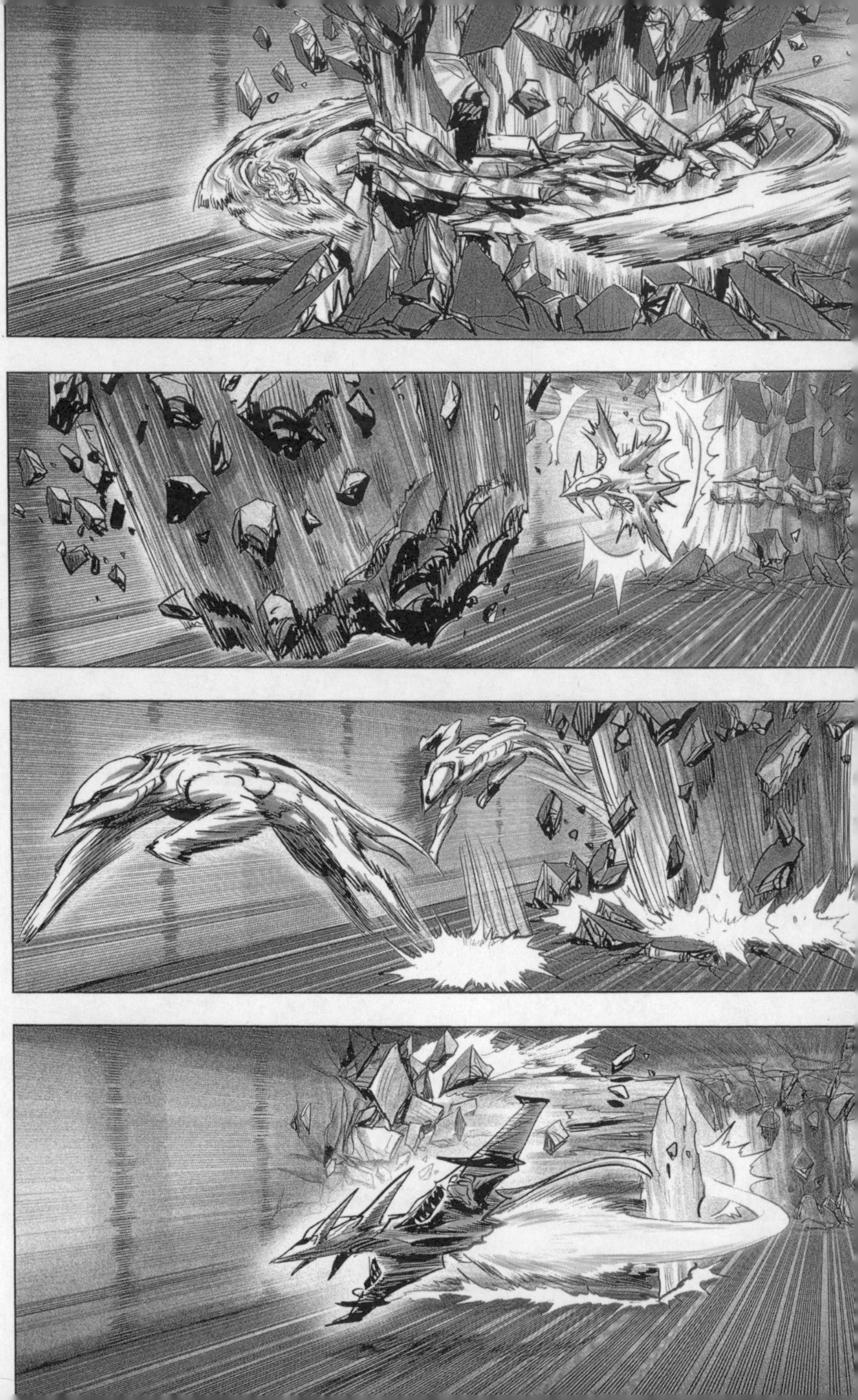

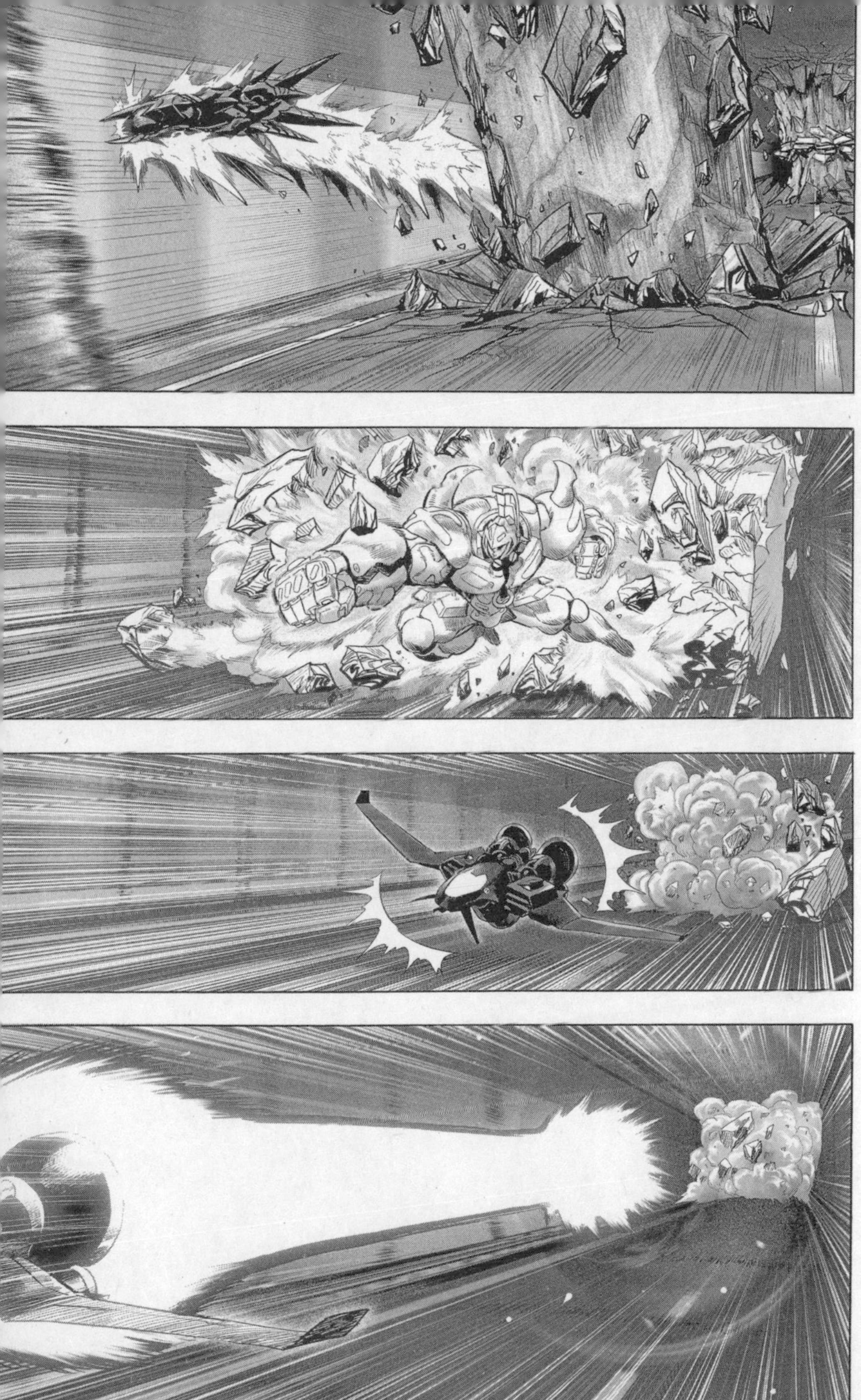

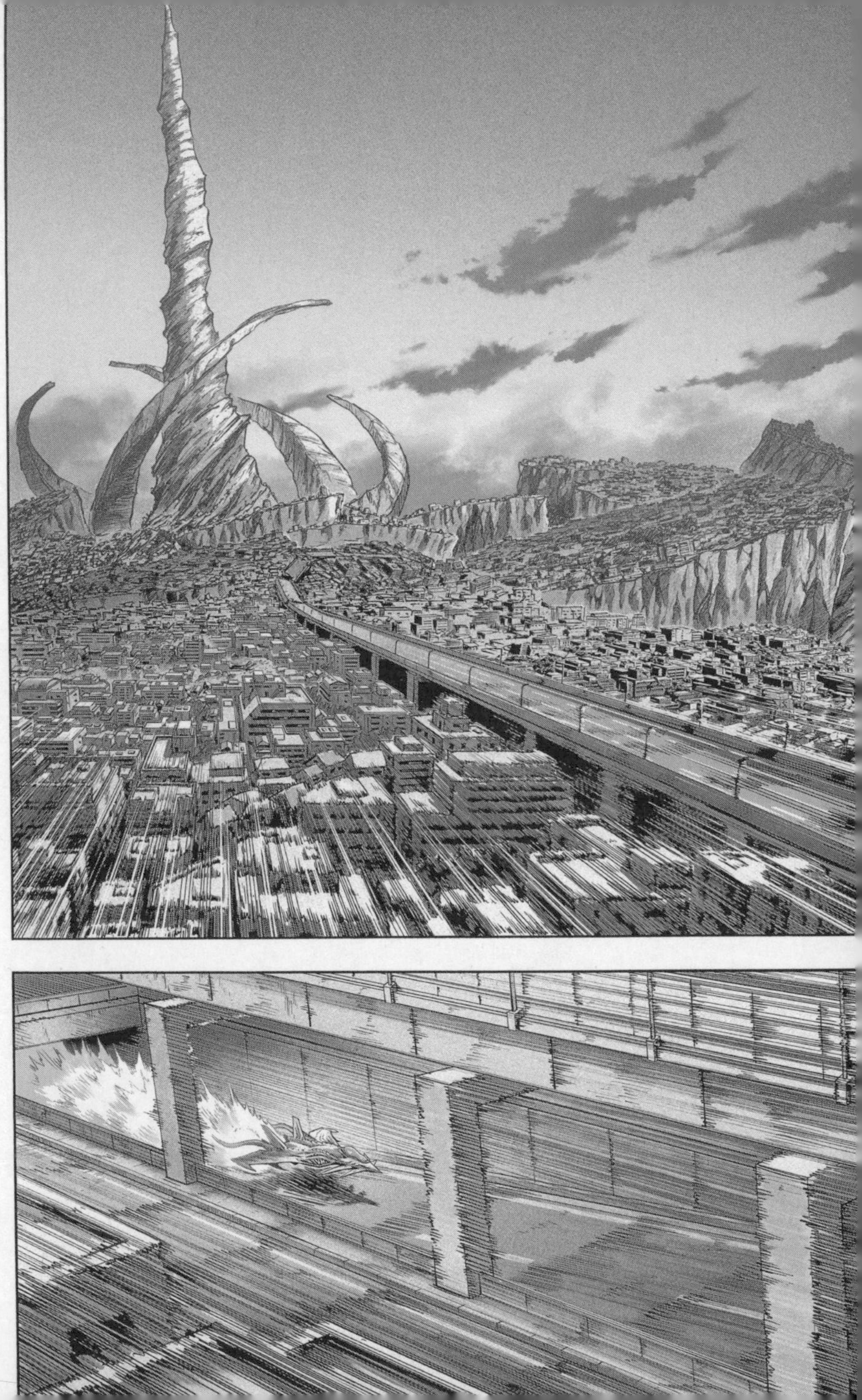

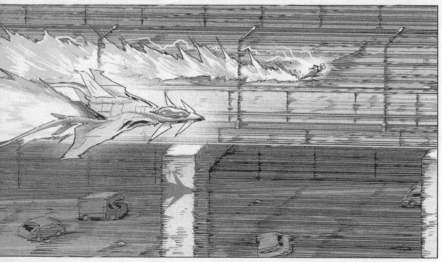

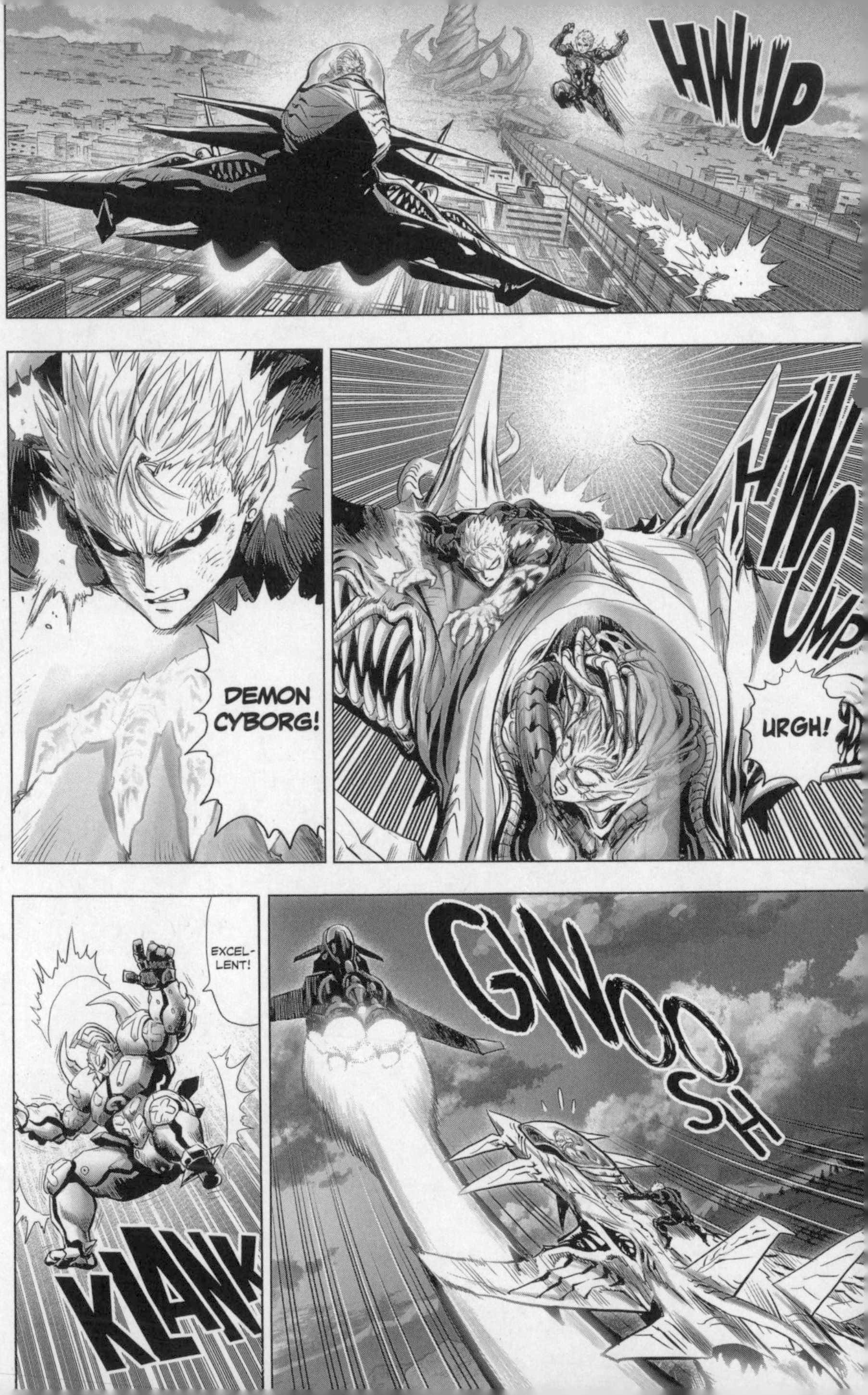
HWUP
HWOMP
URGH!
DEMON CYBORG!
GWOOOSH
EXCEL-LENT!
KLANK

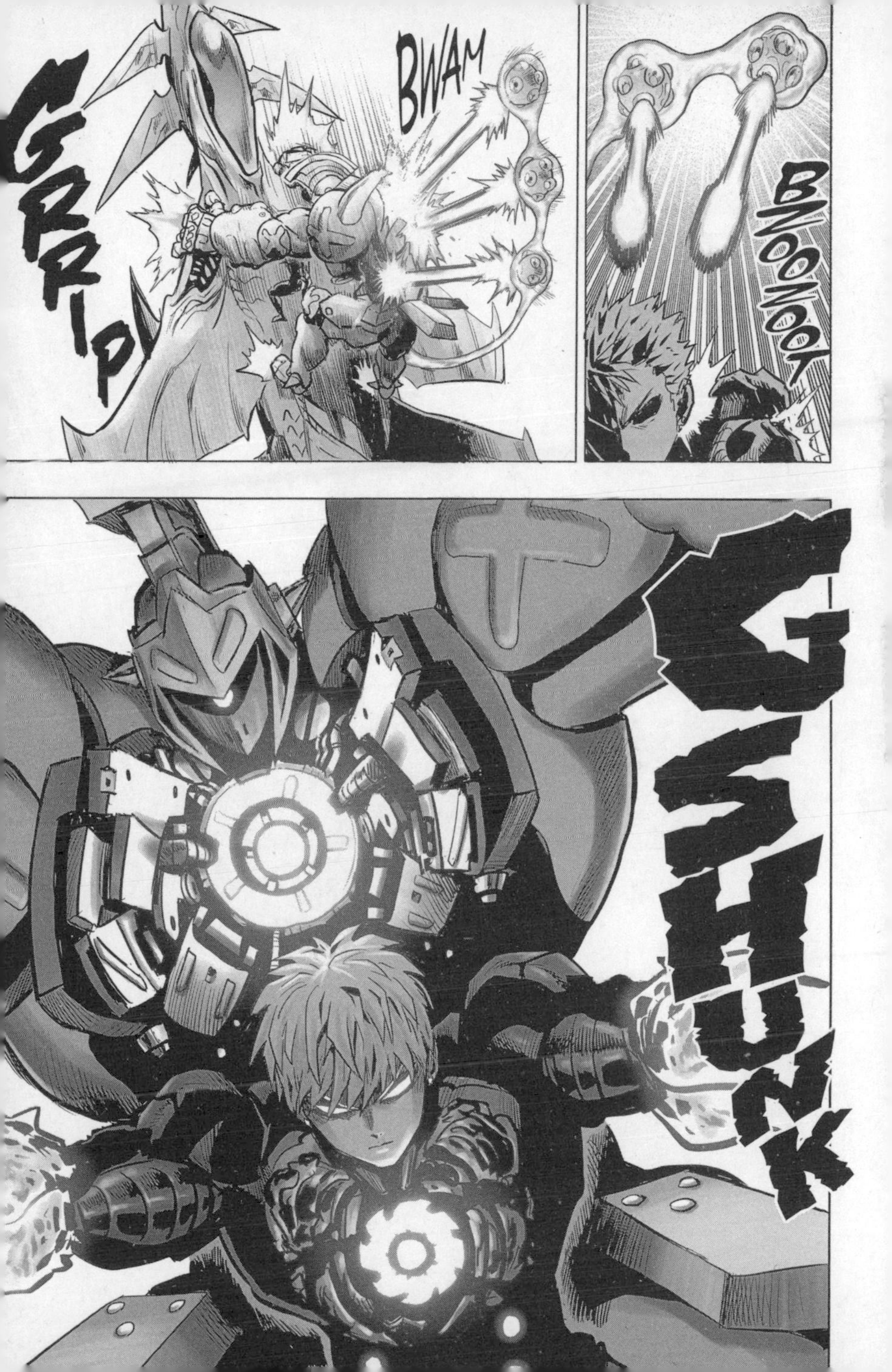
BZOOZOOT
BWAM
GRRIP
GSHUNK

PUNCH 143: **INTO THE ABYSS**

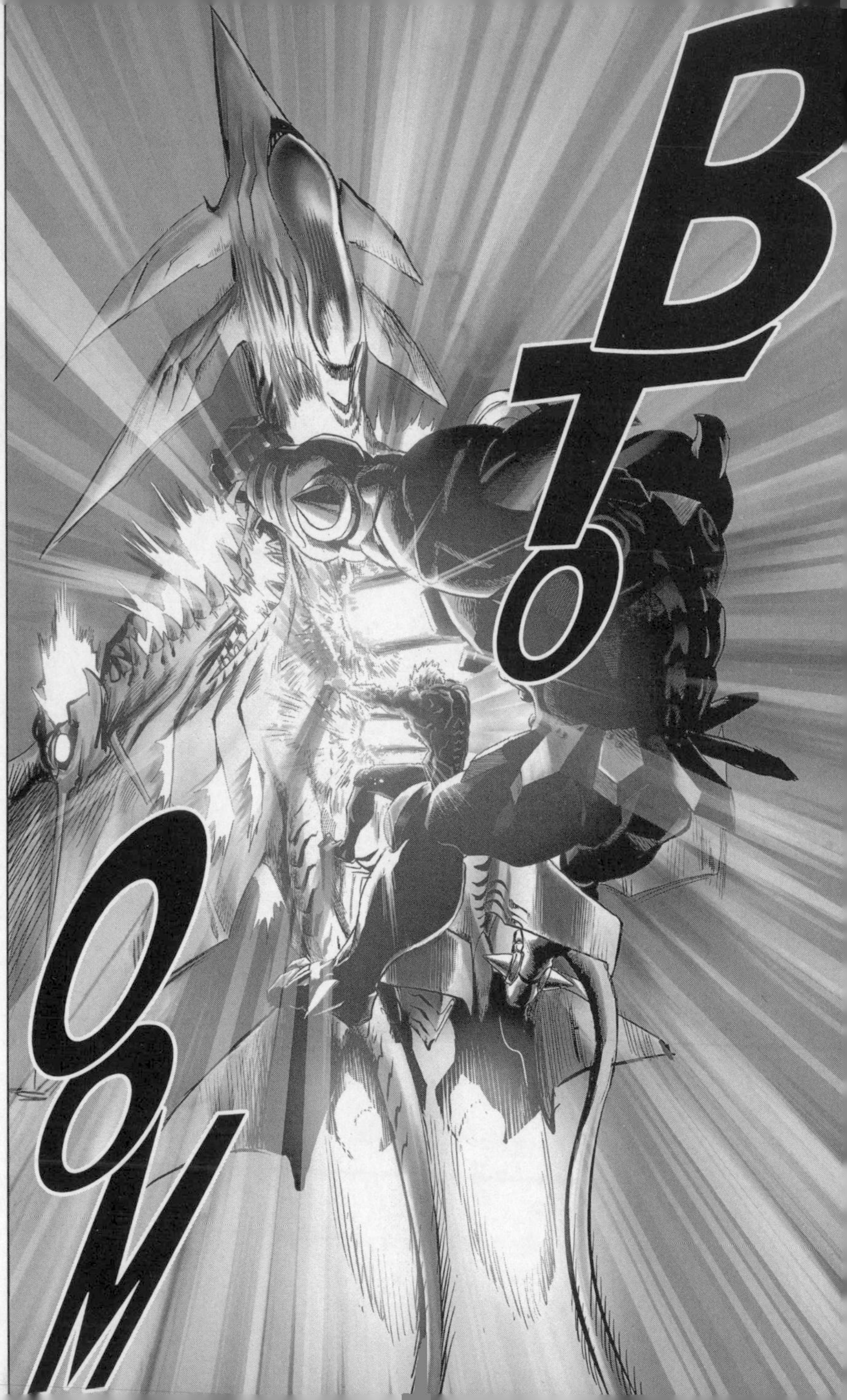
BTOOOM

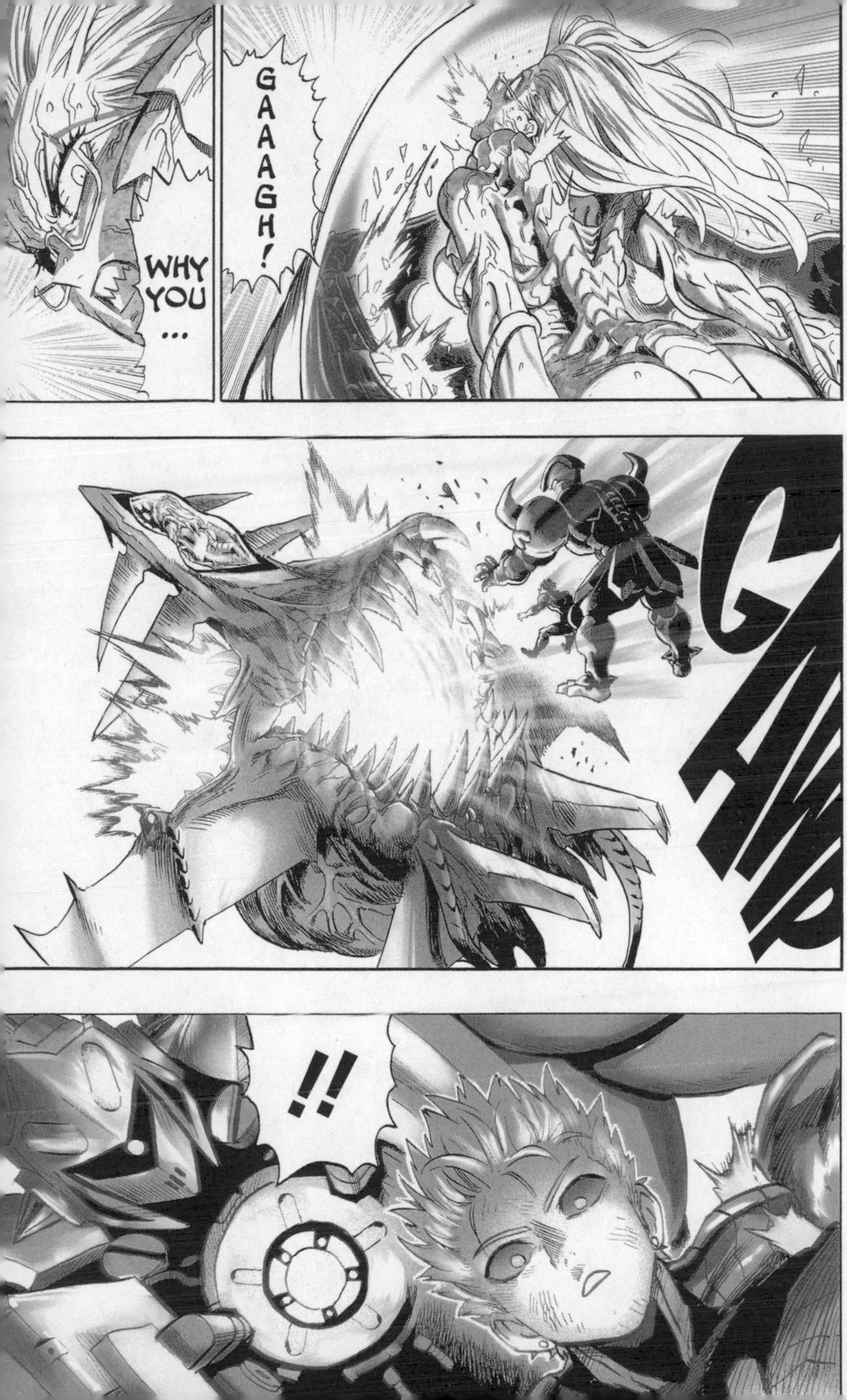
GAAAGH!
WHY YOU ...
!!

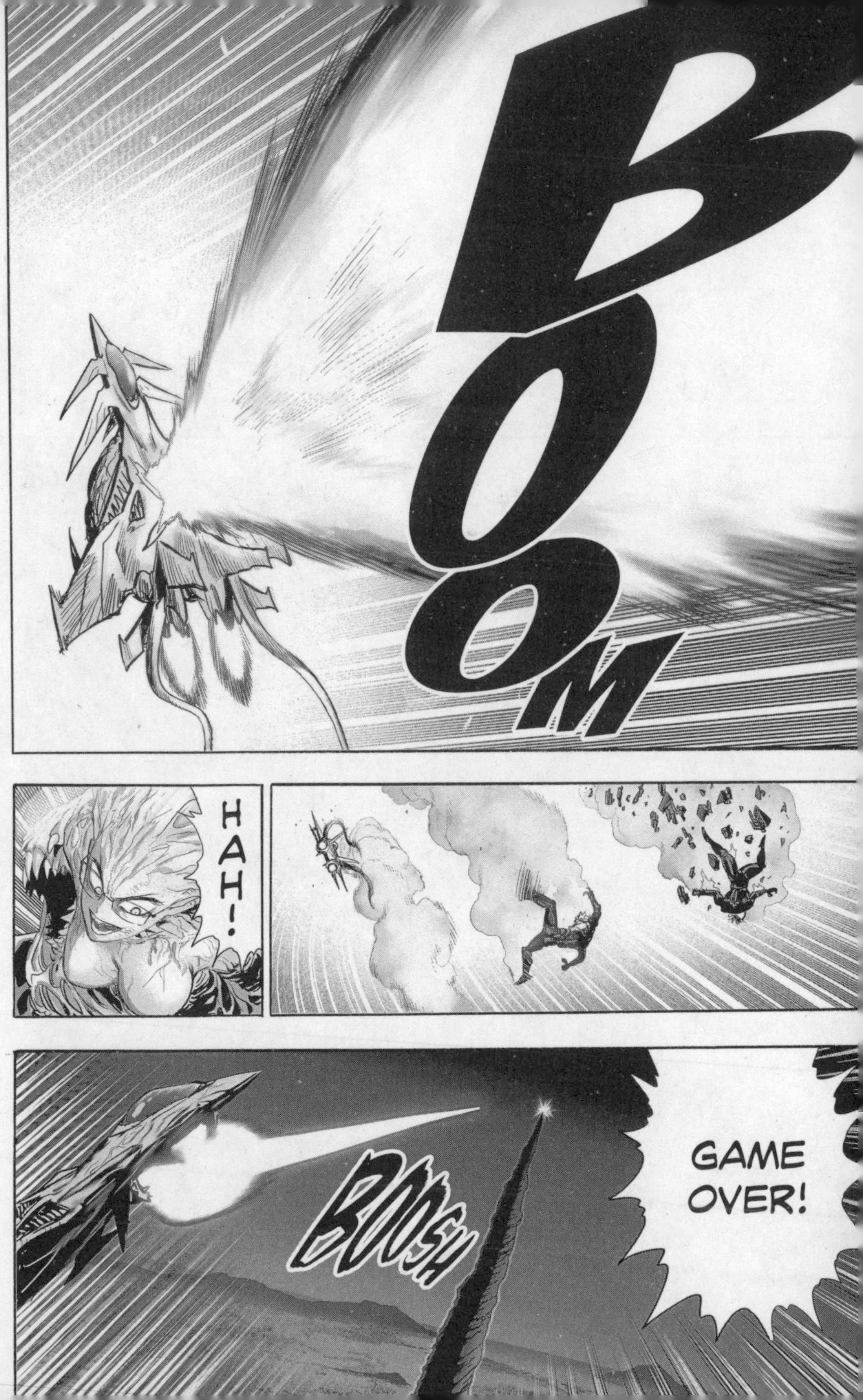
BOOM
HAH!
BOOSH
GAME OVER!

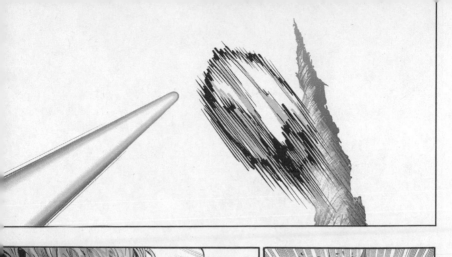

?!

BOOM

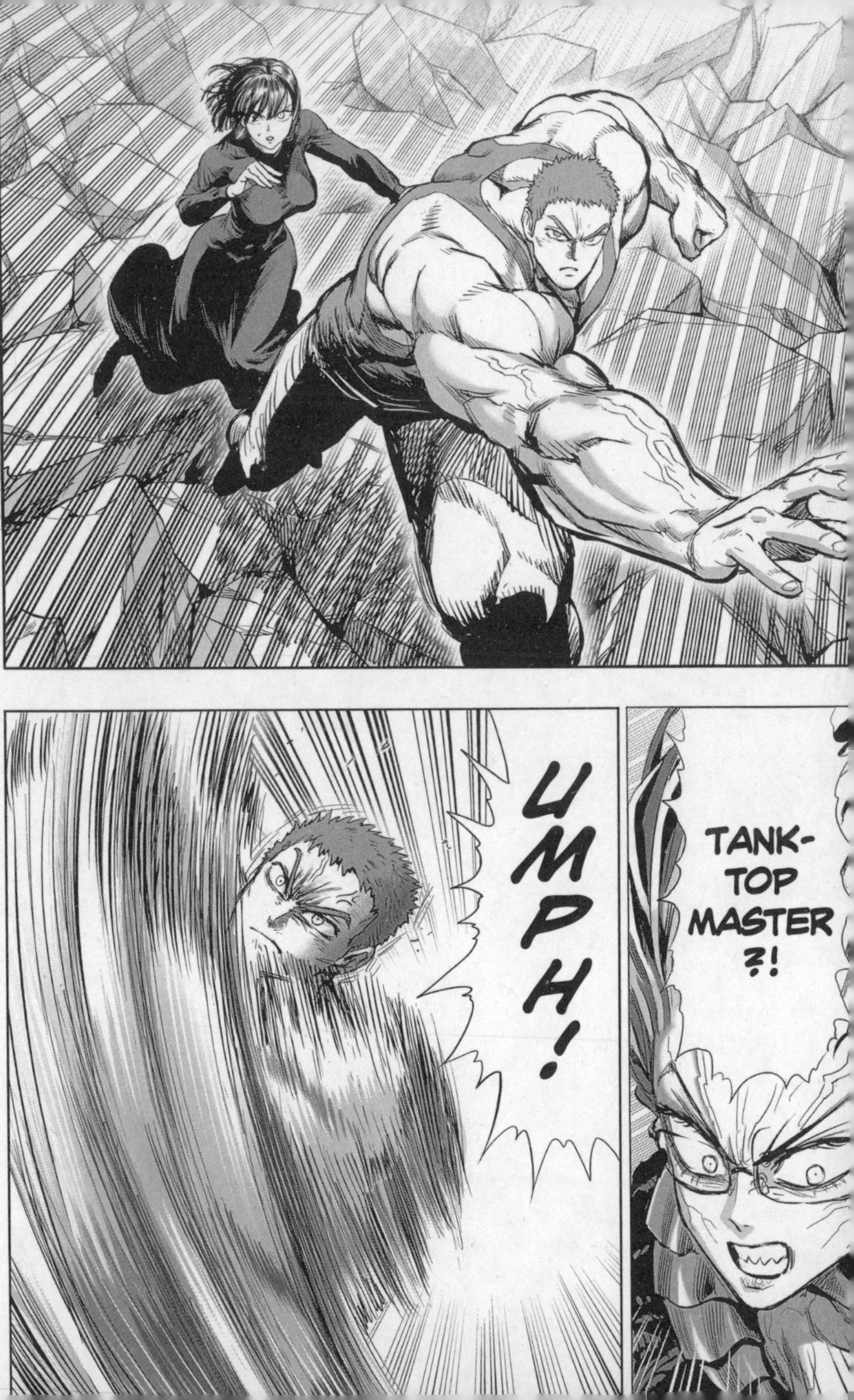
TANK-TOP MASTER ?!
UMPH!

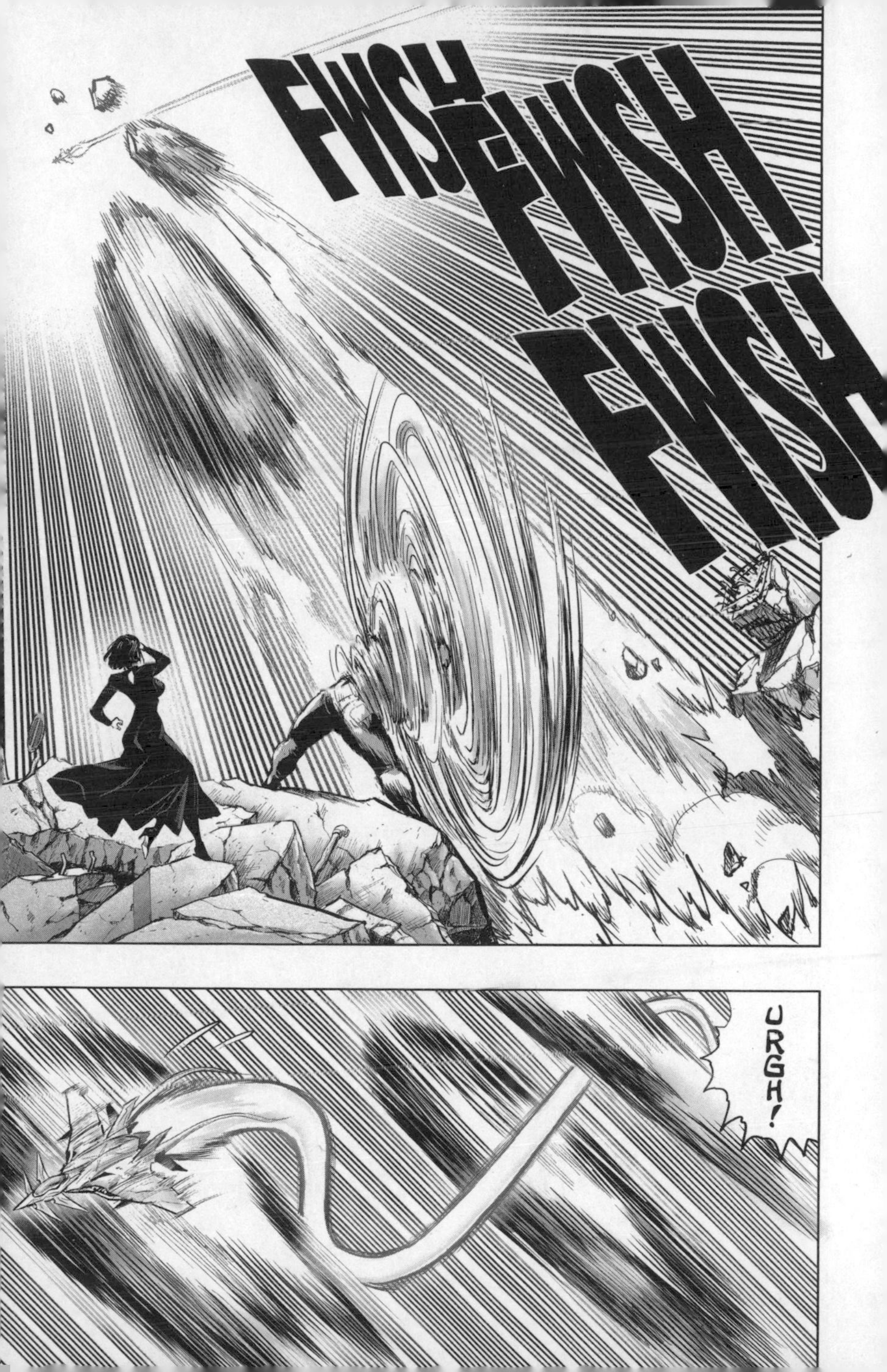
FWSH
FWSH
FWSH
FWSH
URGH!

UH... YOU'RE WELCOME.

BUT I DIDN'T DO ANYTHING TO THE TANK TOP...

THANKS, MISS BLIZZARD!

MY TANK TOP IS SUDDENLY PROVIDING INCREASED AGILITY! I DIDN'T KNOW YOU HAD THAT POWER!

WOO OOO

DEMON CYBORG...

KSHNK

I WANT TO COMBINE WITH YOU AND INTEGRATE OUR POWER CORES FOR MAXIMUM OUTPUT.

I'M RUNNING LOW ON ENERGY.

...I REQUEST YOUR ASSISTANCE.

...ARE YOU WITH ME?

IT MAY NOT WORK, BUT...

THEN HERE GOES!

VREEEEEET

CAUTION

POWER CORE NEAR DEPLETION

YES, I AM WITH YOU.

VMMM

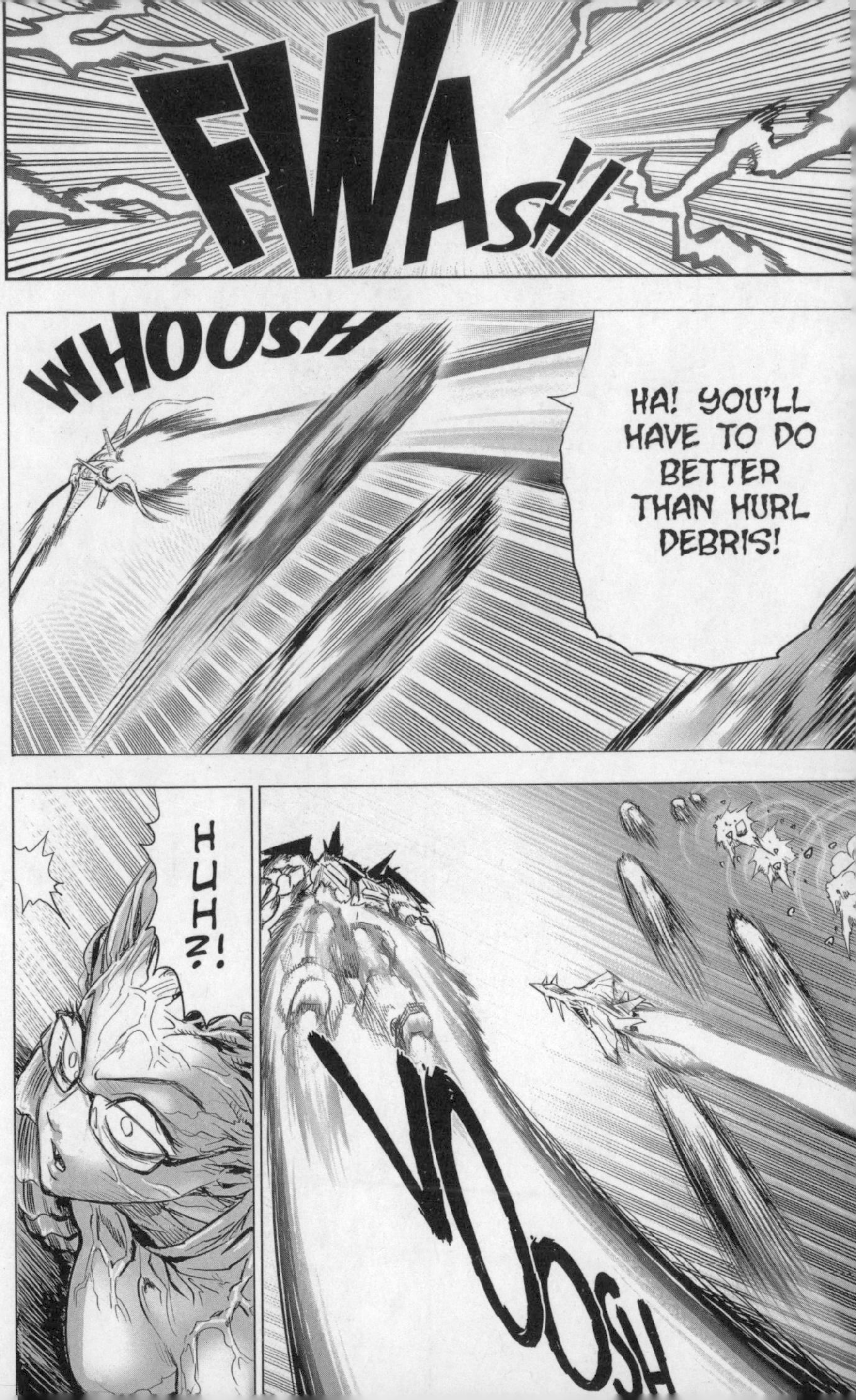
FWASH
HA! YOU'LL HAVE TO DO BETTER THAN HURL DEBRIS!
WHOOSH
VOOSH
HUH?!

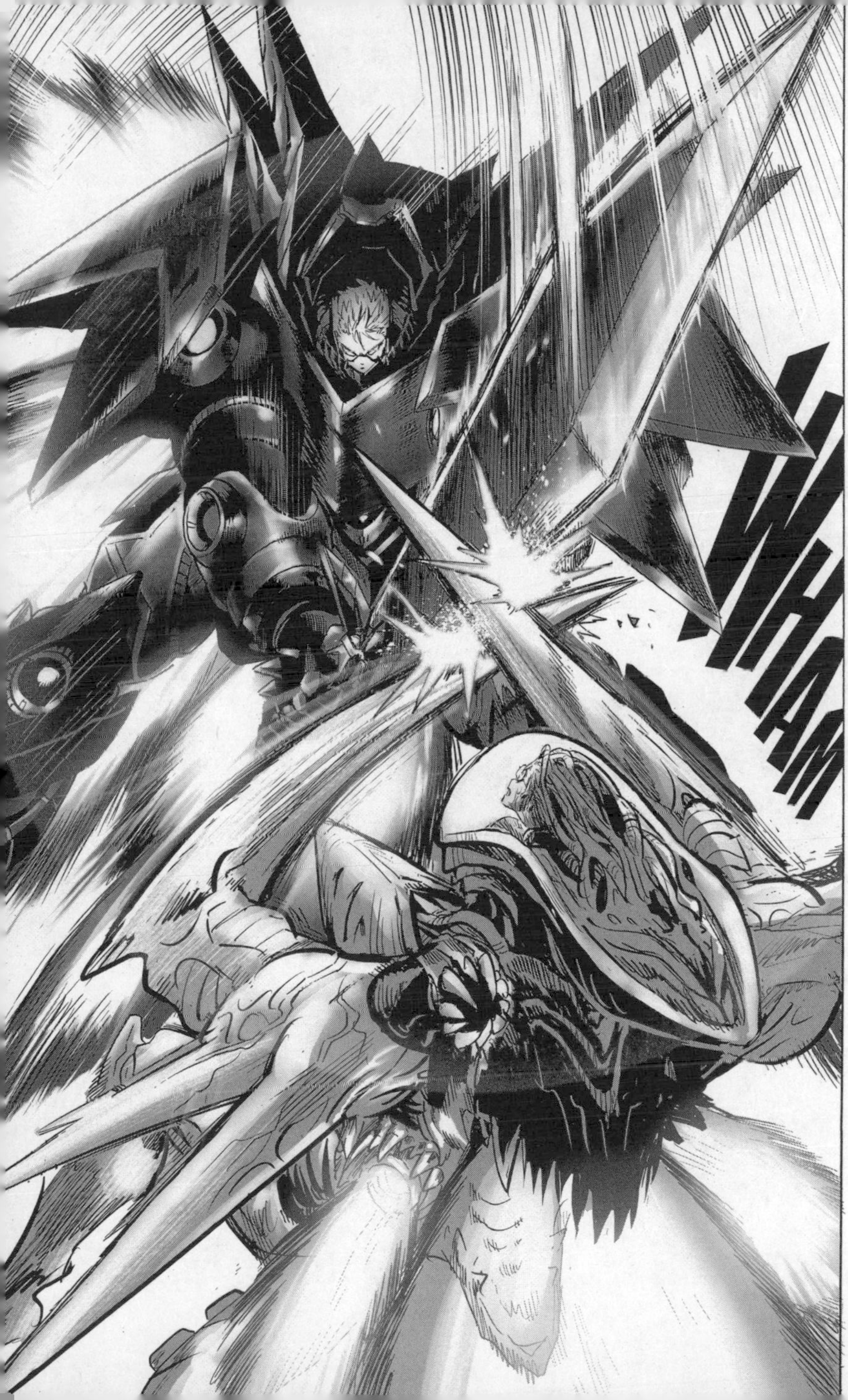
WHAM

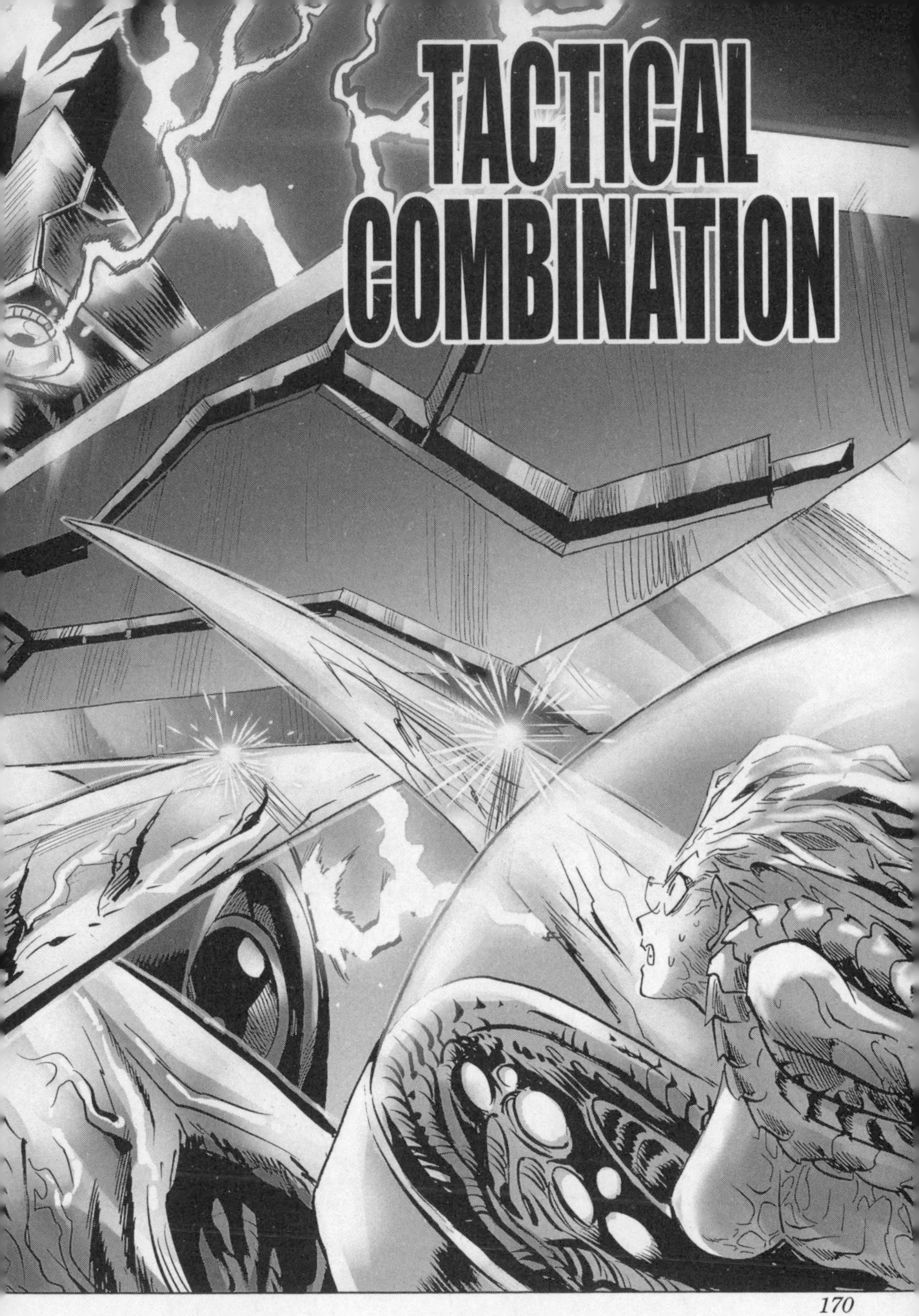
TACTICAL
COMBINATION

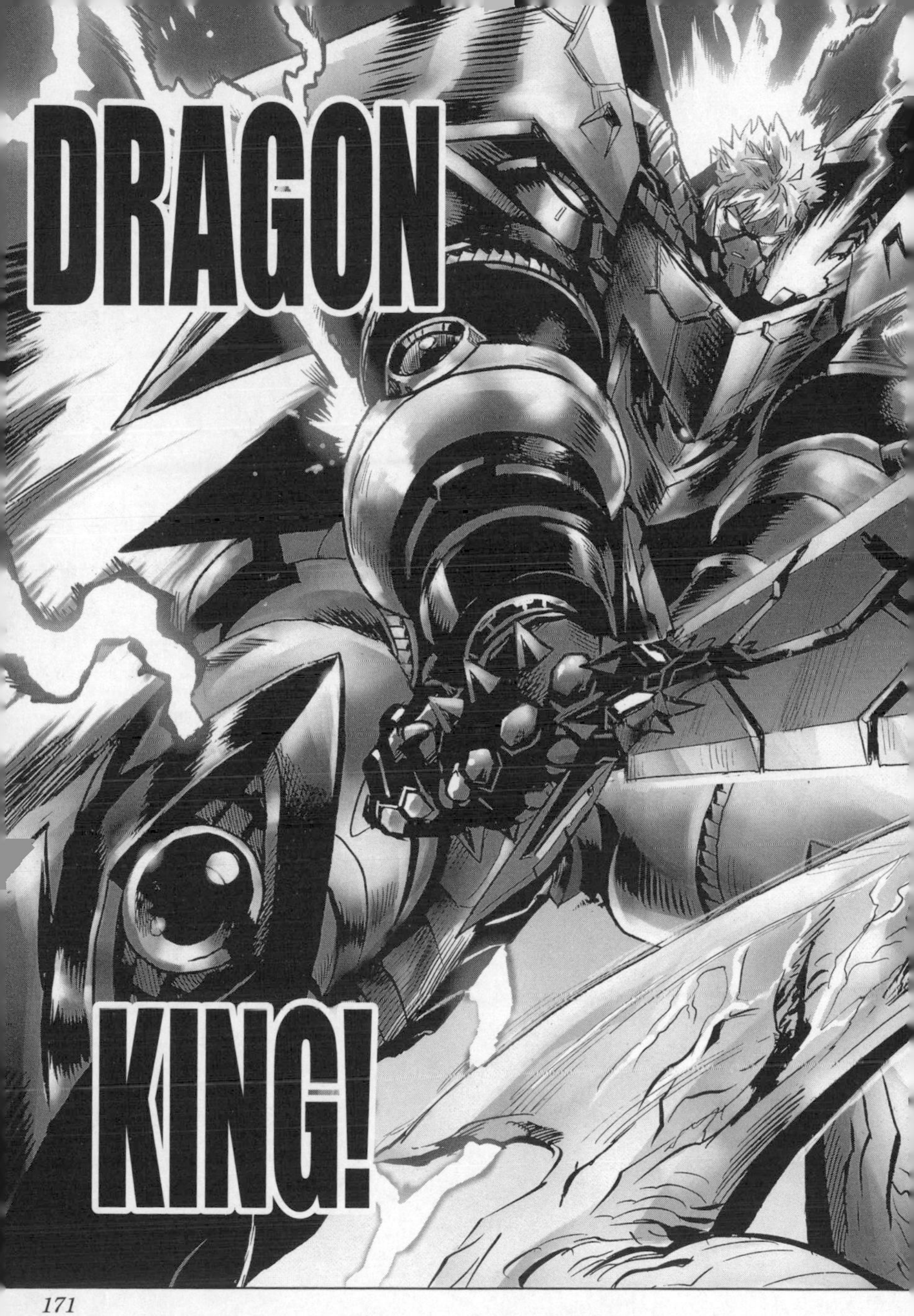
DRAGON
KING!

AT MY SIGNAL, SEPARATE IMMEDIATELY! UNDERSTOOD?

DRIVE KNIGHT, MY CORE COULD EXPLODE AT ANY MOMENT!

...PIECES OF JUNK!

YOU...

NOW'S YOUR CHANCE!

SHE STOPPED MOVING!

UMPH!

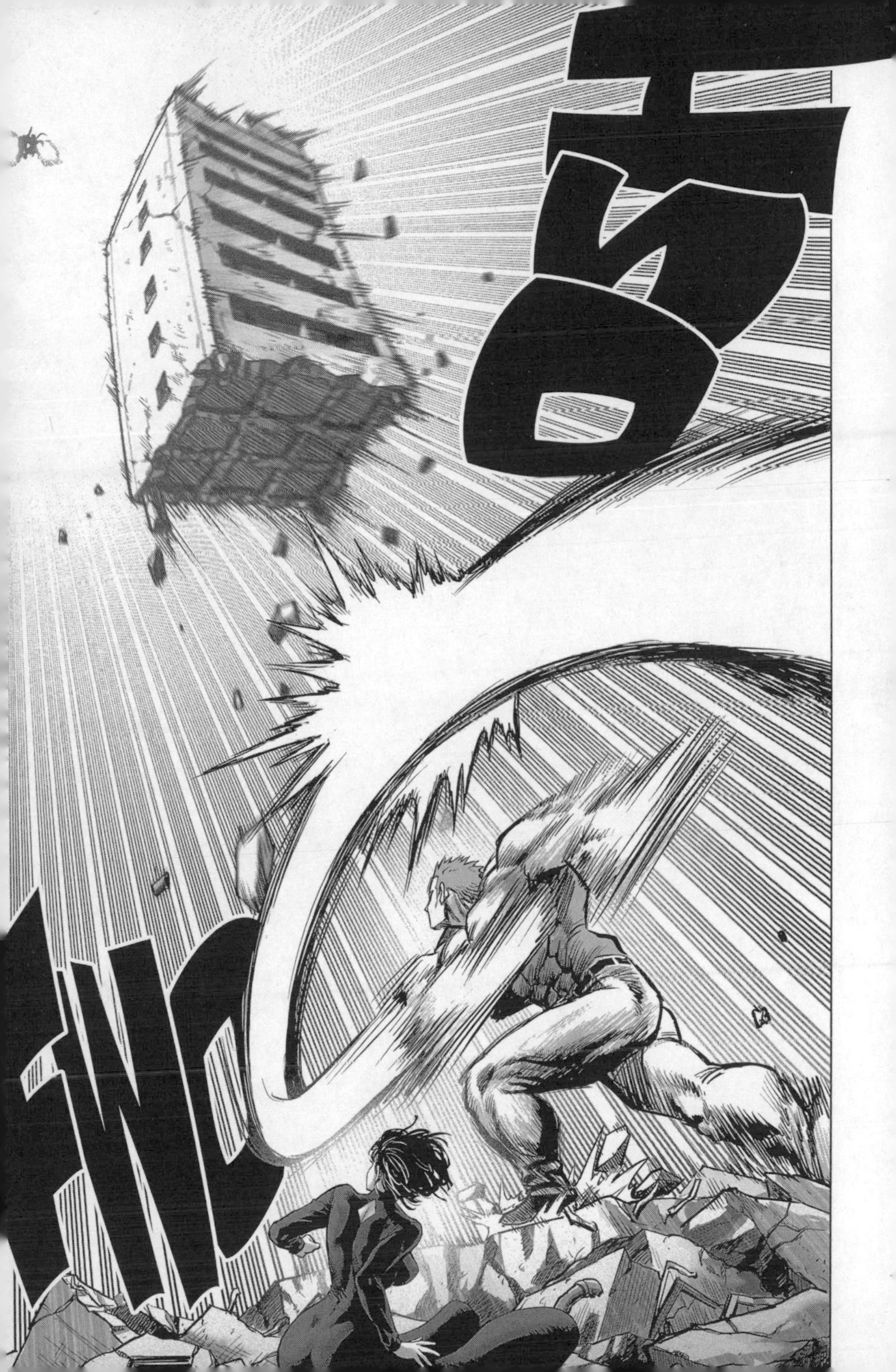

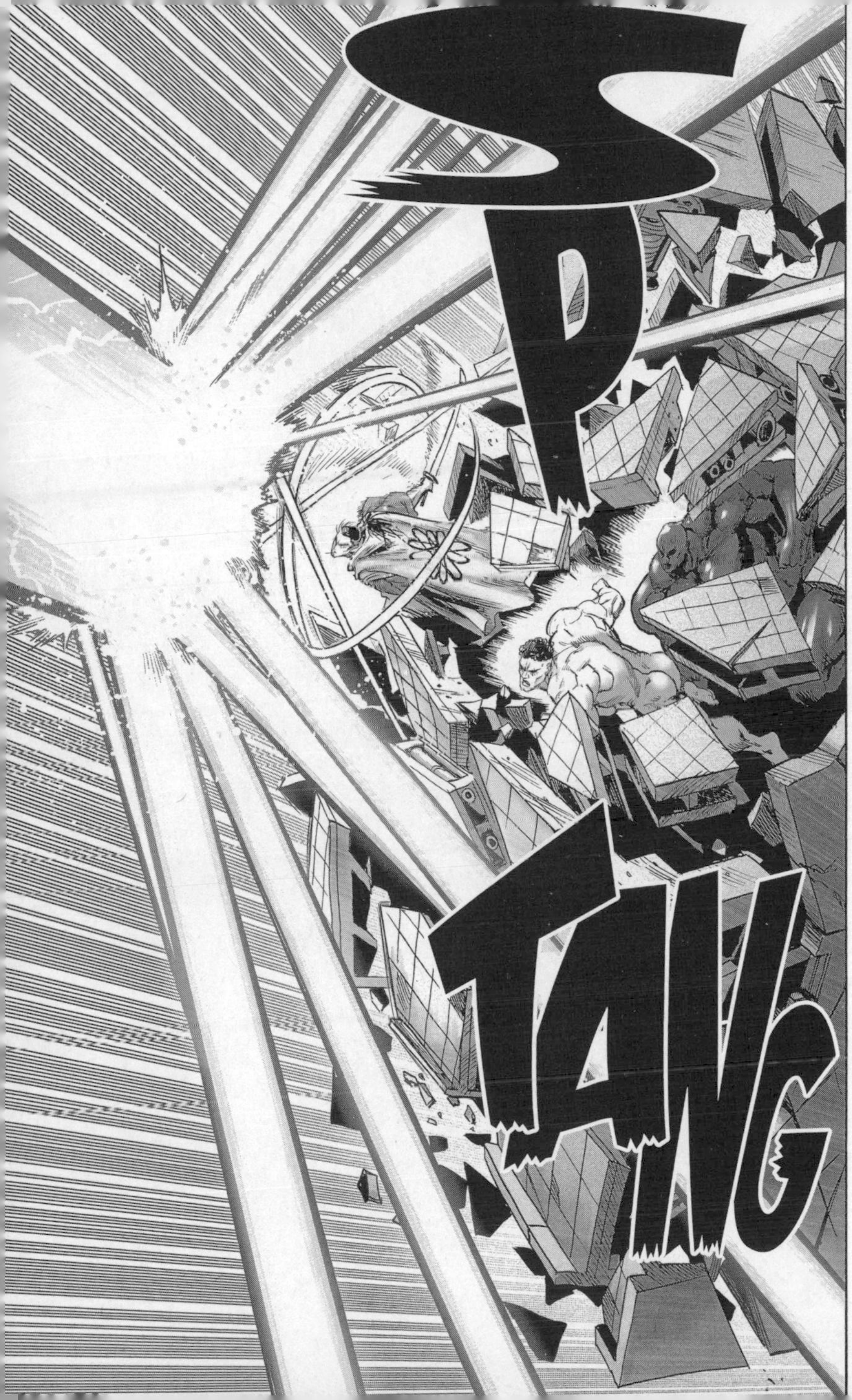
SPTANG

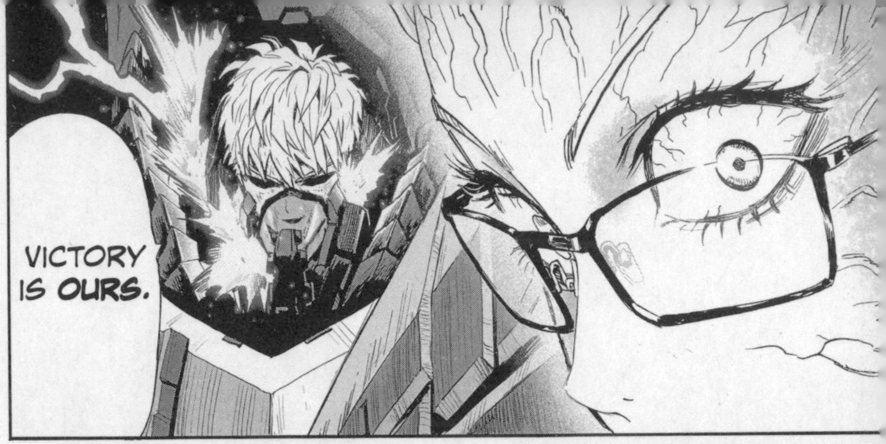
VICTORY
IS OURS.
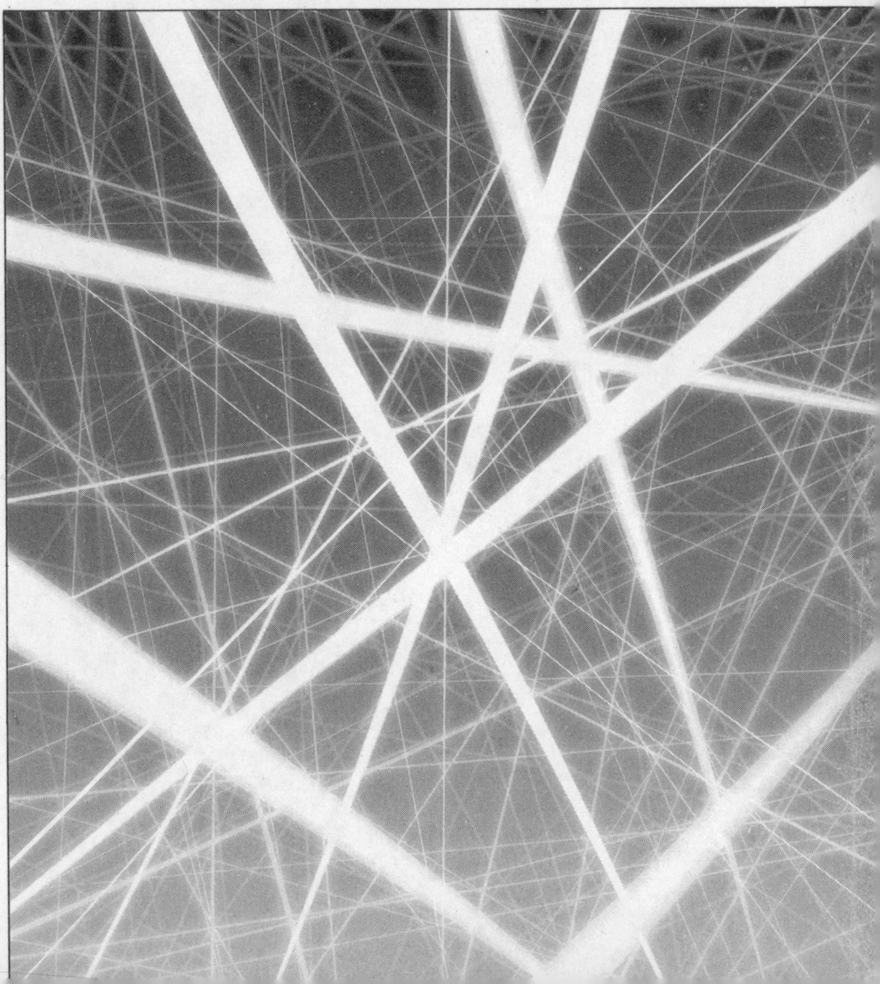

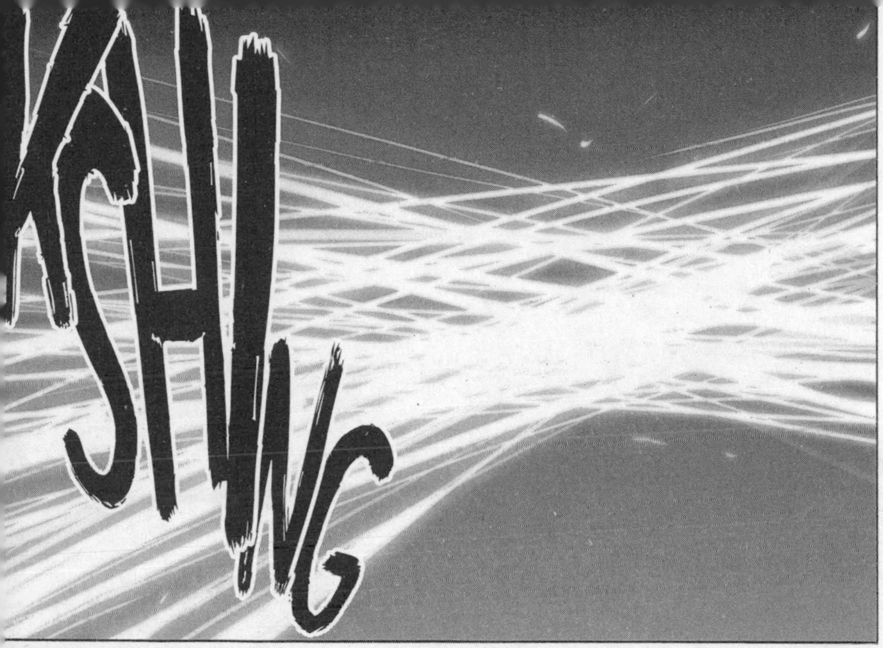
KSHING

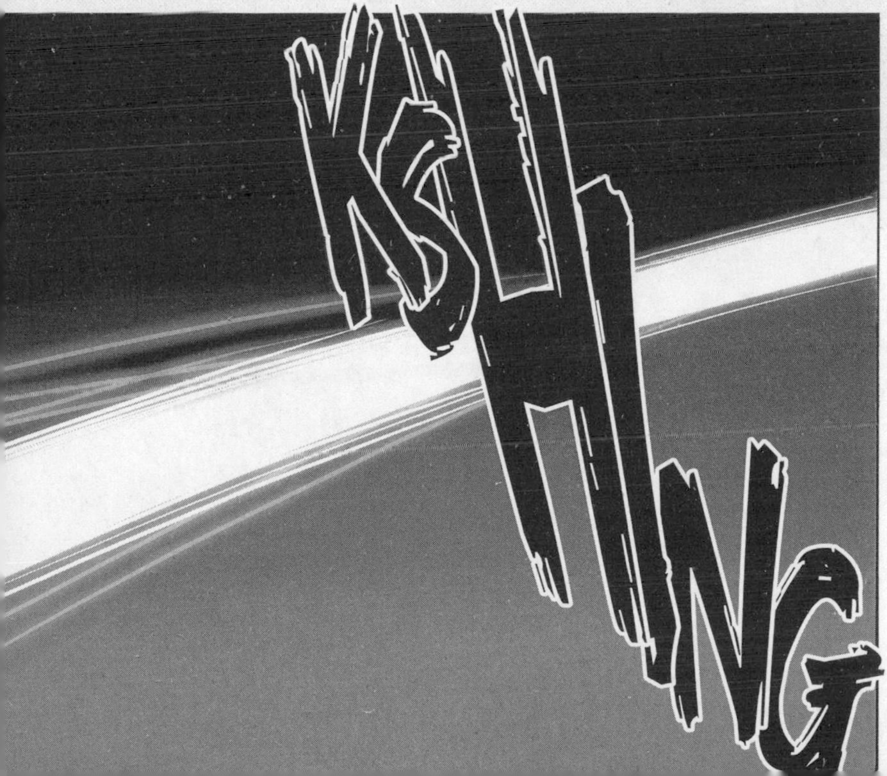
KSHHING

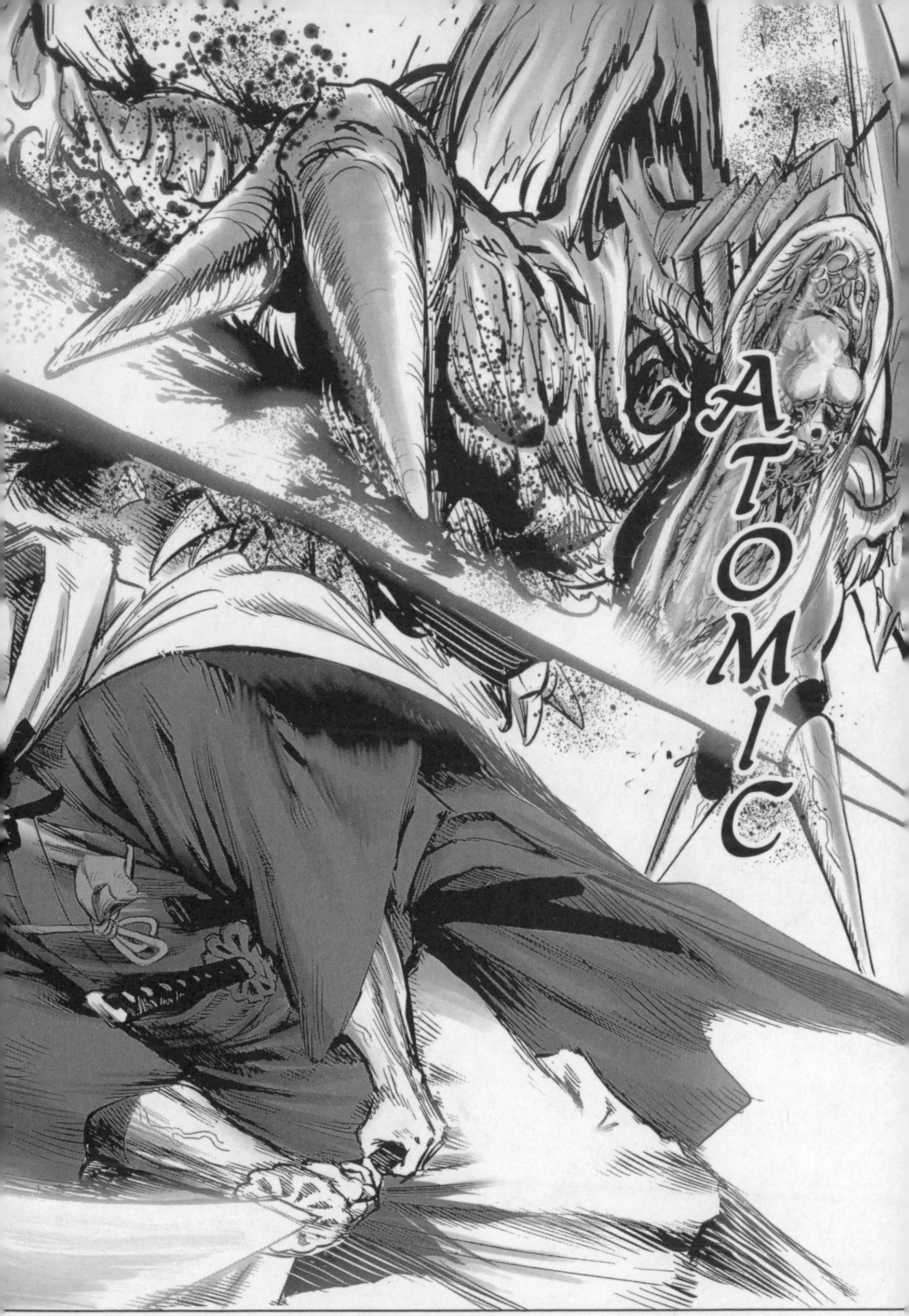
ATOMIC

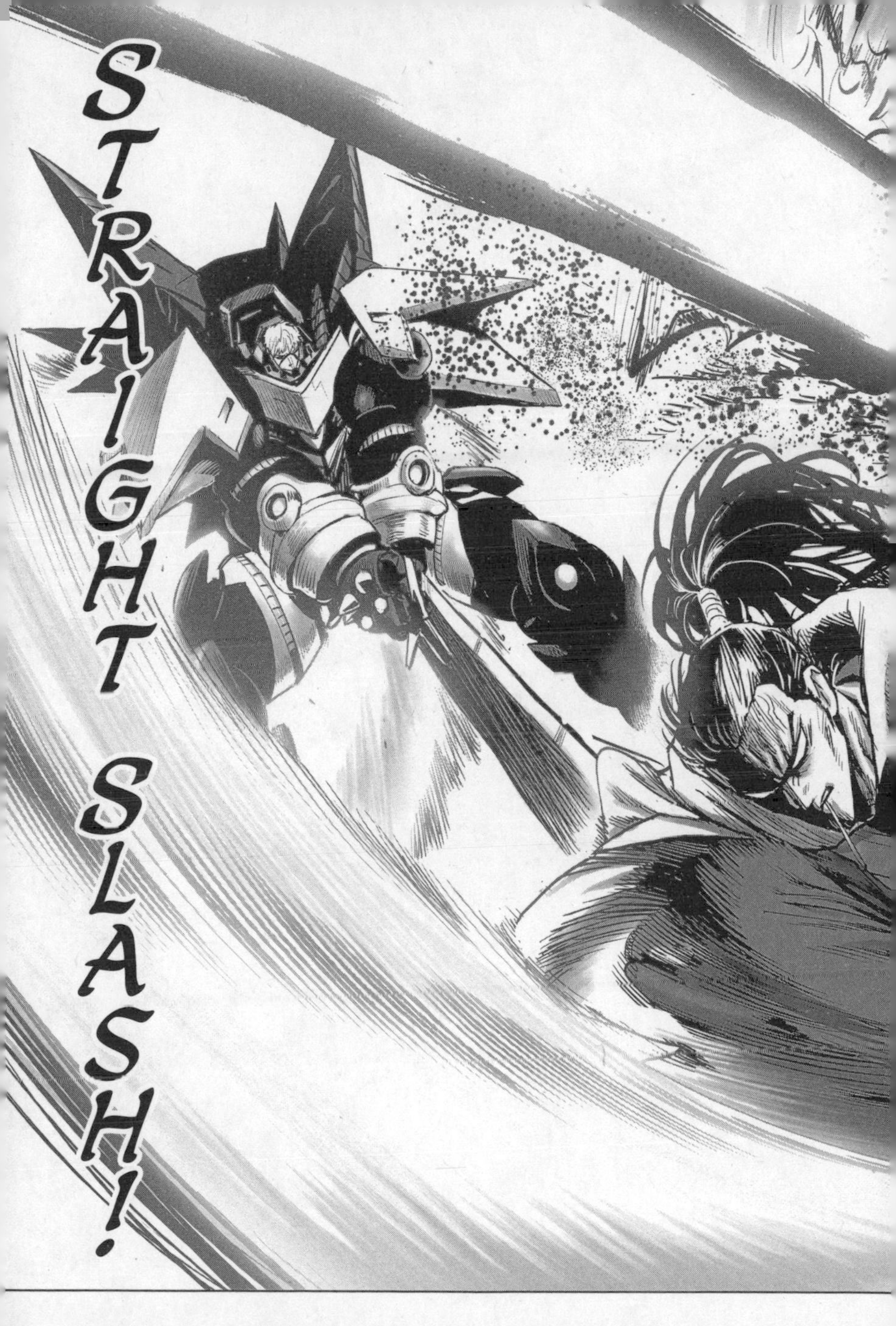
STRAIGHT SLASH!

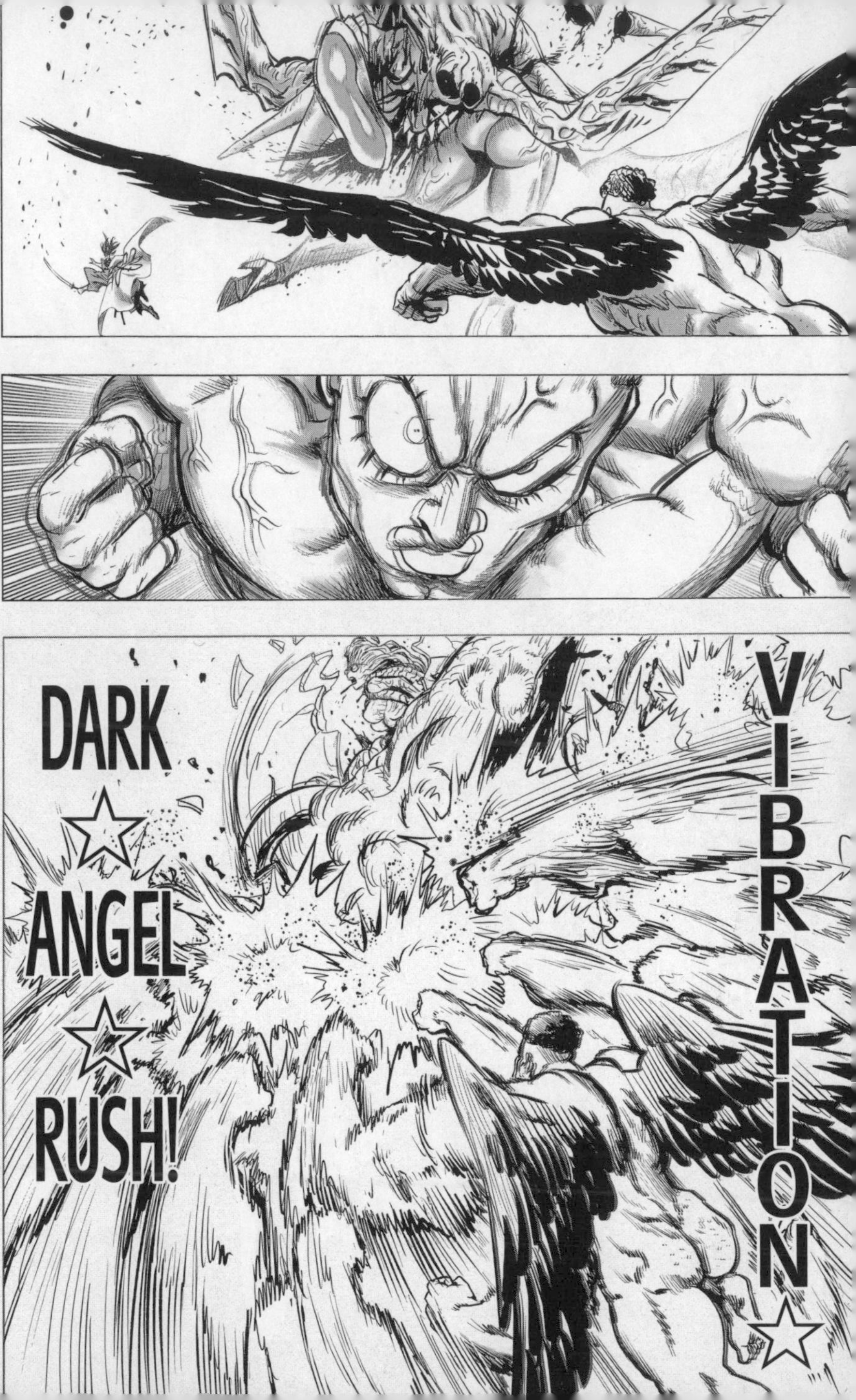
VIBRATION☆
DARK ☆ ANGEL ☆ RUSH!

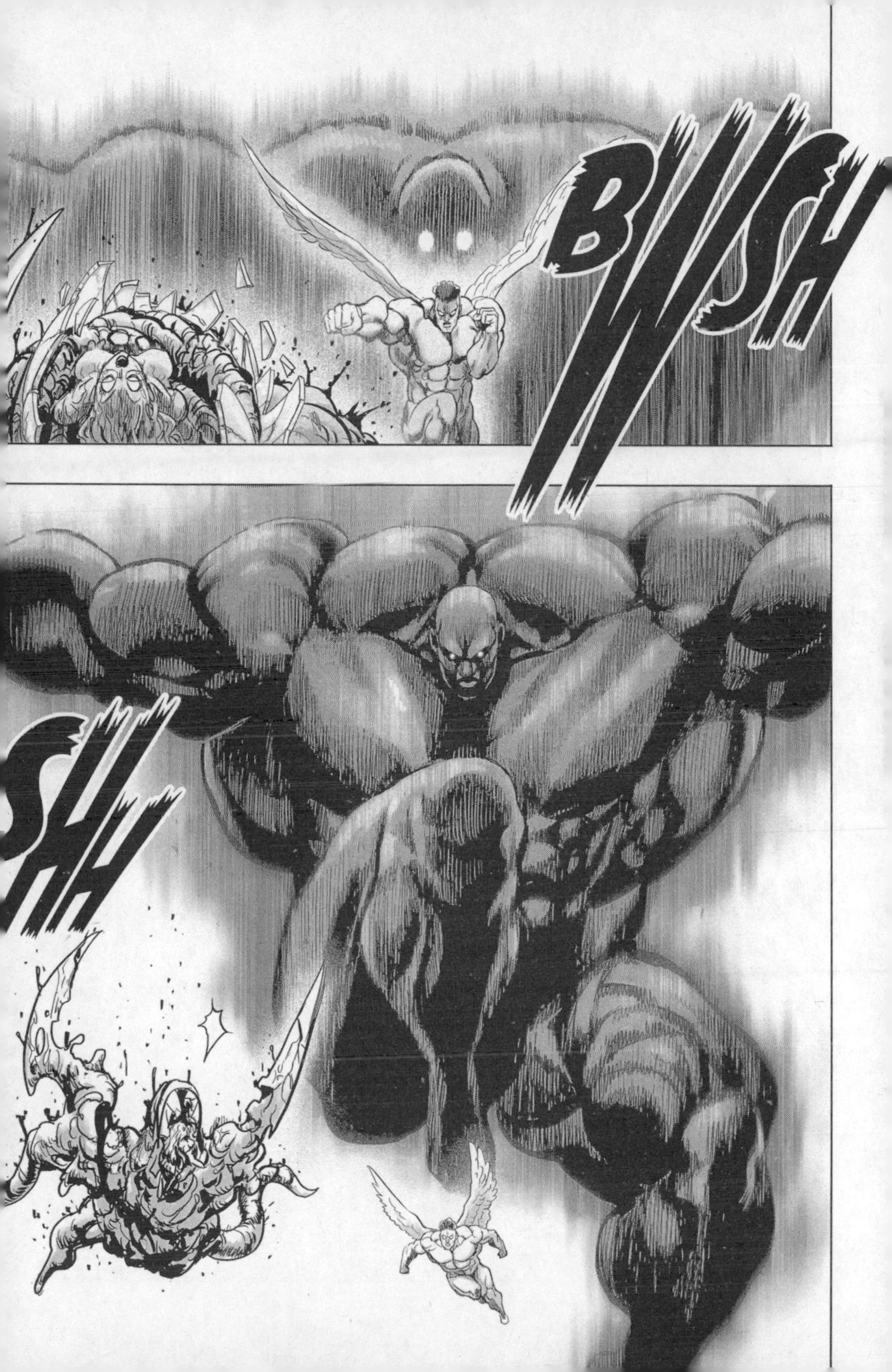
BWSH
SHH

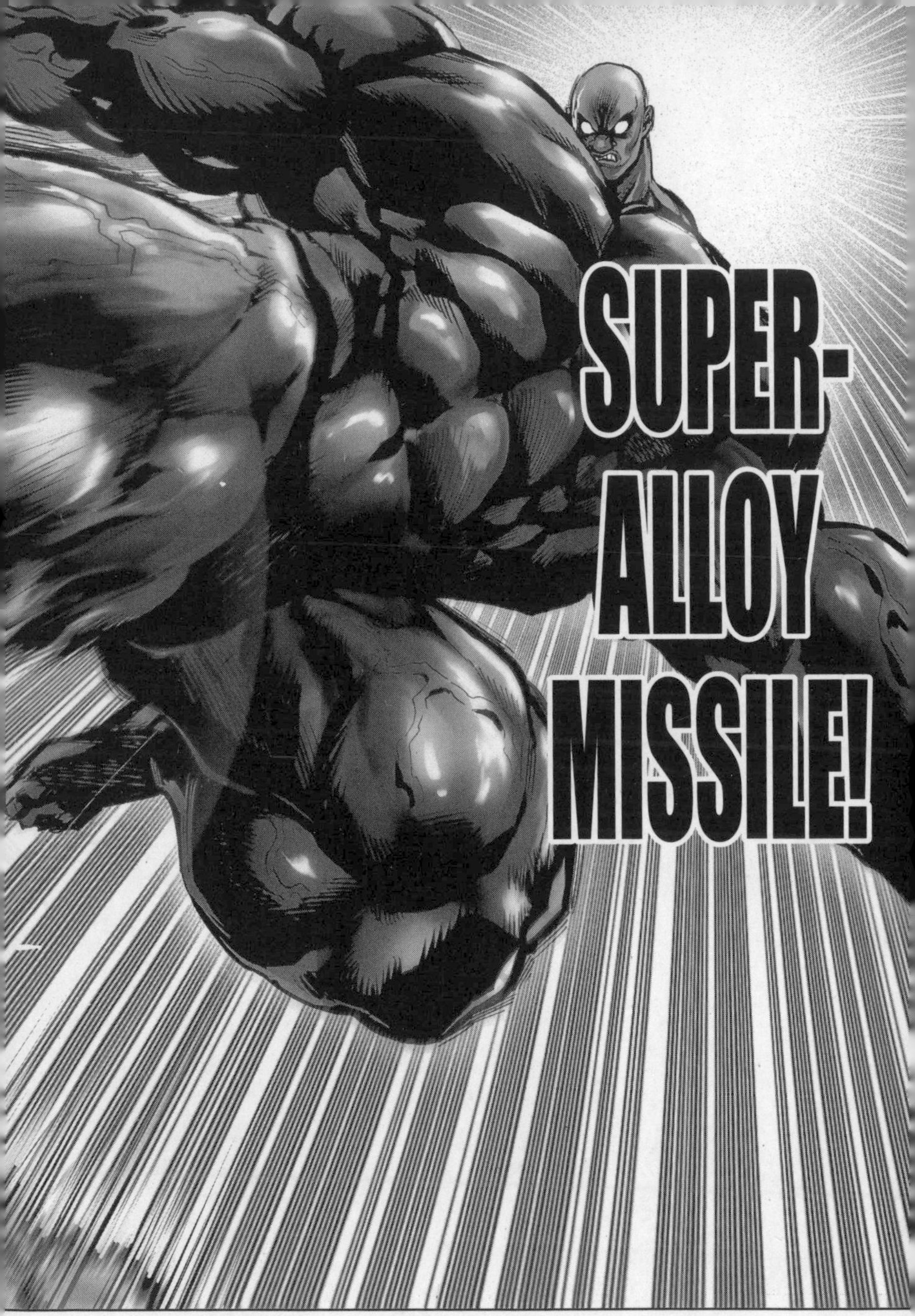
SUPER-
ALLOY
MISSILE!

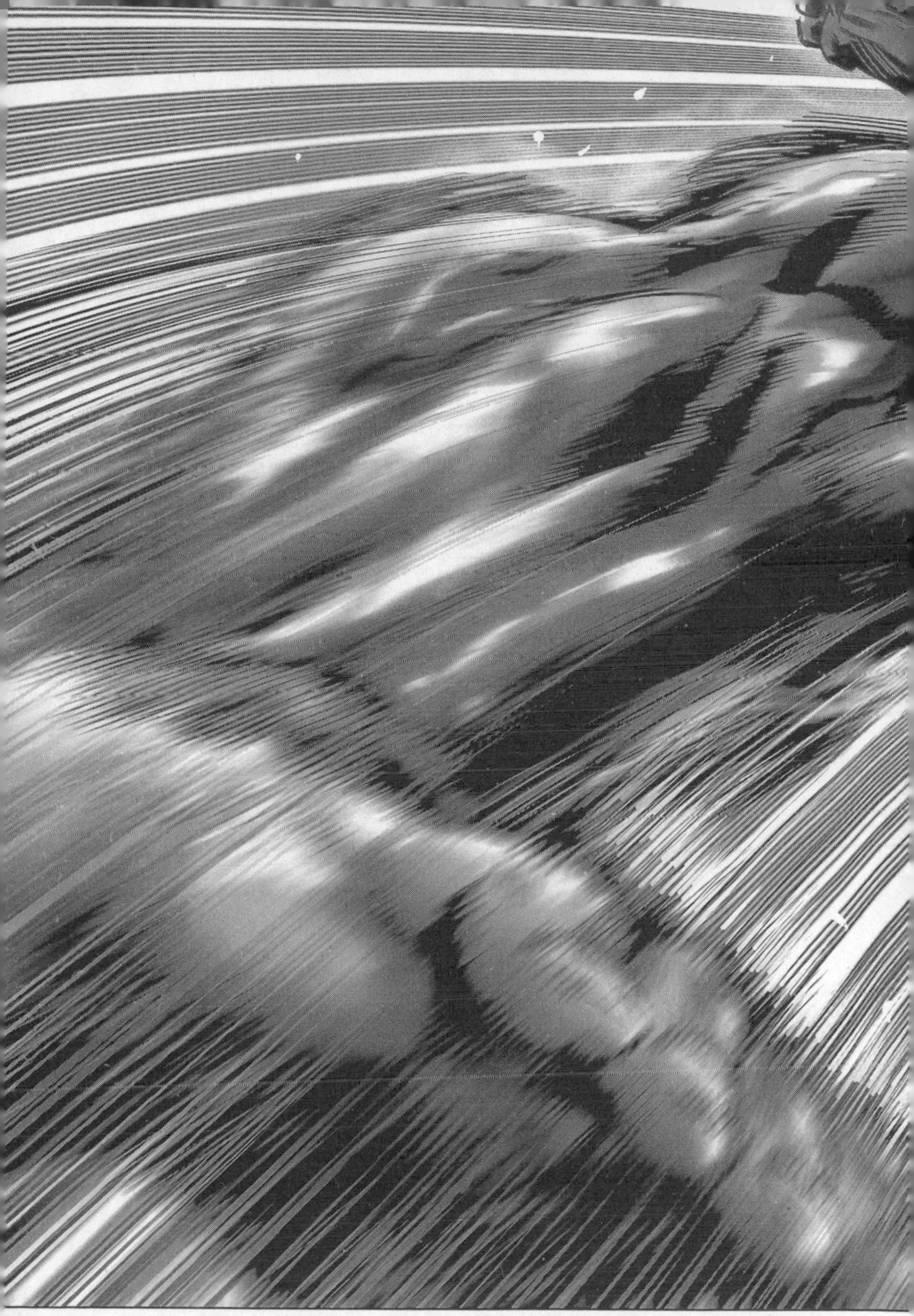

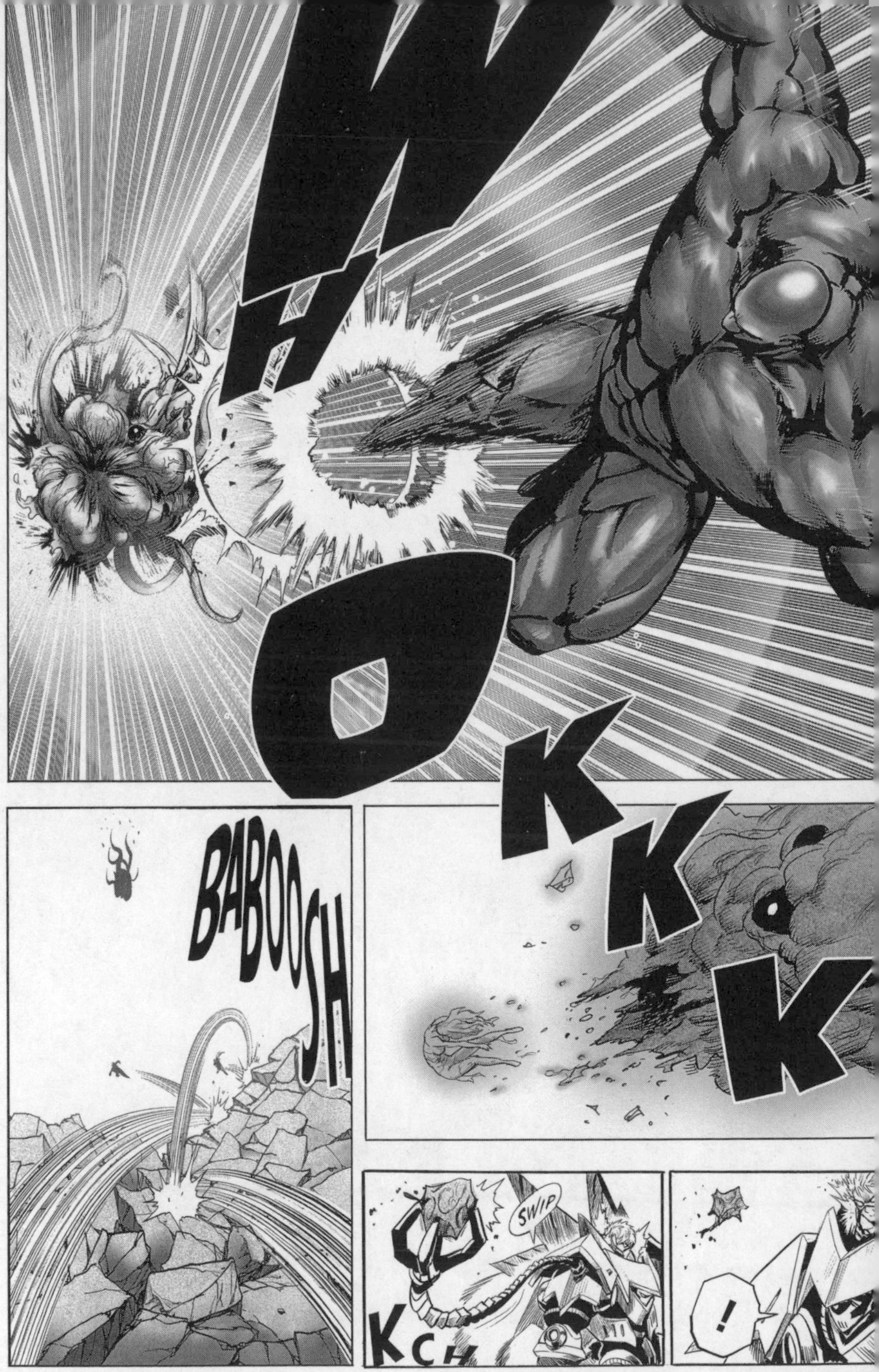
BABOOSH
!
SWIP
KCH

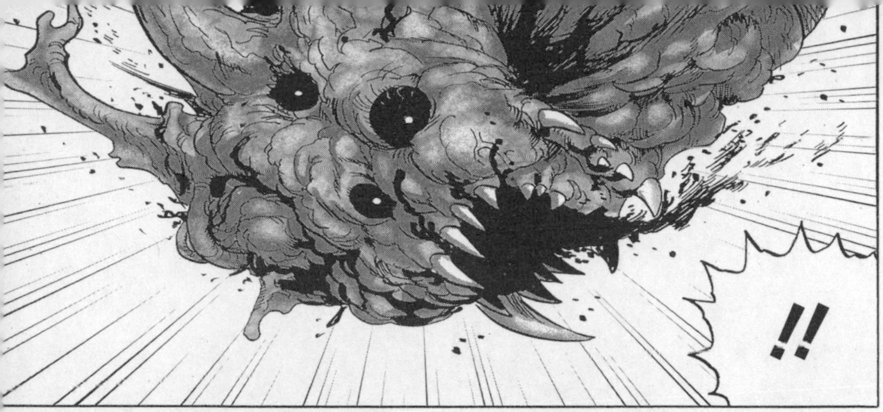
!!

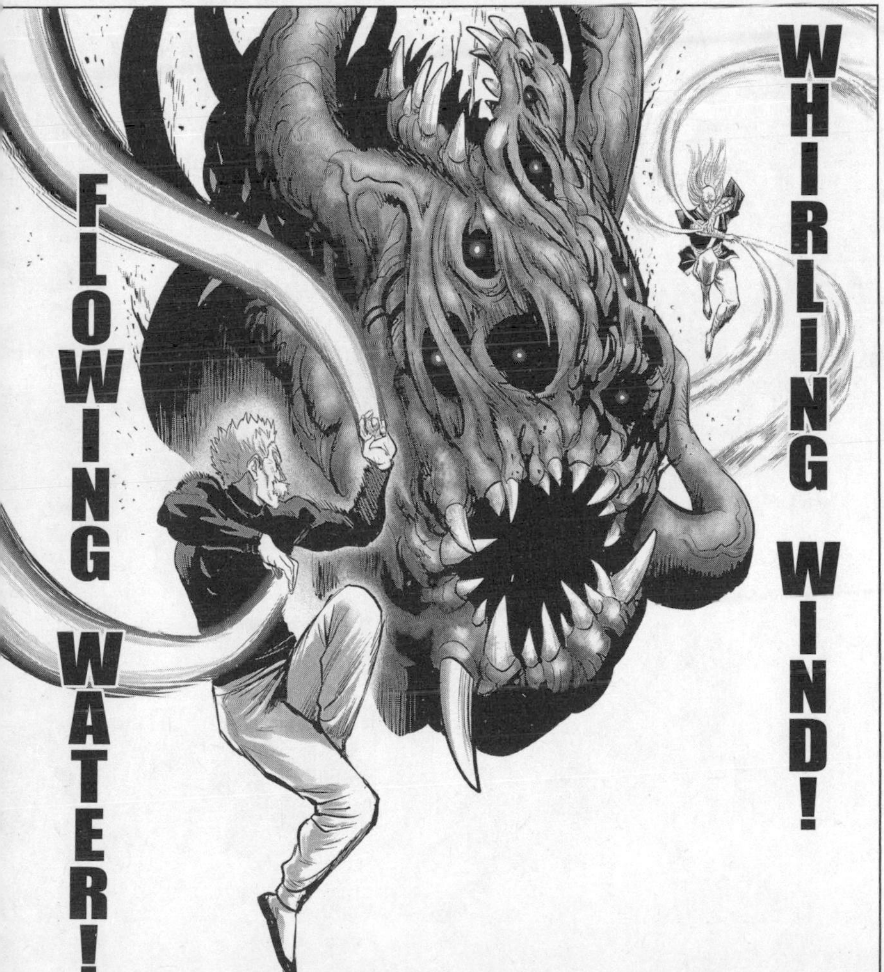
WHIRLING WIND!
FLOWING WATER!

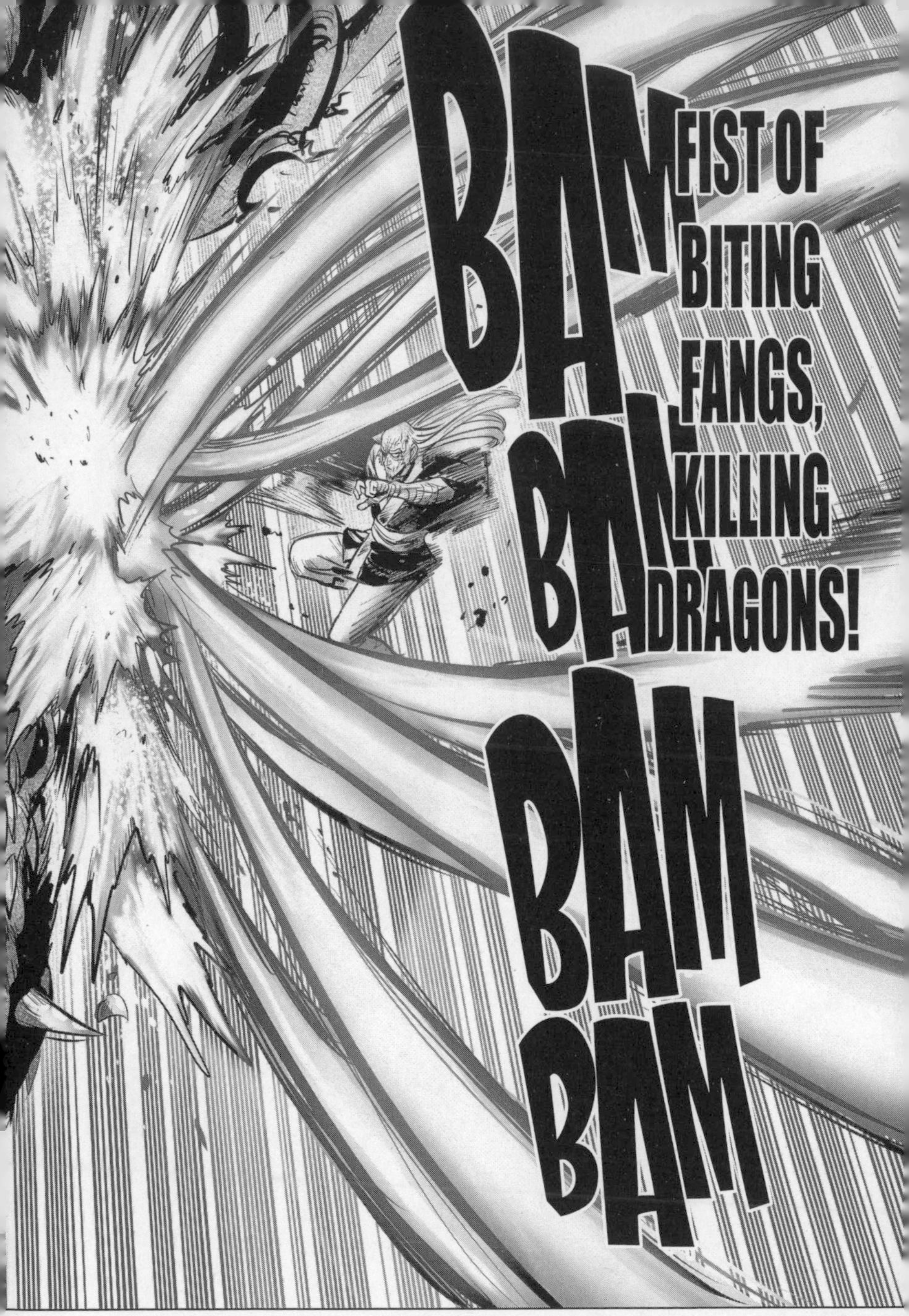
FIST OF BITING FANGS, KILLING DRAGONS!
BAM BAM BAM BAM

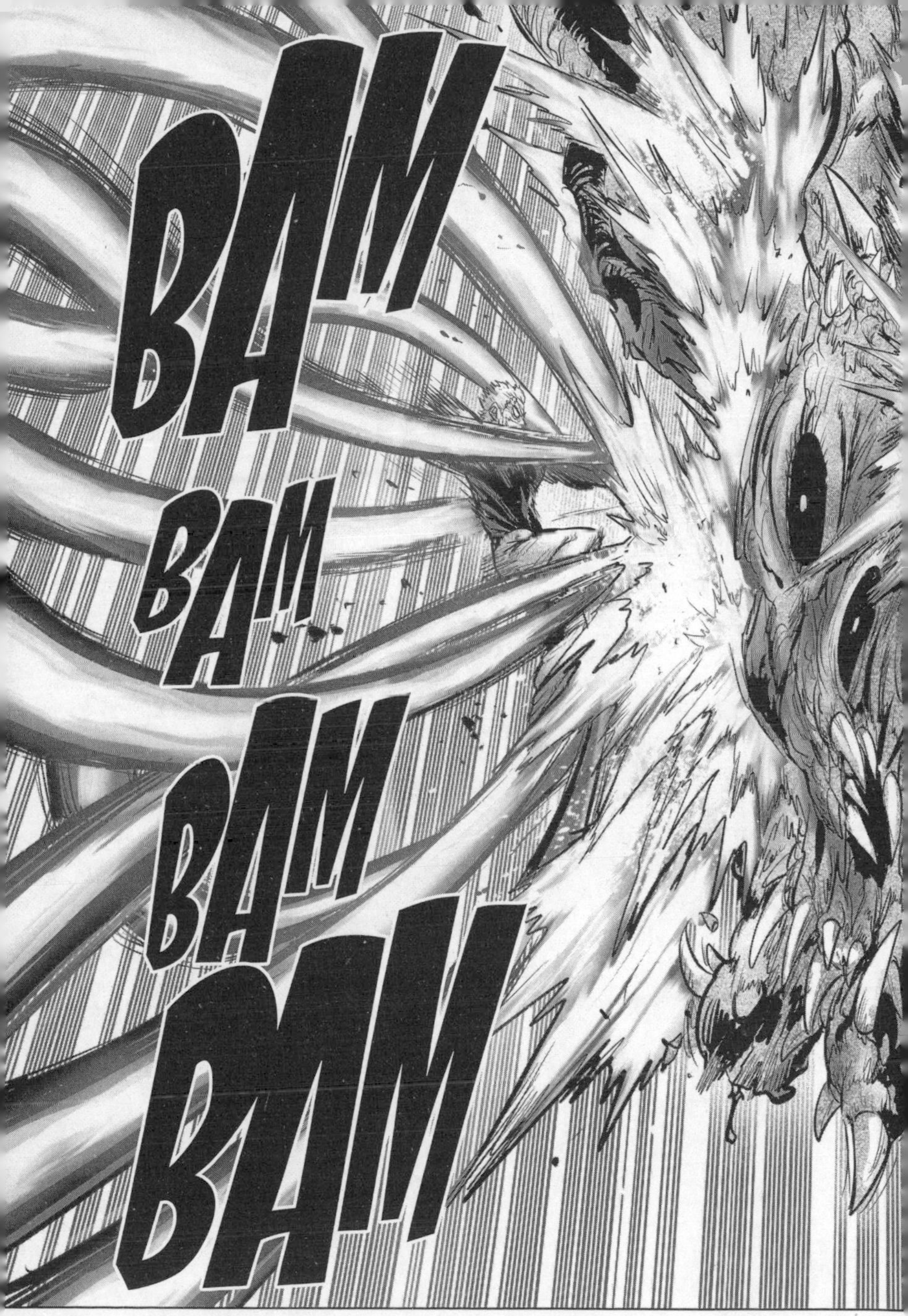
BAM
BAM
BAM
BAM
BAM

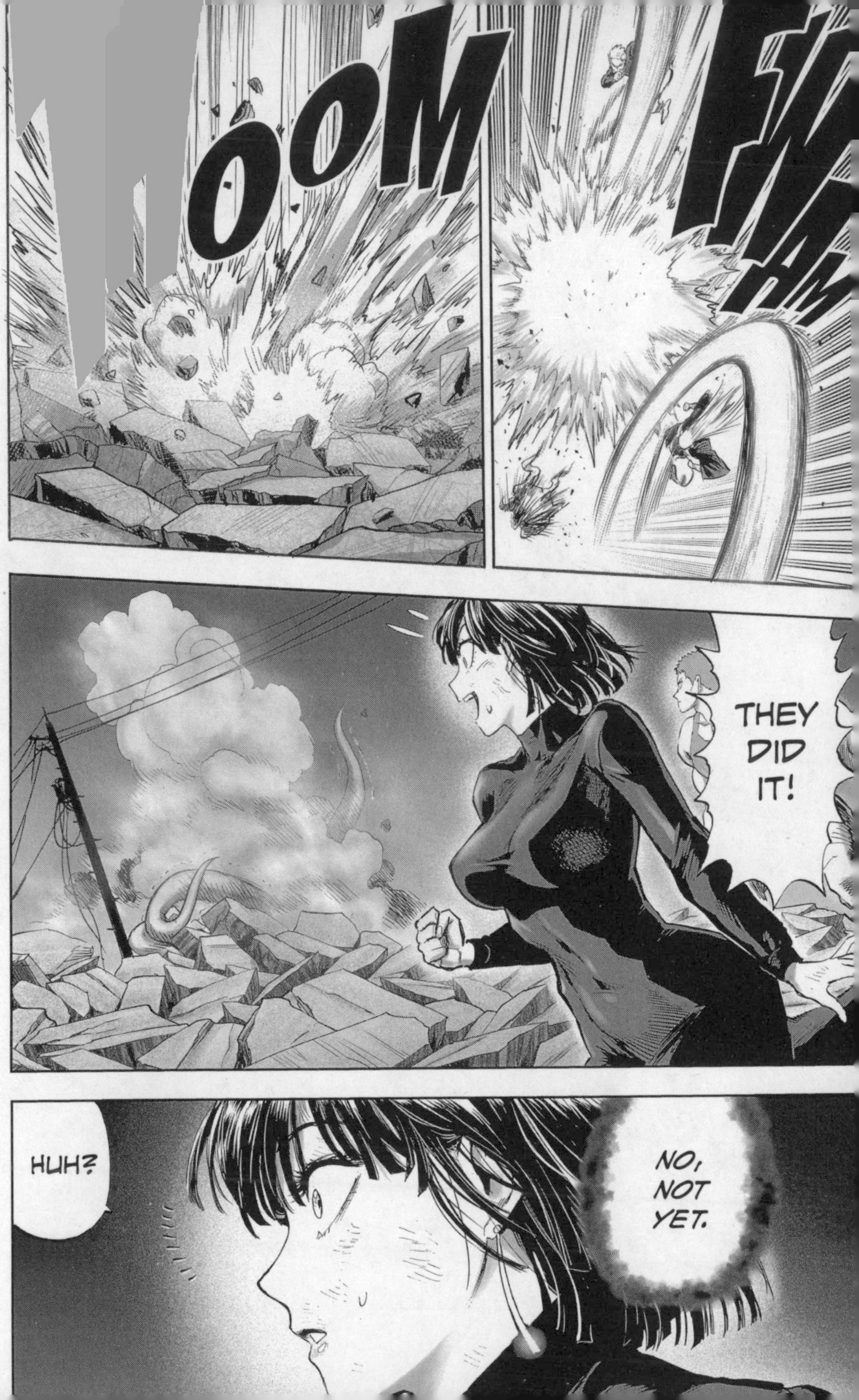
THEY DID IT!
NO, NOT YET.
HUH?

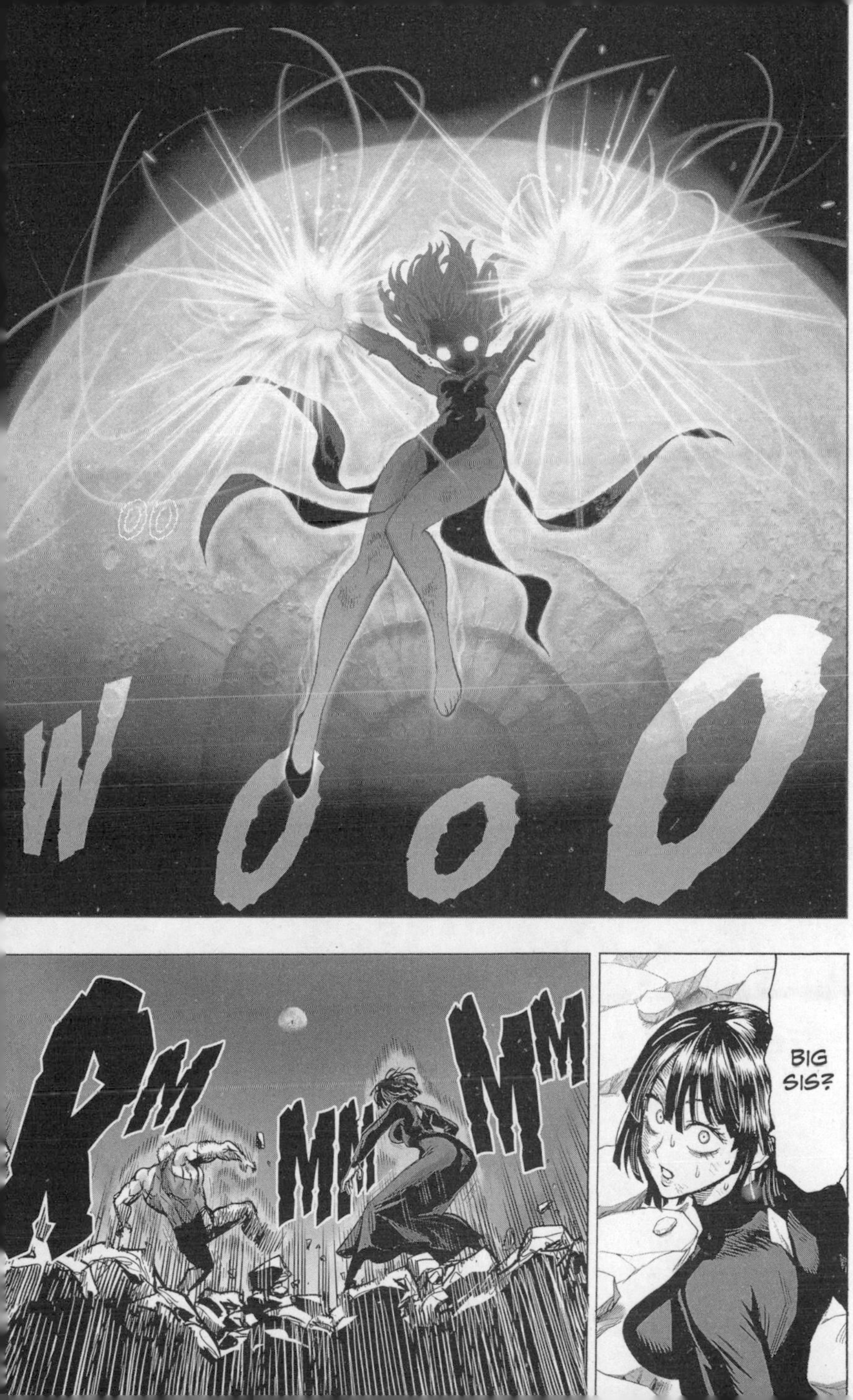
OO
WOOO
BIG SIS?
DMMMMMM

GOOD! JUST A LITTLE MORE!

OH, YOU MEAN THIS?

IF ONLY IT COULD BE MOVED...

NO, THERE'S SOMETHING IMMENSELY HEAVY THERE.

CAN'T YOU GET **YOURSELF** OUT NOW?

WHAT **IS** THIS?

WHEW!

CRUNK

YES, THANKS!

BETTER NOW?

TOSS

SHOULD I **PULL** YOU?

W-WHAT IS THIS THING?

UGH!!

YIKES!!

NO, STAY BACK!

YOU MIGHT BREAK SOMETHING!

K THUNK!

I'M IN A DELICATE SITUATION HERE!

TCH!

RMMM

MORE INTENSE RUMBLING ...

RMMM

WAH!

RMMM

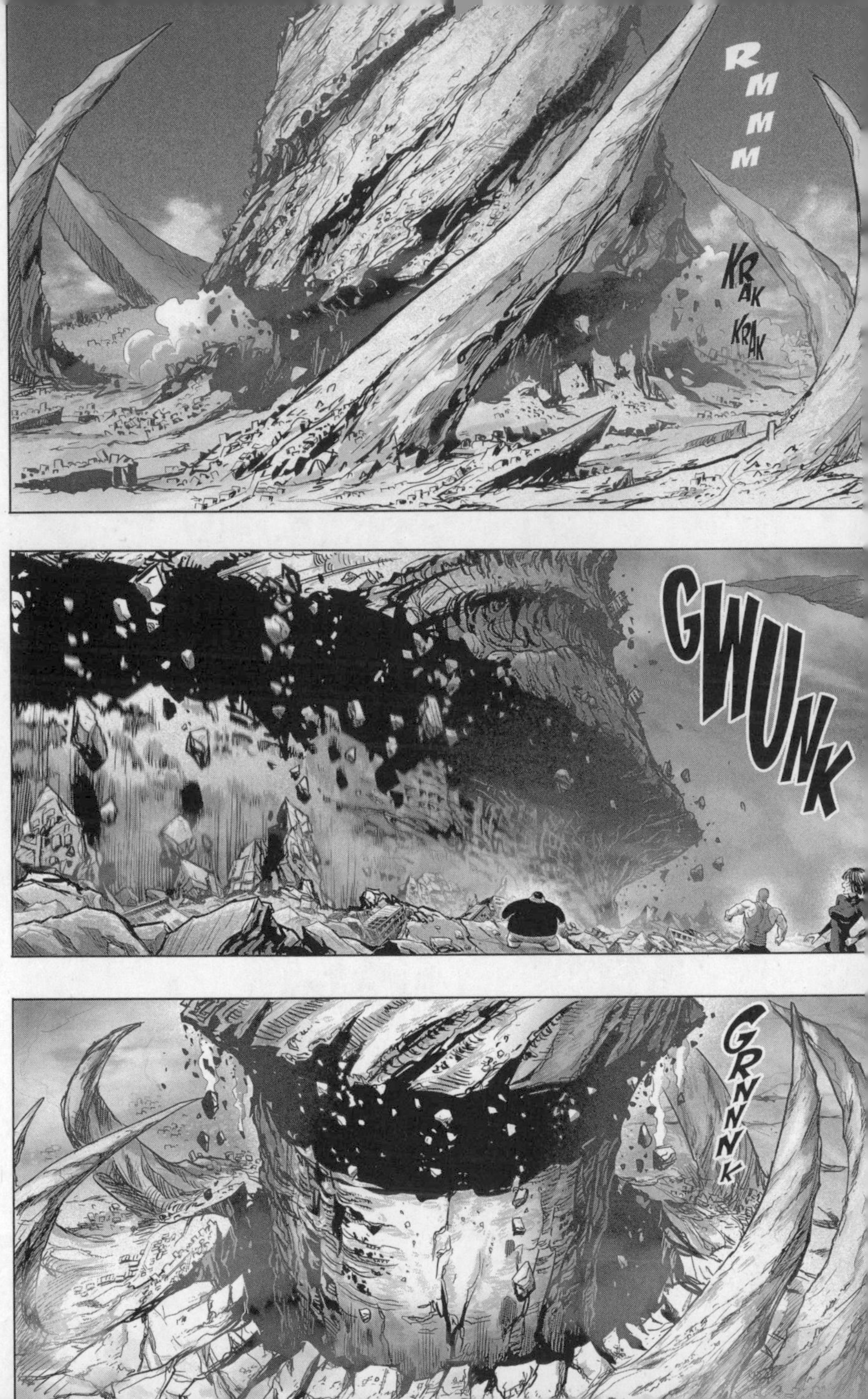
RMMM
KRAK
KRAK
GWUNK
GRNNNK

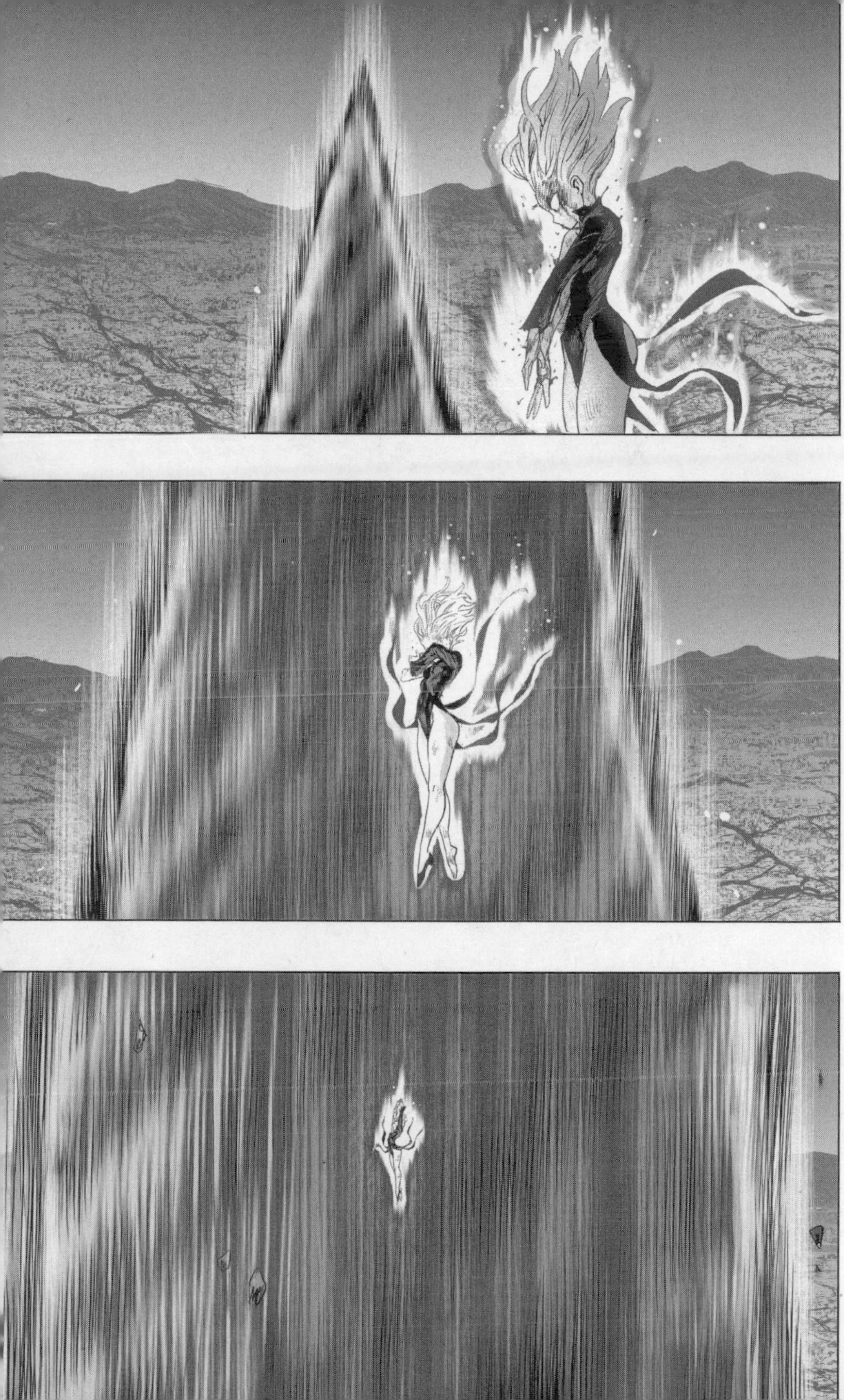

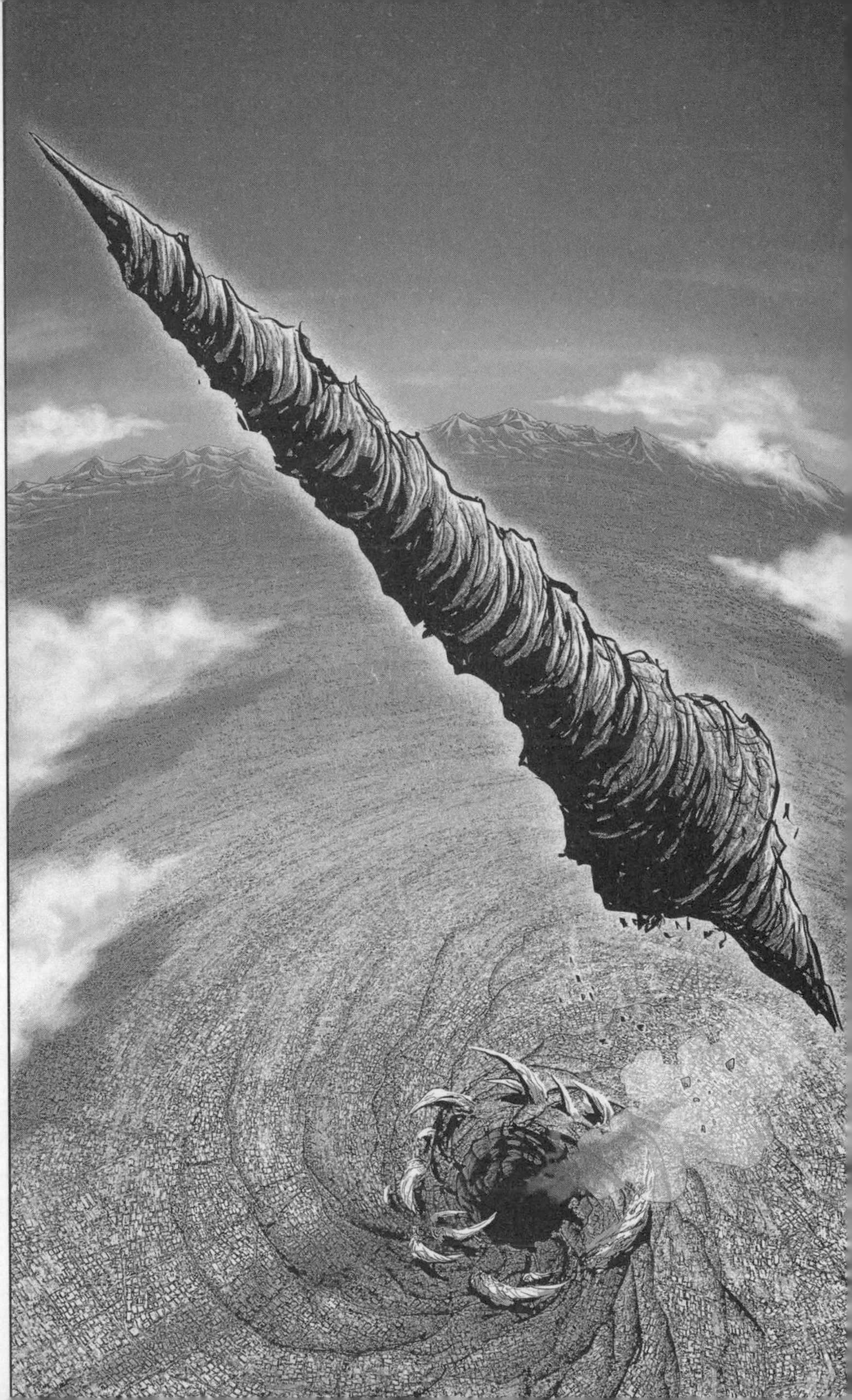

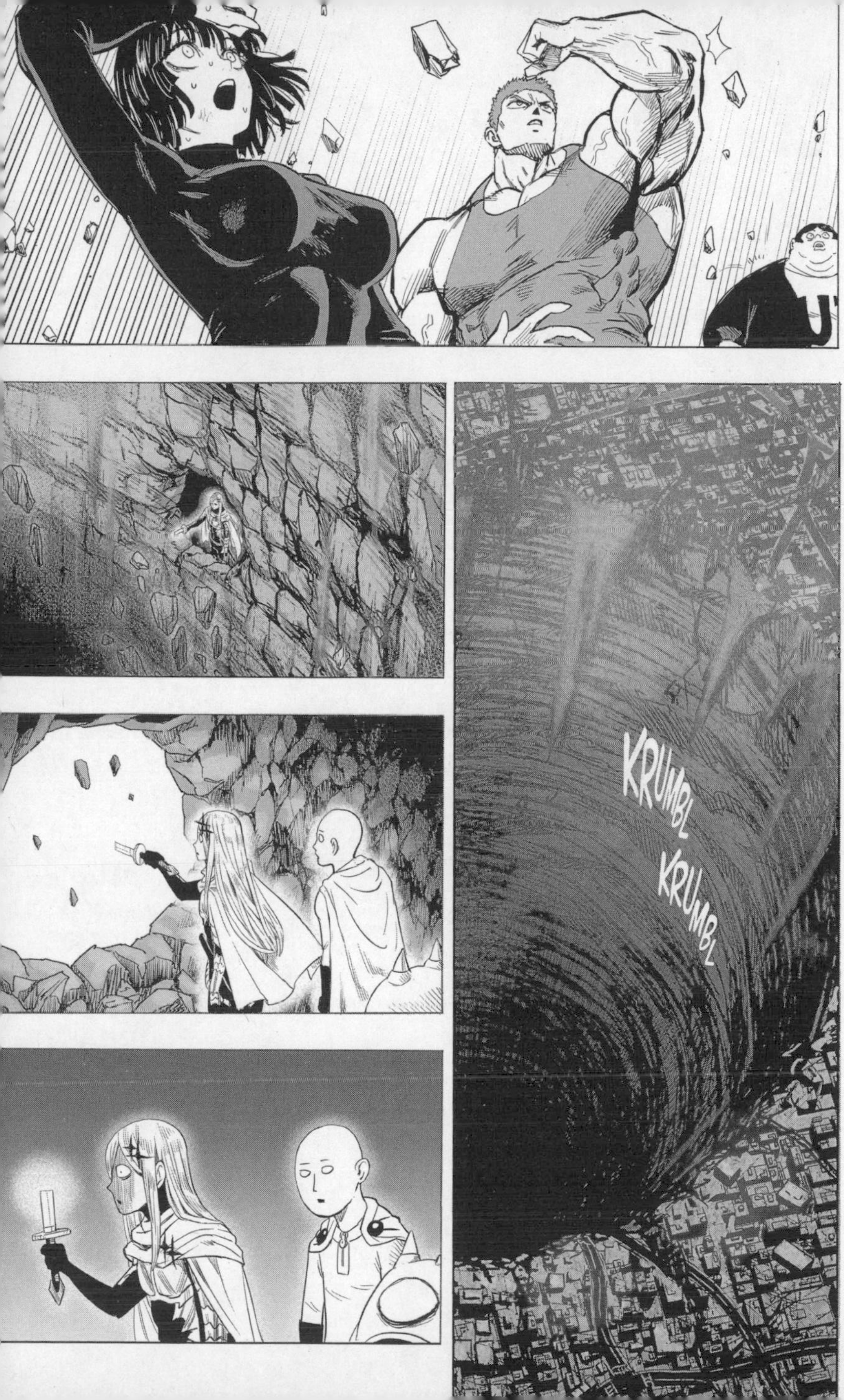
KRUMBL
KRUMBL

FLASH-
KILL...

RR Rr R M

Flash-
kill

WELL,
BOULDERS
AREN'T
GONNA
BREAK
MY **ARM.**

USE
YOUR
HEAD..

**THAT'S
WHAT YOU
WERE
WORRIED
ABOUT
BREAKING
?!**

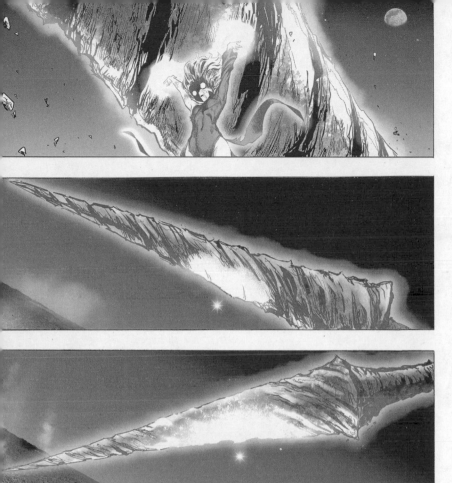

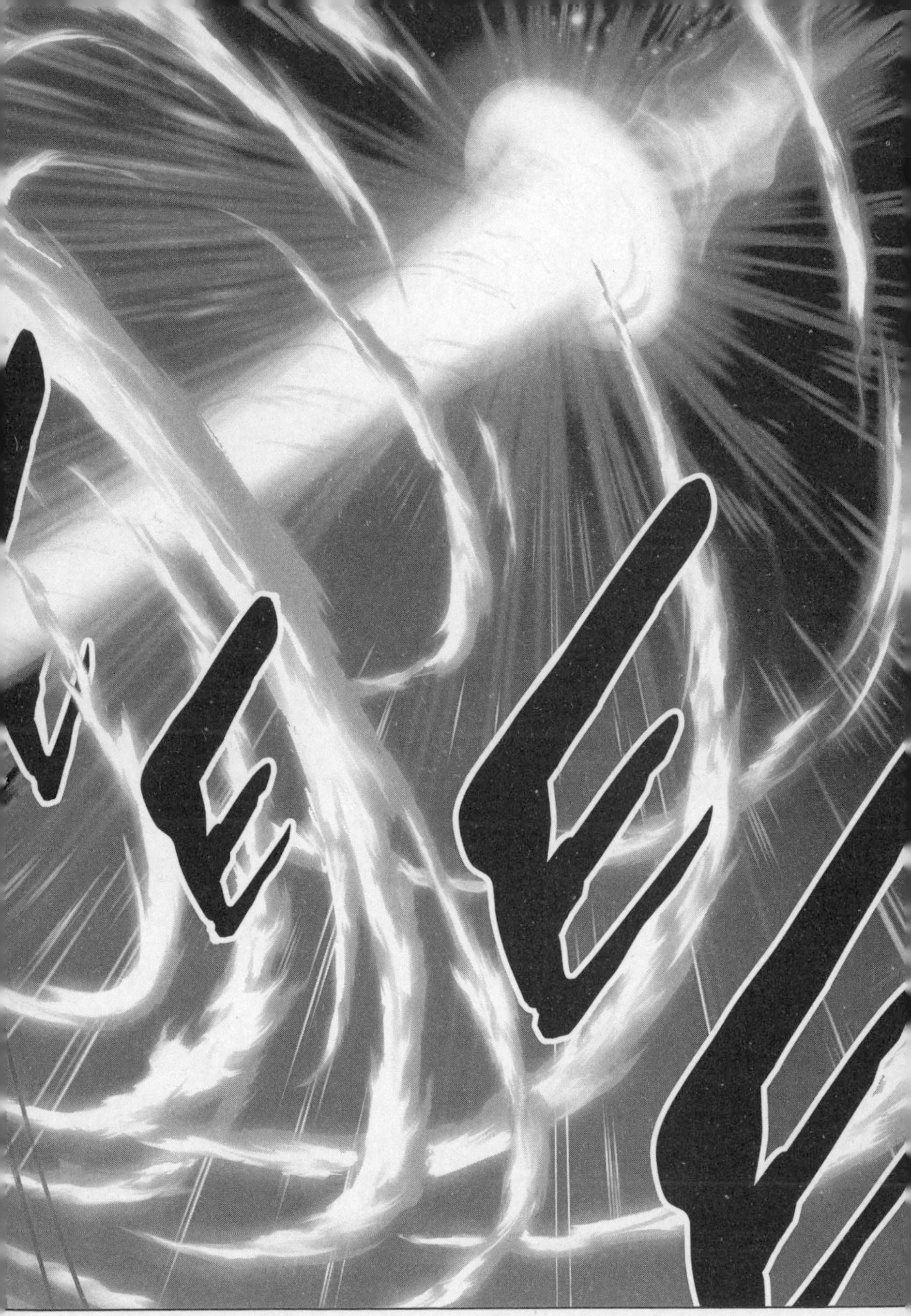

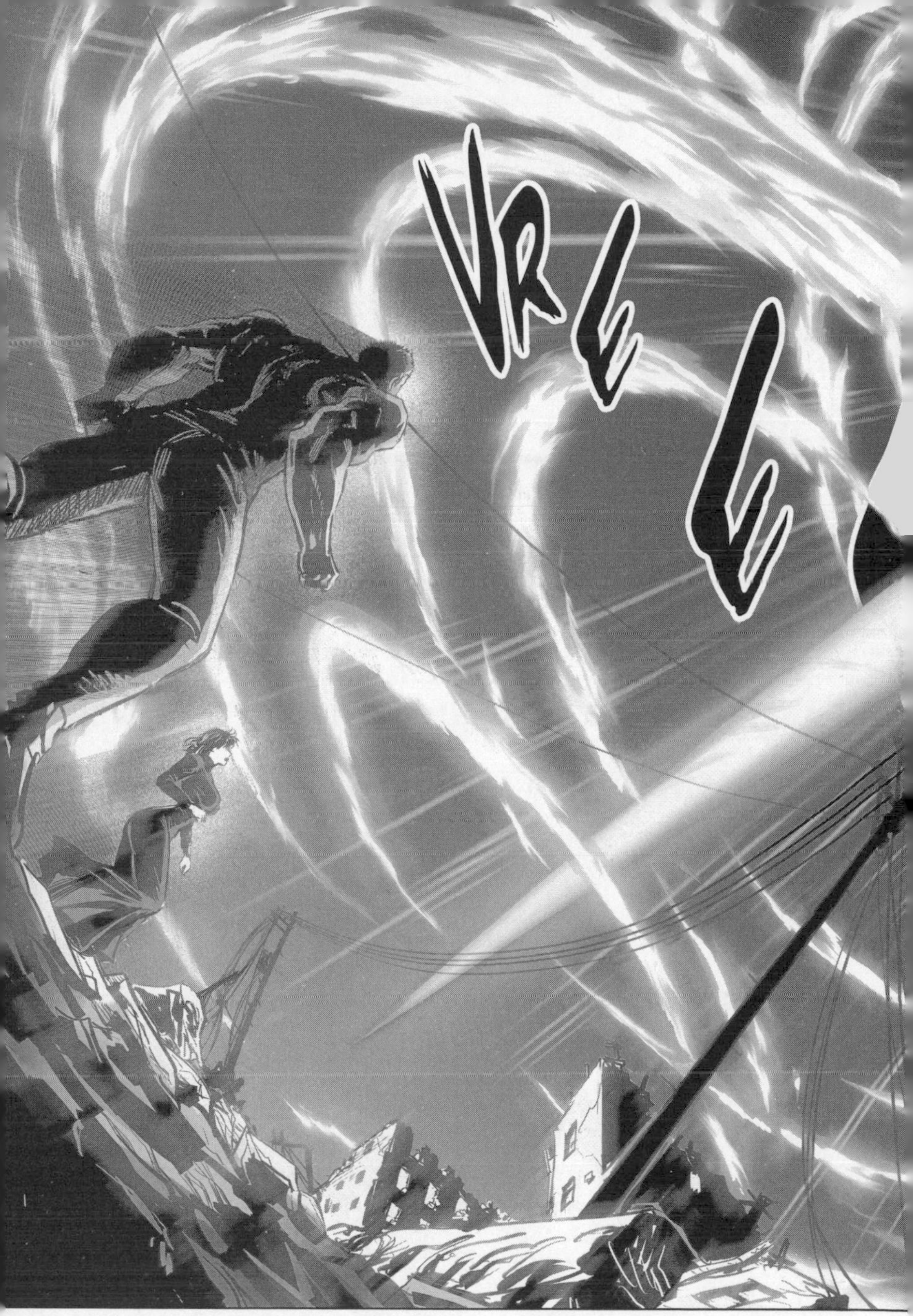
VREEE

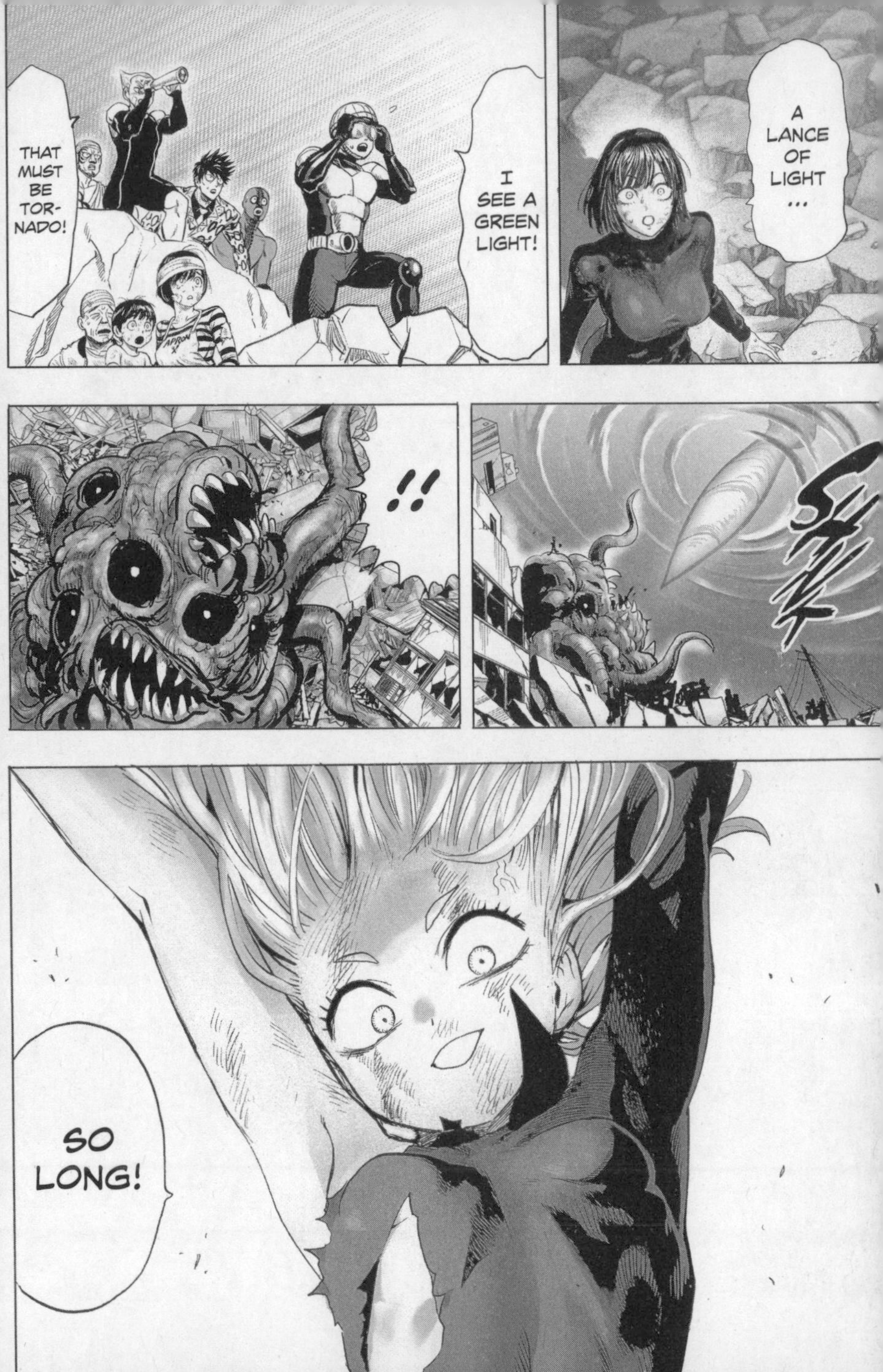

A LANCE OF LIGHT ...
I SEE A GREEN LIGHT!
THAT MUST BE TOR-NADO!
SHNK
!!
SO LONG!

SNEAK

NO.

I SHOULD HAVE JUST BLASTED THE WALL APART IF IT WAS GOING TO BREAK ANYWAY.

ARE YOU INSULTING MY SWORD?

FLASH-KILL SURE DIDN'T COME **OUT** IN A FLASH!

HM?

...

THIS'S MY CHANCE TO SLIP AWAY!

GWUP

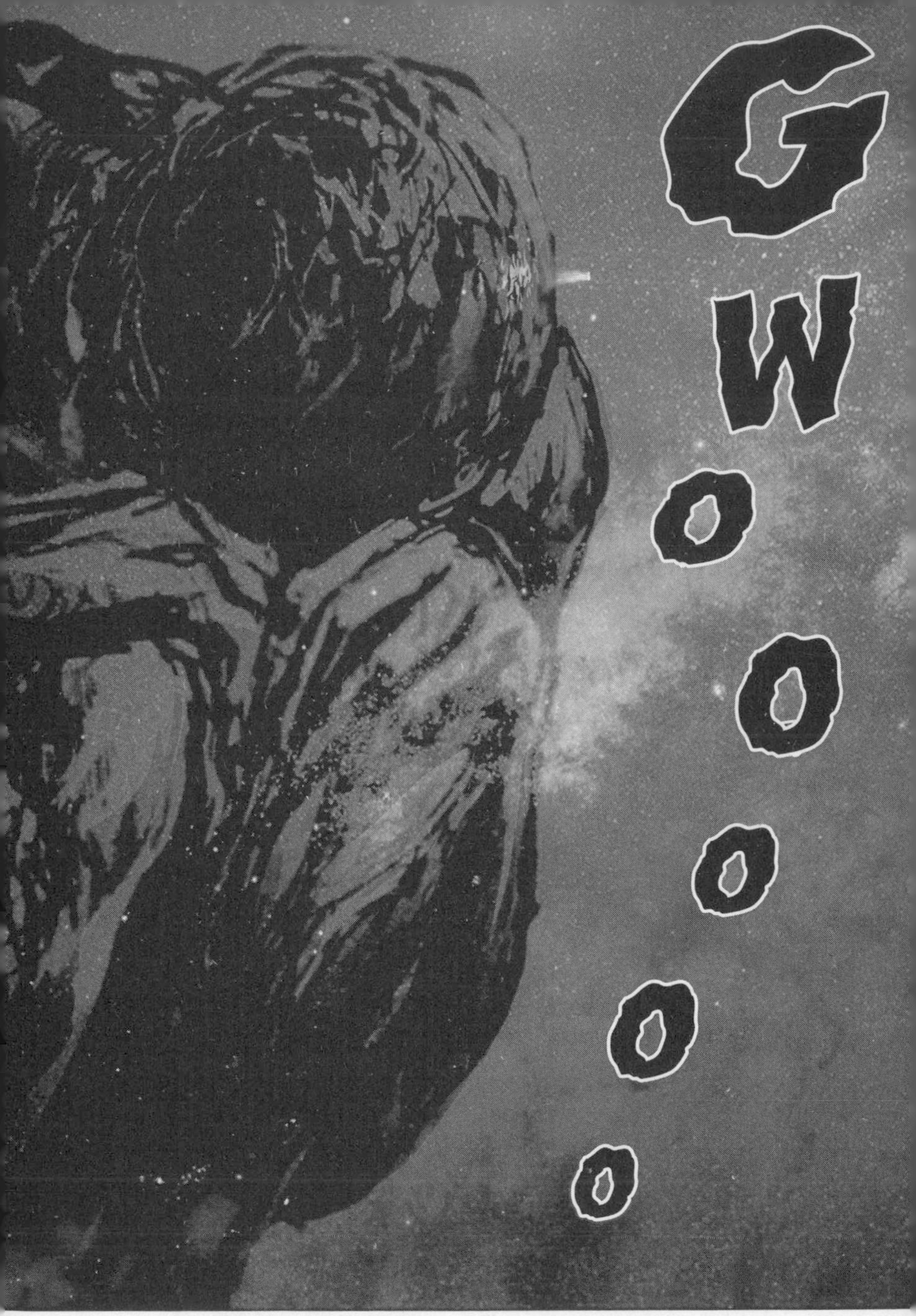
GWOOOOO

The reason for that is Watchdog Man, who operates out of Watchdog Man Plaza in the heart of City Q.

This city has the lowest total casualties caused by monster attacks, earning it a reputation as the safest city.

...City Q is peace-ful.

Yet again today...

I'M SLEEPY.

YAWN

BONUS MANGA: SENSE OF SMELL

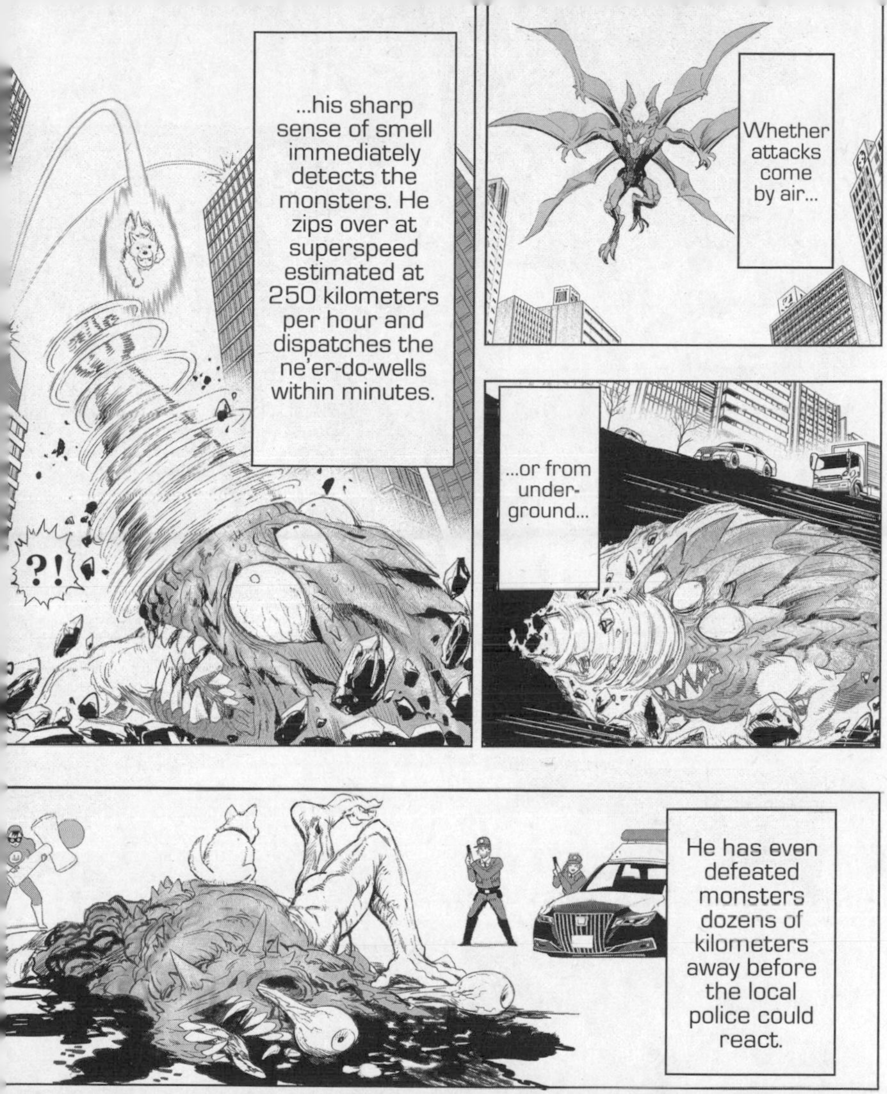
Whether attacks come by air...
...or from under-ground...
...his sharp sense of smell immediately detects the monsters. He zips over at superspeed estimated at 250 kilometers per hour and dispatches the ne'er-do-wells within minutes.
?!
He has even defeated monsters dozens of kilometers away before the local police could react.

That day, attacks came from multiple monsters estimated to be threat level Demon.

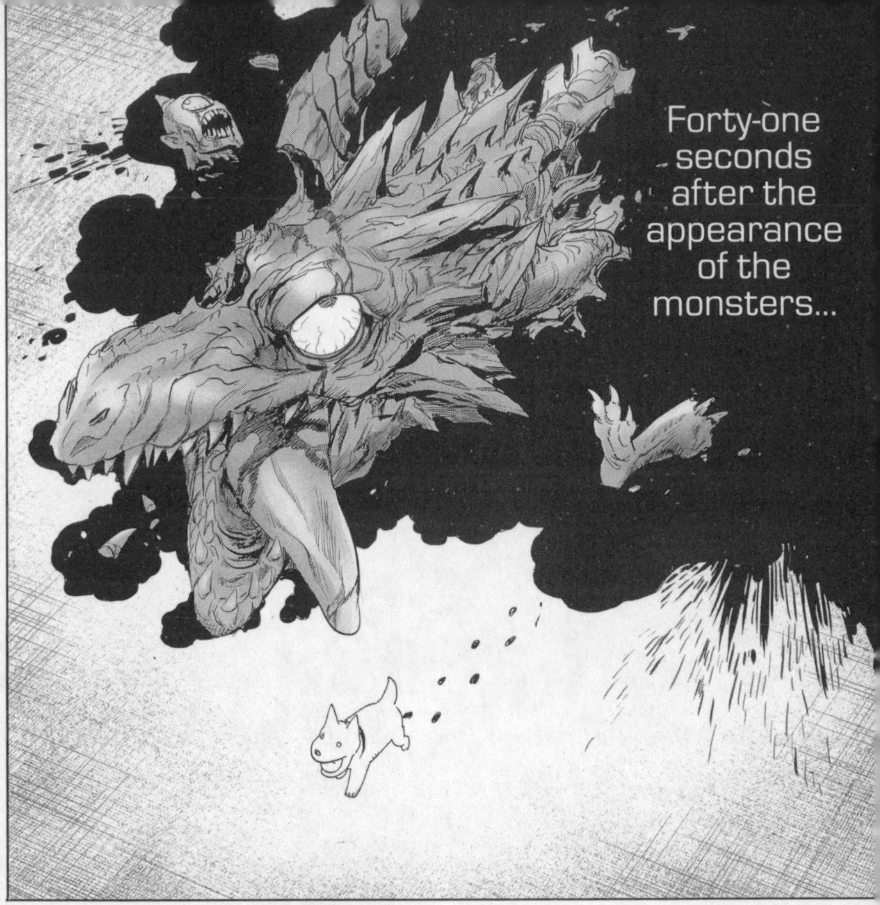
Forty-one seconds after the appearance of the monsters...

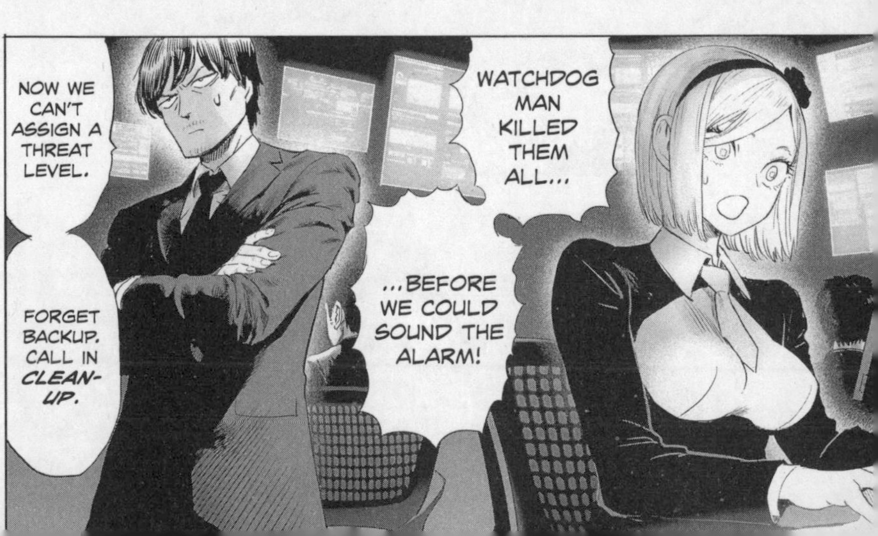
WATCHDOG MAN KILLED THEM ALL...
...BEFORE WE COULD SOUND THE ALARM!
NOW WE CAN'T ASSIGN A THREAT LEVEL.
FORGET BACKUP. CALL IN *CLEAN-UP*.

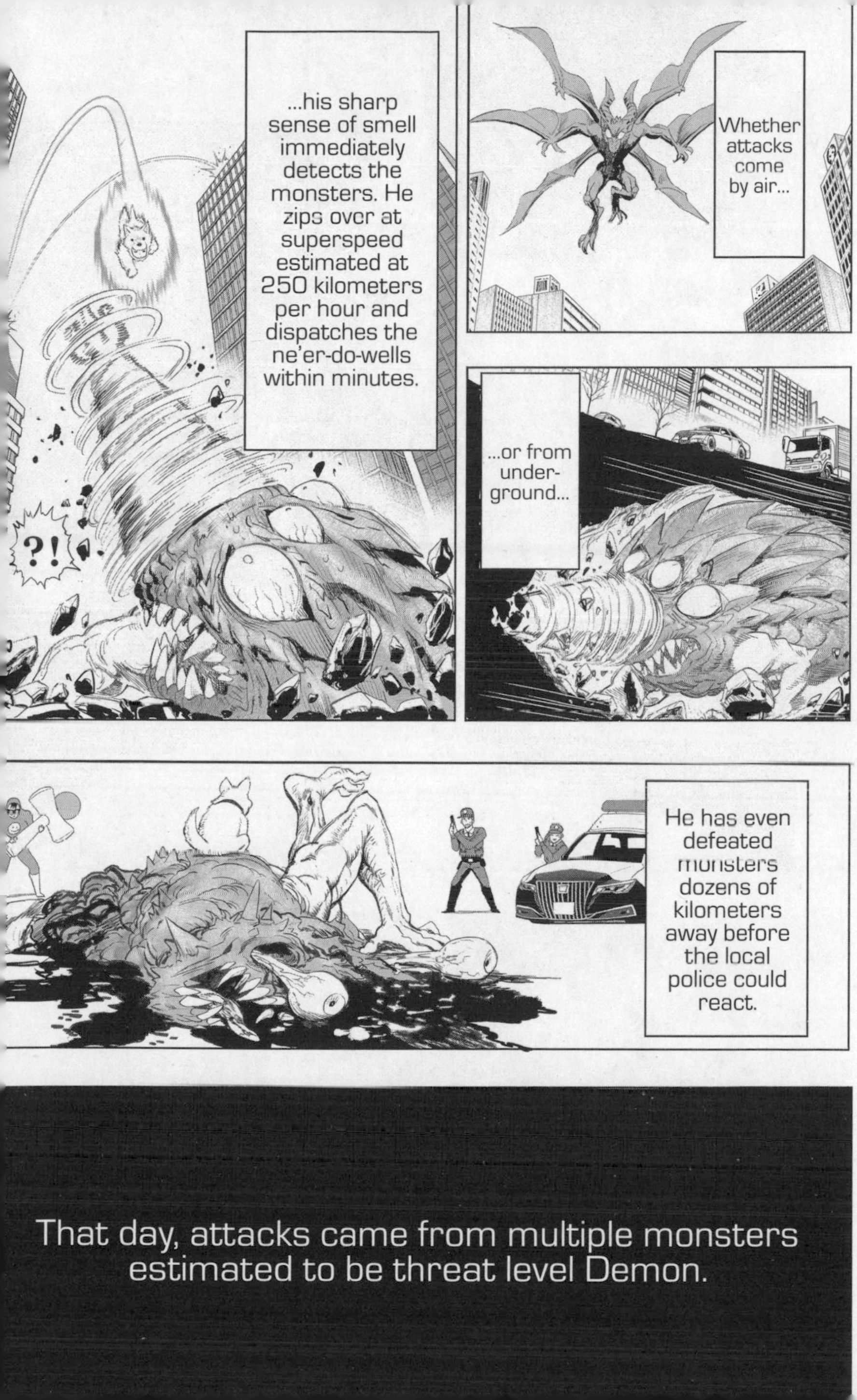
Whether attacks come by air...
...or from underground...
...his sharp sense of smell immediately detects the monsters. He zips over at superspeed estimated at 250 kilometers per hour and dispatches the ne'er-do-wells within minutes.
?!
He has even defeated monsters dozens of kilometers away before the local police could react.
That day, attacks came from multiple monsters estimated to be threat level Demon.

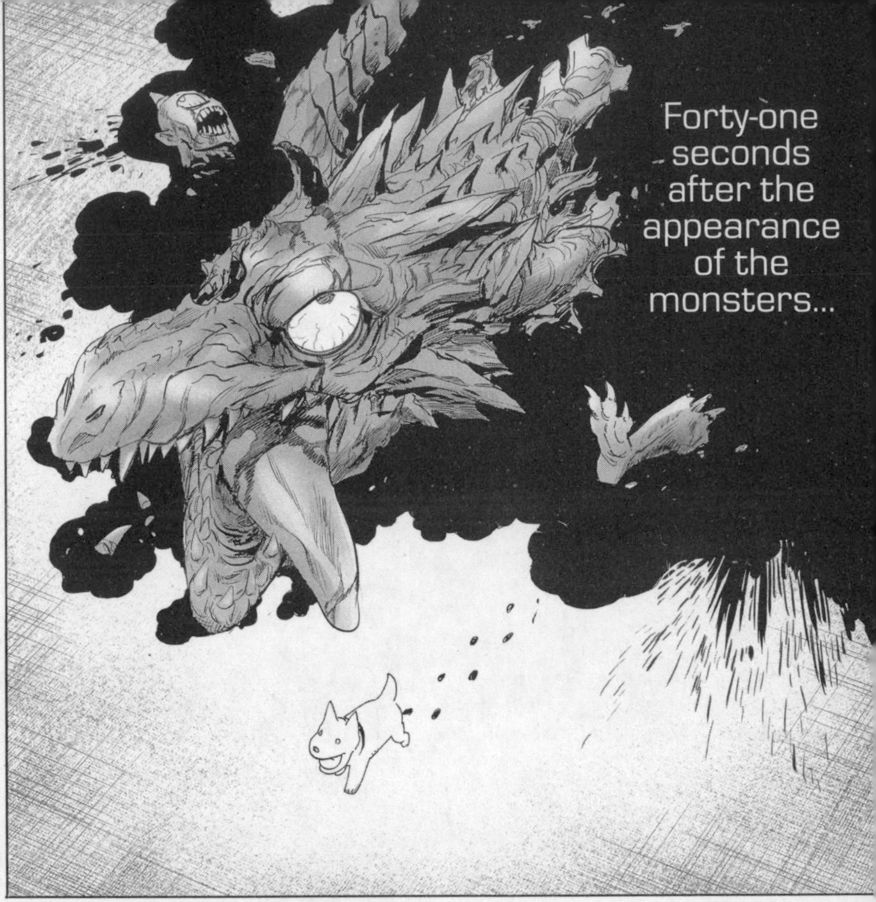
Forty-one seconds after the appearance of the monsters...

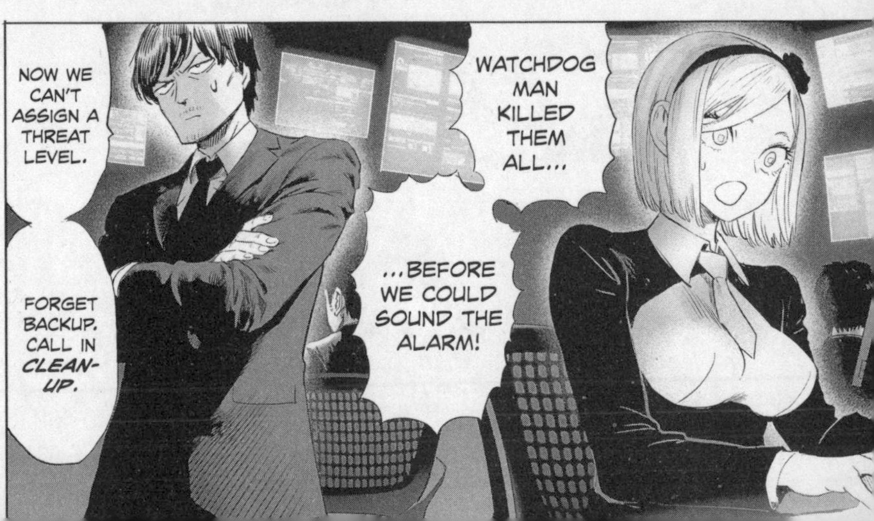
WATCHDOG MAN KILLED THEM ALL...
...BEFORE WE COULD SOUND THE ALARM!
NOW WE CAN'T ASSIGN A THREAT LEVEL.
FORGET BACKUP. CALL IN *CLEAN-UP*.

Yet again today, City Q is peaceful thanks to Watchdog Man.

...his full power.

And still no one knows...

28 Into the Abyss (End)

ONE-PUNCH MAN
VOLUME 28
SHONEN JUMP EDITION

STORY BY | ONE
ART BY | YUSUKE MURATA

TRANSLATION | JOHN WERRY
TOUCH-UP ART AND LETTERING | JAMES GAUBATZ
DESIGN | PAUL PADURARIU
EDITOR | JOHN BAE

ONE-PUNCH MAN © 2012 by ONE, Yusuke Murata
All rights reserved.
First published in Japan in 2012 by SHUEISHA Inc., Tokyo.
English translation rights arranged by SHUEISHA Inc.

Printed in the U.S.A.

Published by VIZ Media, LLC
P.O. Box 77010
San Francisco, CA 94107

10 9 8 7 6 5 4 3 2 1
First printing, May 2024

viz.com

PARENTAL ADVISORY
ONE-PUNCH MAN is rated T for Teen and
is recommended for ages 13 and up. This
volume contains realistic and fantasy violence.
ratings.viz.com